The International Gourmet Cookbook

Jules J. Bond

The
International
Cookbook
Gourmet

CASTLE BOOKS
Secaucus, N.J. 07094

Acknowledgments
The publishers gratefully acknowledge the
following sources for permission to reproduce the
illustrations in this book:
American Egg Board
American Lamb Council
Amstar Corp. (Domino Sugar)
Best Foods
Blue Nun Wines
Bosphorous East Restaurant
Budapest Restaurant
Food and Wines From France, Inc.
Free Lance Photographers Guild
Gonzales Byass Sherry
Mrs. Herbst's Bakery
House of Rufino Wines
Italian Tourist Office
Japanese National Tourist Organization
Josh Konecky
The McIllhenny Co. (Tabasco)
Moet & Chandon Wines
National Live Stock & Meat Board
National Macaroni Institute
The National Rice Council
Pickle Packers International
H. Roth & Sons
Sarge's Delicatessen
Schieffelin & Co.
Spanish Green Olive Commission
Tio Pepe Spanish-Mexican Restaurant
Turkey Information Service
United Dairy Industry Assoc.
U.S. Dept. of Commerce – National
   Marine Fisheries Service

Line drawings by Nicole Rigby – New York Post

Designed by Harold Franklin and Roy P. Jensen

Library of Congress Catalog Card Number: 79-53778

ISBN 0-89009-298-2

Manufactured in the United States of America

Introduction

The culinary horizon has widened as international travel has increased, introducing the world's great dishes to millions of people who love fine food — and want to learn how to prepare it at home.

The International Gourmet Cookbook contains 600 recipes, carefully selected, not only for those who have traveled widely, dined and wined in many countries but for everyone who enjoys preparing and savouring dishes of the great cuisines of the world. Indeed, this book takes you on a global cook's tour with easy-to-follow recipes.

These 320 pages introduce a great many ways, familiar and exotic, to prepare dishes from more than 25 countries. Appetizers and soups, egg and cheese dishes, fish and seafood specialties, meats and poultry, rice and pastas, vegetables and salads, sauces and delicious, easy to prepare, desserts from all over the world.

Over 160 of these recipes are lavishly illustrated, not only to whet your appetite but also to guide you in preparing and presenting them in a most attractive manner.

The table of contents indicates the complete coverage, the recipes themselves reflect the truly international scope of this volume. Delicious specialties from the provinces of France and Italy, delightful dishes from Spain and Portugal, the best of the splendid cooking of Vienna and Hungary, great dishes of Greece, Turkey and the Middle East. You will find a great variety of mouth-watering recipes from China, Japan, Korea and other countries of the Orient.

Last, but not least, recipes for the great specialties of our own hemisphere, from Maine to Cajun country, from Mexico to South America.

We have not only chosen the most typical and tasty recipes from the many countries represented in this volume, but we have also carefully avoided dishes calling for ingredients hard to find in markets or the average food shop. Many dishes were chosen with the high-cost-of-living in mind. While there are a number of recipes for the festive table, requiring more expensive foods, you will find in this book a great number of splendid dishes which can be prepared at moderate cost.

The recipes are concise: clear and easy to follow. The ingredients — with a few exceptions — can be found on most store shelves. The glossary explains some less familiar terms and suggests substitutes for some of the harder to find ingredients.

This book was created for all those who would like to bring variety to the kitchen and dining table, with ease and success.

JULES J. BOND

Glossary

Bean Curd (Tofu) is made from fresh soy beans and is sold in cake form. It is kept in containers of fresh water and will keep for a few days in the refrigerator. Change water daily.

Beurre Manie. One of the easiest and best ways to thicken sauces. Knead equal amounts of butter and flour until smooth. Stir blended mixture into the sauce in small pellets.

Bouquet Garni. A combination of herbs added to stews, soups and stocks for flavoring. The most frequently used combinations are thyme, bay leaf and parsley. Tie fresh sprigs of herbs together with a string. If dried herbs are used, tie in a cheesecloth bag for easy removal.

Coconut Milk and Cream, available in cans or bottles in most markets. Can be prepared by placing 1 cup of dried shredded coconut and 1¼ cup water (or half water/half milk) in the bowl of a blender, run at high speed for ½ minute, then strain through muslin or a triple layer of cheesecloth, squeezing out as much liquid as possible.

Creme Fraiche (French heavy cream). French heavy cream is considerably thicker than American heavy cream. A simple way to approximate French heavy cream is to:

Add one teaspoon of buttermilk to a cup of heavy cream. Blend and heat gently in a saucepan until lukewarm, about 85 degrees. Pour in a glass or porcelain container and let it stand at room temperature until the mixture thickens, this can take anywhere from 6 to 36 hours, depending on the room temperature. Stored in the refrigerator, creme fraiche will keep for a week.

Daikon. Giant white radish, available in many Oriental food stores, used often grated for flavoring.

Dashi. A clear broth, is the basis of nearly all Japanese soups and sauces. It is prepared by boiling 3 tablespoons dried flaked bonito and a 2-inch square of dried seaweed (kombu) for 3 or 4 minutes in 6 cups of water. Let stand for a few minutes, then strain.

There are several excellent brands of instant dashi available in many stores across the country. Instant dashi comes in powder form and needs to be dissolved in hot water.

Julienne cut. Vegetables or meats cut in very narrow strips.

Kombu. Dried kelp (seaweed). Available in Japanese and other Oriental food stores. Sold in dry sheets or ribbons, used to flavor dashi (soup stock) and other preparations.

Kombu is also available in pickled strips, used mostly as garnish.

Mirin. Japanese sweetened rice wine used in cooking. If unavailable substitute Sherry.

Oyster Sauce. Available in bottles or cans in many markets and all Oriental food stores. Can be approximated by mincing 1 dozen oysters. Strain their liquid into a small pan, add the minced oysters, cover and simmer for 20 minutes. Strain the liquid through a fine sieve, discard the oysters. Add 1½ tablespoons soy sauce to the strained liquid, cool and refrigerate.

Seaweed. *See Kombu, above.*

Toasted Sesame Seed. Place 1 cup sesame seed and 1 teaspoon salt in a skillet, brown and toast seeds slowly until they are toast-colored and puffed. Stir constantly while toasting. Remove from fire, sprinkle with salt. Place in a mortar or in a blender and pound or blend until the seeds are pulverized. Bottle tightly.

Tofu. *See Bean Curd, above.*

White Sauce. To make this basic white sauce, melt 2 tablespoons of butter in the top of a double boiler over simmering water. Add 2 tablespoons of flour, stir until blended, add salt and pepper to taste and a pinch of grated nutmeg. While stirring constantly slowly add one cup of milk, stir for about 5 minutes until thickened and smooth, then cook over simmering water for 5 more minutes.

Basic metric conversions

Solid measures

15 grams	=	½ ounce
25 grams	=	1 ounce
50 grams	=	2 ounces
125 grams	=	4 ounces
225 grams	=	8 ounces
450 grams	=	1 pound
1 kilogram	=	2 pounds 2 ounces

Liquid measures

25 millilitres	=	1 fluid ounce
50 millilitres	=	2 fluid ounces
125 millilitres	=	4 fluid ounces
150 millilitres	=	5 fluid ounces
300 millilitres	=	10 fluid ounces
600 millilitres	=	1 pint
1 litre	=	1¾ pints

Contents

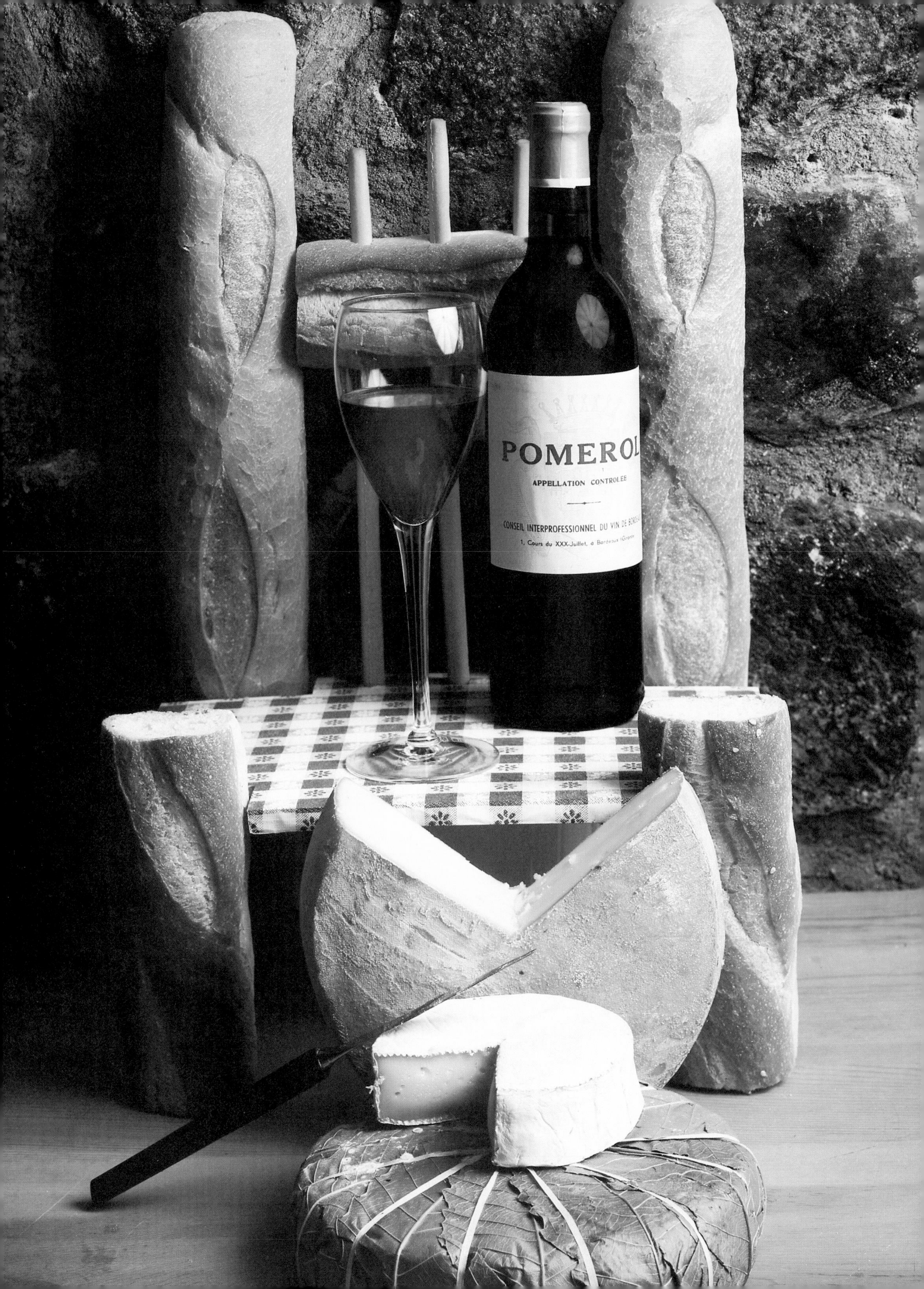
POMEROL
APPELLATION CONTROLEE

Appetizers

Greek Salad ▷

For Six
1 heart of romaine lettuce, shredded
1 Boston lettuce, shredded
1 heart of escarole, shredded
2 tomatoes, cut in wedges
1 medium cucumber, peeled and sliced
1 green pepper, seeded and cut in rings
sliced onion to taste
anchovy rings to taste
black olives
feta cheese, cut in small cubes

Dressing:
¼ cup olive oil
3 tbsp. lemon juice
salt and pepper to taste
1 clove garlic, crushed
1 tsp. oregano
1 tsp. dried mint leaves

Combine oil, lemon juice, salt, pepper, garlic, mint leaves and oregano; blend well. Arrange all other ingredients on a serving plate or on individual plates, spoon dressing over salad and serve.

9

Salade Niçoise

For Six

Boston or romaine lettuce
    leaves
2½ cups cooked green
    beans, cut in half
2½ cups cooked waxy
    potatoes, diced
2 cups canned tunafish,
    drained and broken
    into chunks
10 anchovy filets

5 hard-boiled eggs,
    cut in wedges
½ cup black olives,
    pitted
½ cup green olives,
    pitted
strips of canned pimiento
parsley, minced
3 tomatoes, peeled and
    cut into wedges

Dressing

Mix well:
1 tsp. Dijon mustard
½ tsp. dry mustard
salt and freshly ground
    pepper to taste

pinch of sugar
8 tbsp. olive oil
2 tbsp. tarragon
    wine vinegar
1 egg yolk

Mix green beans and potatoes with the dressing and let stand for an hour or so. Line a salad bowl with the crisped lettuce leaves, place the marinated vegetables in the center and the tunafish around them. Pour any remaining dressing over them. Then arrange the tomato wedges and egg wedges around the center. Cover egg wedges with anchovy filets, scatter olives and pimiento and sprinkle with parsley.

Egg Spreads

For Six to Eight

One
2 hard-boiled eggs
¼ cup mayonnaise

1½ tsp. anchovy paste
½ tsp. lemon juice
pinch of cayenne pepper

Three
2 hard-boiled eggs
¼ cup mayonnaise

1 tsp. curry powder
½ tsp. lemon juice

Rub eggs through a fine sieve or strainer, blend well with other ingredients. Chill for several hours.

Proceed as above.

Two
2 hard-boiled eggs
1½ tbsp. grated onion

¼ cup mayonnaise
2 tsp. minced parsley
salt and pepper to taste

Spread these mixtures on rounds of toast or dark bread; top with a slice of pitted olive, or a bit of pimiento, a sprinkle of paprika or a bit of parsley.

Proceed as above.

Baba Ghanoush

About Three Cups
4 medium eggplants
3 cloves garlic, crushed
salt and pepper to taste
½ cup tahini*
tomato slices

4 tbsp. lemon juice
    (or to taste)
2 tbsp. parsley, minced
pinch of cayenne
    pepper (opt.)
parsley

Cook eggplants under a broiler, turn them often and broil until the skin is charred and blistered and the eggplant is soft. Peel and wash the eggplant and squeeze out as much juice as possible. Mash the eggplant or process in a food processor, crush garlic with salt, add to eggplant and beat or process until creamy. Add tahini and lemon juice, a little of each at a time, add minced parsley and cayenne and beat until smooth. Chill, garnish with parsley and tomato slices.

*Tahini is ground sesame seeds. It is a rather thick oil or thin paste, available in all stores specializing in Greek and Middle Eastern foods.

Paella Salad

For Six to Eight

4 chicken breasts, split, boned and skinned
6 tbsp. olive or salad oil
¼ cup dry vermouth or white wine (or chicken broth)
salt
1 lb. shrimp, shelled and deveined
¼ tsp. powdered saffron

2 tsp. lemon juice
2 cups (about) chicken broth
1 medium onion, chopped
1 clove garlic, chopped
1½ cups uncooked rice
1½ cups small Spanish stuffed green olives
1 ripe avocado, sliced
watercress and tomato wedges

If desired, use skin and bones from chicken breasts for making chicken broth. Heat 3 tablespoons oil in large skillet. Add chicken and turn each piece to coat with oil. Add wine and sprinkle with 1½ teaspoons salt. Simmer 10 minutes. Turn chicken; add shrimp and simmer covered, 5 minutes, or until shrimp turn pink, set aside. Pour cooking liquid into large glass measuring cup and skim off fat. Stir in saffron and lemon juice; add enough chicken broth to make 2½ cups.

In same skillet, heat remaining 3 tablespoons oil; add onion and garlic and sauté until tender, stirring occasionally. Add rice and stir until rice turns slightly opaque. Add chicken broth mixture. Bring to a boil; cover, reduce heat and simmer 12 to 15 minutes or until rice is tender. Remove from heat. Cut chicken pieces into 2 or 3 diagonal slices and halve shrimp lengthwise. Add to rice with olives and toss lightly. Season to taste with salt. Cool, then chill. Arrange in salad bowl and garnish with avocado, watercress, tomatoes and lemon wedges, if desired. Serve with ¾ cup mayonnaise seasoned with 1 tablespoon brandy (optional) and 1 teaspoon lemon juice.

Devilled Stuffed Eggs ▷

For Six

6 hard-boiled eggs
3 tbsp. Dijon mustard
salt and pepper to taste
½ cup whipped cream
1 tsp. minced shallots
3 scallions, minced
1 cup mayonnaise
paprika

Cut eggs lengthwise in half. Remove yolks. Rub yolks through a sieve, blend well with 2 tbsp. mustard, salt and pepper. Blend in whipped cream, shallots and minced scallions. Using a pastry bag with a star tube, fill the egg whites with the mixture. Blend mayonnaise with remaining 1 tablespoon mustard, coat the eggs with the mayonnaise, sprinkle with paprika.

Cheddar and Herb Spread

2 cups grated cheddar
   cheese (white Vermont
   preferred)
4 tbsp. heavy cream
2 tbsp. sherry wine
1 tbsp. Cognac
3 tbsp. butter
2 tsp. minced chives

2 tsp. minced parsley
pinch of rosemary,
   crushed
pinch of thyme
1 tsp. dried tarragon,
   crushed
salt and pepper to taste
pinch of mace

Put cheese in top of a double boiler, melt over simmering water, add all other ingredients and blend with a whisk until smooth. Put in crocks, cover and refrigerate for a day or two before using.

Greek Cheese Dip

About One Cup

1 cup feta cheese
2 tbsp. milk
2 tbsp. olive oil

pepper to taste
¾ cup chopped parsley
4 tbsp. chopped dill

Rinse cheese with cold water, drain and crumble. Place cheese in a food processor or blender, add milk, oil, pepper and some of the parsley and dill. Process or blend for a few seconds, add remaining herbs, blend until smooth. Add a little more milk if the mixture is too stiff.

Serve as a dip with raw vegetables, or with crackers, or put some of the mixture on small slices of ham and roll up cigarette shaped.

Bean Spread

About Two Cups

½ cup dried white beans
1 clove garlic, crushed
2 tbsp. fresh lemon juice
6 tbsp. olive oil

1 tsp. paprika
salt and pepper to taste
1 tsp. chili powder
minced parsley

Soak beans overnight in water. Cook beans in water until soft. Drain and rub beans through a sieve. While still warm, add garlic and lemon juice, blend well, then beat in olive oil, paprika, salt, and pepper and chili powder. Put in a serving bowl and sprinkle with parsley.

Cheese and Ale Spread

1 lb. sharp cheddar cheese
¼ lb. roquefort cheese
   (or blue cheese)
1 stick butter
1 cup stale ale
   (or dark porter)

1 clove garlic, chopped
2 tbsp. grated onion
1 tbsp. Worcestershire sauce
1 tbsp. Dijon mustard
Tabasco sauce to taste
2 tsp. lemon juice

Cut cheeses into chunks. Mix with all other ingredients. Put half of the mixture into a food processor fitted with the steel blade or in a blender; process until smooth. Repeat with the other half. Pack spread into crocks and refrigerate for at least 24 hours before serving.

Appetizer Pie

One 9-inch Pie

1 package (8 oz.) cream
   cheese, softened
3 tbsp. sour cream
3 tbsp. pickle liquid (from
   sweet cucumber slices)
½ tsp. garlic salt
few grains pepper
¼ cup chopped sweet
   cucumber slices

3 drops Tabasco sauce
9-inch baked pastry shell
⅔ cup sweet cucumber
   slices
¾ lb. shrimp, peeled,
   deveined and cooked
1 hard-boiled egg, chopped
2 tbsp. red caviar
2 tbsp. chopped boiled ham
1 tbsp. chopped onion

Combine cream cheese, sour cream, pickle liquid, garlic salt, pepper and Tabasco; mix well. Stir in chopped pickles. Spread mixture in pastry shell. Arrange pickle slices, shrimp, egg and caviar in rings over cheese filling, leaving an empty space in the center. Combine ham and onion; place in center of pie. Cover tightly and chill at least 3 hours. Cut in wedges to serve.

Note: Pie can be made in a 9-inch pie plate or quiche pan, as desired.

Crab and Shrimp Chasseur

For Six

1 lb. shelled and deveined
  shrimp
  kgs. (6 oz. each)
  zen king crab meat

  ained
  mushrooms
  cup flour

1½ cups light cream
½ cup dry white wine
1 pkg. (5 oz.) triple cream
  cheese with herbs
  (Belletoile, Tartare or
  Boursin)
salt and pepper
patty shells

Cook shrimp, drain. Thaw crab and drain well. In a chafing dish over direct sterno heat, melt butter and sauté mushrooms for 1 minute. Sprinkle with flour. Gradually stir in cream and wine. Stir constantly until sauce bubbles and thickens. Add cheese, a small piece at a time, stirring after each addition until sauce is smooth. Stir in shrimp and crab meat. Remove from heat and place over hot water to keep warm. Reheat until piping hot. Season to taste with salt and pepper. Spoon mixture into patty shells.

Pizza à la Garibaldi ▷

For Four

uncooked bread dough sufficient
  for 1 medium sized loaf
½ cup olive oil
1 cup grated Parmesan cheese
2 cups stuffed green olives
1 cup black olives, pitted
12 anchovy filets, drained
2 cups tomato sauce (p. 248)
1 tbsp. dried marjoram

Roll out the dough into a 12-inch round, leaving the outer rim a little thicker than the center. Generously oil a baking sheet and put the dough on it. Sprinkle the dough with a little olive oil and with the grated cheese. Place the stuffed green olives, the black olives and anchovy filets neatly on the dough. Top with tomato sauce, sprinkle with marjoram and a little more olive oil. Bake in a preheated 400⁰ oven for 25 minutes.

Drunken Chicken

For Four

2 whole chicken breasts,
  boned
water
2 scallions, chopped

1 clove garlic, crushed
2 slices fresh ginger root
2 tsp. salt
sherry

Put water, scallions, garlic, and ginger root in a saucepan
and bring to a boil. Add chicken breasts, cover and simmer
for 10 minutes. Remove from heat and let stand covered for
15 minutes. Drain chicken, remove and discard skin. Sprinkle chicken with salt and put in a jar with tight fitting
cover. Fill jar with sherry, enough to cover the chicken, and
refrigerate for 3 to 4 days. Before serving, drain and cut into
bite size cubes. Serve cold.

Eggplant Caviar

For Four

4 small or 1 large eggplant
1 small onion
3 green or sweet red
  peppers seeded
salt and pepper to taste

2 tbsp. lemon juice
1 large clove garlic,
  crushed
1 cup olive oil
sliced tomatoes
black olives

Put eggplant under a broiler or roast in hot oven until the
skin is black and the eggplant soft and cooked. Cover eggplant with a damp cloth for about 10 minutes, then peel off
charred skin. Put eggplant, peppers and onion through a
grinder, season with salt and pepper, add lemon juice and
garlic. Then add, while beating constantly, the oil in a thin
stream. Add more lemon juice, salt and pepper if needed.
Chill well, garnish with tomato slices and black olives.

Lipto Cheese Spread

About One Cup

½ lb. cream cheese
2 tsp. paprika
1 tsp. prepared mustard
1 small onion, grated
3 anchovy filets, mashed

½ tsp. crushed caraway
  seeds
1 tsp. capers, drained
  and chopped
¼ cup beer

Press cheese through a strainer and blend well with all
other ingredients. Let stand for a few hours or overnight
before serving. Serve on squares of dark bread.

If you have a food processor, put all ingredients in the
bowl and process with the steel blade for a few seconds.

Note: This spread is made in Hungary with a rather
sharp sheep cheese. Some cheese stores carry a very similar imported sheep cheese, "brindza". If you can buy
brindza, use it instead of cream cheese but add a quarter
pound of butter to the mixture.

Lebanese Salad (Tabbouleh)

For Six

1 cup bulgur (cracked
  wheat)
2½ cups chopped broad
  leaf (Italian) parsley
2 tbsp. fresh mint leaves,
  chopped

6 scallions
3 firm ripe tomatoes
3 tbsp. fresh lemon juice
  (or to taste)
½ cup olive oil
salt and pepper to taste

Place bulgur in a bowl, cover with cold water and let soak
for one hour. Drain and squeeze out as much water as possible.

Chop scallions (green and white parts). Chop 2 tomatoes. Combine bulgur with scallions, mint leaves, chopped
tomatoes, lemon juice and oil. Chill well. Garnish with
remaining tomato cut in wedges.

◊ Boereks
Triangles

Unfold the sheets in a package of phyllo dough and place them on a slightly dampened towel. Cut the stack lengthwise into 4 rectangular strips, each about 3 inches wide. Cover with a slightly dampened towel to prevent drying out. Take one strip at a time, brush the sheet with melted butter. Place a teaspoon of filling near the narrow edge of the strip, fold one corner over the filling to shape a triangle. Then fold the triangle over again, and continue doing so until the whole strip has been folded into a triangle. Tuck the end of the strip into the triangle and butter the edge to make it stick together. Put on oiled baking sheets, brush the triangles with melted butter and bake at 350⁰ for about 25 minutes until golden brown.

Cigarette Shaped

Cut strips a little wider than for triangular boereks, butter the strips, place a little filling at the narrow end of the strip, fold both long edges towards the middle to cover the filling, then roll up like a cigarette. Butter edge to make it stick together. Place rolls close together on oiled baking sheets and brush the tops with melted butter. Bake at 350⁰ for 25 minutes until golden brown.

Meat Filling

About 45 Boereks
½ lb. ground lamb
  (or beef)
1½ tbsp. butter
1 medium onion, grated
1 small clove garlic,
  crushed
1 tsp. paprika

1 tbsp. tomato paste
1 egg, lightly beaten
½ cup parsley, chopped
2 tbsp. fresh dill, chopped
salt and pepper to taste
2 tbsp. water
½ lb. phyllo sheets
melted butter

Heat 1½ tablespoons butter in a skillet, sauté meat and onion until lightly browned, add garlic, tomato paste, paprika and 2 tablespoons water, blend and cook 5 minutes longer. Remove from heat, blend in egg, parsley, dill, salt and pepper. Fill desired shape and bake, see above.

Cheese Filling

About 45 Boereks
6 oz. feta cheese
6 oz. cream cheese
6 oz. farmer cheese or
  1 cup pot cheese
2 eggs, lightly beaten
2 tbsp. milk

1 tbsp. Worcestershire sauce
½ cup parsley, chopped
¼ cup fresh dill, chopped
pinch of grated nutmeg
pepper to taste
melted butter
½ lb. phyllo sheets

Blend cheeses, eggs, milk and Worcestershire sauce until smooth, mix in all other ingredients. Fill desired shape and bake, see above.

Chicken Liver Terrine

For Six to Eight
4 tbsp. butter
1 lb. chicken livers
½ tsp. dried thyme
1 small bay leaf

salt and pepper to taste
1 tbsp. minced shallots
¼ cup port wine
¾ cup butter, softened
3 egg whites, beaten stiff

Heat 4 tablespoons butter in a skillet, add chicken livers, thyme and bay leaf; season with salt and pepper and sauté over high heat for about 2 minutes, stirring a few times. Add shallots, cook another minute or two. Remove from heat, discard bay leaf. Reserve six chicken livers and put remainder in a bowl. Pour port wine over the livers and let stand for 1 hour, then mash livers with a fork or in a mortar into a smooth paste. Rub the paste through a fine sieve (or use a food processor to do the entire procedure). With a wooden spoon beat the softened butter into the paste, correct seasoning. Fold beaten egg whites into the mixture. Fill a 1½ quart terrine or loaf pan with half the liver mixture. Distribute the reserved whole livers on top and cover with remaining liver mixture. Cover with a lid or aluminum foil, chill for 24 hours.

Crab a la Russe ▷

For Four
2 quarts water
2 onions, chopped
2 carrots, chopped
sprig of thyme, 1 bay leaf, 2 sprigs
    parsley tied together
¼ cup vinegar
salt to taste
6 peppercorns
12 hard-shelled crabs
1½ cups mayonnaise
2 tbsp. capers
1 tbsp. tomato purée

Heat the water in a kettle, add onions, carrots, herbs, salt and pepper and vinegar. Bring to a rolling boil and boil for 5 minutes. Add crabs. Bring to a boil again and simmer for 10 minutes. Drain and cool the crabs, open them, pick out all the meat. Reserve 4 of the empty shells. Flake the crabmeat and blend it with ½ cup mayonnaise.

Stuff the 4 crab shells with the crabmeat and sprinkle a few capers over each shell. Stir the tomato purée into the remaining mayonnaise and serve it in a sauceboat.

Della Robbia Brie

Place a wheel of Brie (weighing about 2 pounds) on a round cheese board or serving platter 3 or 4 inches larger than the Brie itself to allow space for an attractive arrangement of frosted Tokay, Concord and green grapes, slices of red and golden delicious apples, and slices of Anjou and Bosc pears, to create a colorful Della Robbia effect. Arrange platter in advance and keep chilled. About one hour before serving, place platter on table to serve as centerpiece. By the time you are ready for dessert, the cheese will have reached room temperature, and be ready for serving. To serve, cut cheese from center to outer rim into long, thin triangular wedges (about one-inch at rim). Place it on the dessert plate with a small bunch of grapes, 2 - 4 slices of fruit, a few unsalted pecans and 2 - 3 thin slices of French baguette.

To frost grapes: Cut individual portions of grapes from the main bunch. Dip them into lemon juice or slightly beaten egg white, then granulated sugar. Chill 15 - 20 minutes, then repeat process.

Terrine of Pork and Veal

For Eight
2 lbs. lean pork
2 lbs. shoulder of veal
    (boneless)
2 tsp. salt
pepper to taste
½ tsp. allspice (ground)
¼ tsp. mace

1 pinch powdered ginger
1 large carrot, peeled
    and chopped
1 onion stuck with
    4 whole cloves
2 cups dry white wine
2 envelopes unflavored
    gelatin

Put meats in a pot with cold water and bring to a boil. Drain, rinse meat under running cold water. Return meats and all other ingredients except gelatin to the pot, add water to cover and simmer over low heat about 2 hours. Remove the meat and chop it coarsely. Boil the broth until it is reduced to 4 cups, then strain through a fine sieve. Return the liquid to the pot, add the chopped meat and simmer for 15 minutes. Correct the seasoning. Soften the gelatin in a little cold water, pour meat and broth into it, blend and chill until well set. Unmold and cut into slices. Garnish with fresh parsley.

Onion Tart

For Four
1 recipe pate brisée
4 large onions
3 tbsp. butter
1 cup heavy cream
1 cup milk

4 eggs
1 cup grated Swiss cheese
salt and white pepper
¼ cup fine white
    breadcrumbs

Make the pate brisée and let rest for an hour. Cook onions in butter in a heavy saucepan over low heat for about 10 minutes or until they are soft. Do not let them brown. Beat the cream together with the milk, eggs and grated cheese. Season to taste with salt and pepper. Roll out the pastry to ⅛ inch thick, line with it a 9-inch pie plate or a flan ring placed on a baking sheet. Spread the onions on the pastry and pour egg mixture over the onions. Sprinkle with breadcrumbs. Bake in a preheated 350° oven for about 30 minutes. Serve immediately.

◁ Marinated Shrimp with Olives and Mushrooms

For Six
1 lb. fresh, firm
   mushrooms, quartered
1 cup water
⅓ cup olive oil
⅔ cup vinegar
2 tbsp. lemon juice
2 cloves garlic, halved
salt to taste

½ tsp. thyme
½ tsp. black peppercorns
pinch of grated nutmeg
pinch of cayenne pepper
2 bay leaves
¾ cup pimiento-stuffed
   green Spanish olives
2 lbs. medium shrimp,
   cleaned and cooked

Combine mushrooms, water, oil, vinegar, lemon juice and seasonings in a saucepan. Bring to a boil, cover and cook for 5 minutes. Pour into a bowl, add olives and shrimp, toss and cool. Chill for a few hours or overnight before serving.

Note: Do not overcook shrimp. Put them in cold water, bring to a boil and simmer for 1 minute. Let cool in the cooking liquid.

Steak Tartare ▷

For Four
1½ lbs. beef filet or very
   lean top round
4 egg yolks
⅓ cup minced onion
2 tbsp. capers, drained
2 tbsp. parsley, minced
1 tbsp. caraway seed
1 tbsp. paprika
salt and pepper to taste

Trim all gristle and sinews off the meat and grind or mince very fine. Make four patties, arrange them on a serving platter. Make a depression in the center of each patty and drop an egg yolk in each depression. Arrange all other ingredients in neat little piles around the meat, and let each person mix the patty with the egg yolks and other ingredients to taste. Serve with buttered black bread.

Avocado Cream

About Two Cups

1 avocado, peeled and
    pit removed
⅔ cup sour cream
½ cup mayonnaise
2 tbsp. parsley, minced
1 tbsp. paprika

1 tbsp. onion, grated
1 small clove garlic,
    crushed
1 tbsp. lime juice
1 pinch cayenne pepper
salt and pepper to taste

Put all ingredients in a blender or food processor and blend until very smooth. Use as a dip or on fish, cold meats or salads.

Guacamole

For Four

2 ripe avocados
2 medium tomatoes, peeled,
    seeded and chopped
2 tbsp. grated onion
2 green chili peppers
    (fresh or canned), chopped

1 tbsp. olive oil
1 tbsp. lemon juice
1 tbsp. lime juice
salt and pepper to taste
½ tsp. ground coriander
    (opt.)

Mash peeled avocados with a fork, blend in lemon and lime juice, and then all other ingredients.

Cold Ratatouille

For Six to Eight

2 eggplants, peeled,
    cut into 1-inch cubes
    (about 4 cups)
4 zucchini, washed,
    unpeeled, cut into 1-inch
    cubes (about 4 cups)
1¼ cups olive oil
2 large cloves garlic,
    minced
3 large firm tomatoes,
    peeled, seeded,
    coarsely chopped

1 large onion, minced
salt and pepper to taste
1 tsp. dried basil, crumbled
1 tbsp. parsley, minced
pinch of thyme
½ cup dry white wine
¼ cup wine vinegar
1 tbsp. lemon juice
    (or to taste)
⅓ cup ripe black olives,
    pitted, chopped
2 tbsp. chives, chopped

Heat oil in a heavy saucepan, sauté eggplant and zucchini for 5 minutes; add onion and garlic, cook gently for 5 more minutes. Add tomatoes, salt, pepper, basil, parsley, thyme, wine, vinegar and lemon juice and black olives; mix well and simmer 5 to 6 minutes longer. Correct seasoning. Pour into a serving dish, chill well. Sprinkle with chives before serving.

Hummus

About Two Cups

1 cup cooked chick peas
    (canned may be used)
juice of 2 lemons
3 cloves garlic, crushed

salt to taste
½ cup tahini*
1 tsp. paprika
1 tbsp. parsley, chopped

Rub chick peas through a sieve, beat in tahini and lemon juice, a little at a time, until smooth. Add garlic and salt and beat again until well blended and smooth. A food pro-cessor or electric blender will greatly simplify the preparation and produce a smoother dip. Put ingredients in the processor or blender and blend until smooth. When serving, sprinkle with paprika and parsley. Use as a dip or spread on toast fingers or crackers.

*Tahini is ground sesame seeds. It is a rather thick oil or a thin paste, available in all stores specializing in Greek and Middle Eastern food.

Pate Brisée

For a Nine inch Tart
2 cups sifted all-purpose
   flour
1 whole egg
½ tsp. salt
3 tbsp. heavy cream
¾ cup sweet butter

Place the flour in large bowl and make a well in the center. Put the whole egg, salt, cream and butter into it. Gradually blend the flour into the other ingredients. Knead the pastry until smooth. Chill in the refrigerator for at least 2 hours before rolling out.

Piquante Anchovies

For Four to Six
2 cans anchovy filets
½ small clove garlic,
   crushed
2 tbsp. minced parsley
1 tbsp. minced shallots
1 tsp. lemon juice
1 tsp. wine vinegar

Drain the oil off the anchovies, combine oil with all other ingredients and blend well. Separate anchovy filets and arrange them on a serving dish, spoon the oil mixture over them and let stand for an hour or two before serving.

Ham Mousse

For Six
½ lb. cooked ham
8 tbsp. butter
1 cup heavy cream
salt and pepper to taste
pinch of dried thyme
2 tbsp. pimiento, diced
   small
pinch of mace
2 envelopes unflavored
   gelatin
½ cup Madeira wine
   (Sercial)
1 cup chicken broth
¼ cup Armagnac or
   Cognac

Grind ham with the finest blade of the grinder or use a food processor, then blend well with softened butter. Blend in cream, salt and pepper, thyme, mace and pimiento. Bring the chicken broth to a boil, soften the gelatin in the Madeira and then add to and dissolve in the hot broth. Cool the broth, blend in with the ham mixture, then add the Cognac. Blend once more. Correct the seasoning, pack into a mold and refrigerate.

Baked Scallops ⇨

For Four
1 ½ lbs. bay scallops (or sea
　scallops cut in half)
1 large egg
1 tbsp. water
½ tsp. tarragon
1 small clove garlic, crushed
¼ tsp. basil
salt and pepper to taste
dry breadcrumbs
4 tbsp. melted butter

Beat egg until light and creamy, add water, herbs, garlic, salt and pepper, blend well. Coat scallops with egg mixture, then roll in breadcrumbs. Put them in a shallow buttered baking dish, sprinkle with melted butter and bake in 450° oven for about 8 minutes. Serve on hot toast, garnish with lemon wedges and parsley.

⇧ Stuffed Grape Leaves

About Thirty Pieces
2 large onions, minced
2 tbsp. water
1 tsp. salt
⅔ cup long grain rice
¾ cup olive oil
1 tbsp. fresh mint, chopped
1 tbsp. fresh dill, chopped
　(save stems)

½ cup parsley, chopped
　(save stems)
2 tbsp. lemon juice
2 tbsp. pine nuts
2 tbsp. currants
salt and pepper to taste
12 oz. jar of grape leaves
1 cup water

Put onions in a saucepan, add 2 tablespoons water and 1 teaspoon salt, cover and simmer for 10 minutes. Remove from fire, mix with rice, add ½ cup oil, mix well. Add mint, dill, parsley, 1 tablespoon lemon juice, pine nuts, currants, salt, pepper; blend. Wash grape leaves to remove all brine, separate leaves. If leaves are very large, cut them in half. Place 1 tablespoon filling on the rough side of each leaf, fold leaf from the sides of the middle, covering the filling, and roll up tightly. Arrange dill and parsley stems in the bottom of a saucepan, add remaining oil and lemon juice. Place rolls on top of the stems, close together, top with more layers of rolls. Pour water over the rolls, cover them with wax paper and place a plate over the wax paper to weigh the rolls down. Cook over gentle heat for about 1 hour, until all water has been absorbed and rice is cooked. Add more water during cooking if needed. When cooked, remove from pan and cool. Serve garnished with lemon wedges.

Quiche Lorraine

For Six to Eight
1 recipe pate brisée (p. 27)
½ lb. lean bacon slices
2 tbsp. butter
4 egg yolks, beaten
   lightly

2 tbsp. flour
1 cup heavy cream
1 cup milk
salt and pepper to taste
¼ tsp. grated nutmeg
⅓ lb. sliced Swiss cheese

Line a 9-inch pan with pate brisée and chill thoroughly.

Sauté bacon in butter until it is translucent. Mix the flour with eggs, heavy cream and milk; season lightly with salt, pepper and nutmeg. Line the bottom of the tart pastry with the cheese and bacon slices, pour the egg mixture over them. Cook in a preheated 375⁰ oven for about 25 minutes or until the custard is set. Serve immediately.

Liver Mousse

For Six
½ lb. chicken livers (or
   duck or turkey livers)
5 tbsp. cooking oil
⅓ cup onions, minced
4 shallots, minced
1 clove garlic, minced
pinch of mace
small pinch of allspice

small pinch of powdered
   ginger
pinch of dry thyme
1 bay leaf
salt and pepper to taste
8 tbsp. butter
1 cup heavy cream
¼ cup Cognac
1 envelope plain gelatin

Sauté livers in oil over high flame for 4 minutes. Then add onions, garlic, shallots, spices and herbs and season with salt and pepper. Cook another 3 minutes. Remove bay leaf and discard. Rub everything else through a fine sieve or place in the bowl of a food processor and chop fine with the steel blade. Blend in the butter, then the heavy cream. Soften gelatin in a tablespoon of cold water, then dissolve in a couple of spoonfuls of hot water; add gelatin and Cognac to liver mixture, blend again and pack in a mold. Refrigerate well.

Braised Endive Vinaigrette

For Four
4 medium endives
½ cup water
½ tbsp. lemon juice
1 tbsp. oil

1 tsp. sugar
salt and white pepper
1 tbsp. parsley, minced
Vinaigrette sauce (p. 315)

Trim root end of endives, remove any loose leaves, wash and put in a casserole. Add water, lemon juice, oil, sugar, salt and pepper. Bring to a boil, cover and simmer for about 45 minutes. Remove endives, let cool and squeeze out most of the cooking liquid. Shape them, put in a serving dish, cover with Vinaigrette sauce, sprinkle with parsley.

Leeks Vinaigrette

For Four
6 medium sized leeks
Vinaigrette sauce (p. 315)
1 tsp. Dijon mustard

1 tbsp. parsley, minced
1 tsp. chives, chopped
1 tsp. shallots, very
    finely minced

Trim leeks, use the white part only. Cut them lengthwise in half and wash carefully under running water. They are usually quite sandy. Simmer them in salt water for about 45 minutes until tender. Remove, drain well and cool. Mix Vinaigrette sauce with mustard, add herbs and shallots, blend and cover leeks with the sauce. Let stand for an hour before serving.

Mexican Corn and Chicken Salad

For Six
3 cups diced cooked chicken
4 medium ears sweet corn
1 cup diced, green pepper
1 tomato, peeled, seeded,
    diced

1 tbsp. lemon juice
⅓ cup mayonnaise
1 tsp. chili powder
cayenne pepper to taste
salt and pepper to taste
2 hard-boiled eggs, sliced

Cook corn in water to cover with 1 teaspoon salt and lemon juice. Cook for 5 minutes — long enough to set the milk of the corn kernels. Drain, cut corn from cob and chill. Combine with diced chicken, green pepper, tomato, mayonnaise, chili powder, cayenne, salt and pepper. Chill, put in a serving bowl, garnish with egg slices.

Chicken on Skewers

For Six
1 chicken breast, skinned
    and boned
½ lb. lean bacon, cut in
    1-inch squares
4 water chestnuts, sliced
    very thin

3 tbsp. soy sauce
1 tbsp. sherry
1 tbsp. brown sugar
¼ tsp. hot mustard
1 tsp. shredded ginger
1 scallion, minced
1 clove garlic, crushed

Combine all ingredients except chicken, water chestnuts, bacon and glaze. Marinate the chicken breast in this mixture for 3 hours. Then remove from marinade, pat dry and slice very thin, across the grain. Thread alternating pieces of chicken, bacon and water chestnuts on small skewers, brush with glaze and broil or deep fry.

Glaze:
2 tbsp. honey

1½ tbsp. soy sauce
½ tbsp. sherry

◊Chopped Chicken Liver

For Six

1 lb. chicken livers
2 large onions, chopped
4 tbsp. chicken fat

4 egg yolks, hard-boiled
1 small clove garlic, minced
salt and pepper to taste

Wash livers in cold water, pat dry and broil for about 4 minutes until browned on both sides. Sauté onions and garlic in chicken fat until just lightly browned. Grind livers, onions and egg yolks, blend in fat left from frying onions, season with salt and pepper.

Shrimp Paté

For Six to Eight

2 cups shrimp, cooked,
  shelled, deveined
3 tbsp. lemon juice
2 tsp. dried dill leaves
salt and white pepper
  to taste

2 dashes Tabasco sauce
  (or to taste)
1 small clove garlic,
  chopped
pinch of grated nutmeg
½ cup olive oil

Place all ingredients except oil in a food processor or blender, add oil gradually, process until smooth.

Nachos   ⬦

Nachos are served as appetizers with a great variety of fillings. They are small tortillas, crisp fried in deep fat, then spread with fried beans, grilled cheese, chopped sautéed meat or other fillings.

Corn Tortillas

For about 24 Nachos

2 cups masa harina (corn flour)
1¼ cups warm water
1 tsp. salt

Combine masa and salt in a bowl, add water and mix well until dough holds together in a ball. Don't use too much water, the dough should not be sticky. Let dough rest for half an hour. Divide the dough in 16 pieces and shape each into a ball. Put the balls of dough on wax paper or a moist cloth, flatten them slightly with your hand, cover with wax paper or cloth and roll them to the desired thickness. They should be about 6 inches in diameter. Trim evenly before cooking.

To cook tortillas: Heat a soap stone griddle or a cast iron skillet, not greased, over medium heat and cook tortillas for about 2 minutes on each side. They should be still soft and lightly flecked with brown.

Herring Salad

5 marinated (pickled)
  herring filets
1 medium dill pickle,
  chopped
1 medium onion, minced
1 small clove garlic,
  minced
1 medium apple, pared,
  peeled and chopped
3 red radishes, chopped

2 hard-boiled eggs,
  chopped
1 large tomato, peeled
  and diced
4 tbsp. soft white
  breadcrumbs
¼ cup wine vinegar
4 tbsp. salad oil
1 tsp. sugar
pepper to taste

Dice the herring filets, blend well with all other ingredients, chill before serving.

Shrimp and Rice Salad ⇨

For Six

12 oz. peeled cooked shrimp
  (about 2 cups)
2 cups cool cooked rice
1 cup diced celery
½ cup sliced green onions
  with tops

⅓ cup each diced green
  pepper and sweet pickles
2 hard-boiled eggs, diced
⅔ cup mayonnaise
1 tbsp. lemon juice
salt and pepper to taste

Cut shrimp in half lengthwise, if desired. Combine all ingredients and mix well. Chill. Serve on crisp greens and garnish with cherry tomatoes and parsley, if desired.

Garlic Provençale

For Four

¼ cup light olive oil
2 doz. large cloves garlic,
  unpeeled
½ cup dry white wine

salt and pepper to taste
4 anchovy filets
4 slices buttered toast
2 tbsp. minced parsley

Heat oil in a small saucepan, add unpeeled cloves of garlic and sauté over medium heat for 2 or 3 minutes. Add wine, salt and pepper, let come to a boil. Cover and simmer for 15 minutes.

Remove garlic from pan. Squeeze garlic out of the skin onto the toast. (It will pop out quite easily). Spread with a knife. Top each piece of toast with an anchovy filet, spoon some of the wine sauce over each slice. Sprinkle with parsley and serve piping hot.

Falafel

1 lb. dried white beans
2 red onions, minced
2 large cloves garlic,
  crushed
3 tbsp. parsley, minced
½ tsp. ground coriander

1 tsp. ground cumin
1 tsp. paprika
½ tsp. baking powder
2 tbsp. flour
salt and pepper to taste
oil for frying

Soak beans overnight or longer in water to cover. Rub off skins and grind with the fine blade of a meat grinder or better, put in a food processor with all other ingredients except oil. Process or grind and blend to a smooth paste. Spoon out pieces the size of a walnut, flatten into small patties, let stand for half an hour. Fry in hot oil until well browned. Serve with tomato or cucumber salad.

Mushrooms Cote d'Argent

For Six

12 firm white mushroom
  caps, medium to large size
lemon juice
2 doz. large, pimiento-
  stuffed olives
3 cloves garlic, minced

2 anchovy filets, minced
1 tbsp. olive oil
¼ lb. cooked ham, ground
white breadcrumbs
salt and pepper to taste
butter

Remove mushroom stems, wipe the caps gently with a damp cloth. Add lemon juice to 3 cups of water, bring to a boil and blanch the mushrooms for 2 minutes. Drain well. Combine all other ingredients except butter. Fill each mushroom cap heaping full, dot with a small piece of butter and bake in a preheated 425° oven for 10 minutes.

Stuffed Mussels

For Four

2 doz. large fresh mussels	½ cup long grain rice
1 tsp. salt	¼ cup pine nuts
½ cup dry white wine	¼ cup currants
1 cup water	2 tbsp. parsley, chopped
2 large onions, chopped	1 tsp. lemon juice
½ cup olive oil	pepper to taste

Scrub mussels well, remove beard. Place in a saucepan, add water, wine, salt; cover and cook for about 10 minutes until mussels open. Discard any that did not open. Remove mussels from shells, reserve shells. Strain liquid and reserve.

In a skillet sauté onions in olive oil until soft. Do not brown. Add rice, sauté 3 minutes stirring constantly — do not scorch rice. Add one cup of mussel juice, cover and cook gently for 15 minutes. Add all other ingredients except mussels, stir with a fork, cover and cook another five minutes or so until rice is cooked. Mix mussels into the rice and heat through. Fill shells with the stuffing and serve hot or cold.

To make mussel shells more attractive, rub them with a little oil.

Egg-Rice Salad

For Six

⅓ cup sliced green onions
1½ cups sliced celery
⅓ cup sweet pickle relish
3 cups cooked rice
6 hard-boiled eggs, chopped
1 cup mayonnaise
salt and pepper to taste

Combine ingredients. Chill. Fill custard cups or individual molds with salad mixture, pressing down firmly with spoon. Unmold on lettuce leaves. Garnish with ripe olives and tomato wedges if desired.

Garlic Eggs

For Six

1 large clove garlic, crushed
3 anchovy filets, mashed
1 tsp. capers, chopped
1 tsp. chili powder
1 tsp. lemon juice
4 tbsp. olive oil
salt and pepper to taste
6 hard-boiled eggs

Combine all ingredients except eggs and blend well. Quarter the eggs, coat with the garlic sauce.

Mussels in Marinade

For Six

2 qts. mussels
2 tbsp. olive oil
1½ tbsp. minced shallots
1 medium clove garlic,
    minced
4 anchovy filets, mashed

¼ cup dry white wine
½ cup white wine vinegar
1 tbsp. minced parsley
1 small bay leaf
½ tsp. crushed basil
salt and pepper to taste
dash of Tabasco sauce

Scrub mussels, remove beards, put in a saucepan with ¼ cup water. Cover and steam open over high heat. Drain, discard all mussels that have not opened. Remove mussels from shells and reserve.

Heat oil in a saucepan, add shallots and garlic, sauté gently until soft but not browned. Add anchovies, blend well, add wine and vinegar and cook rapidly until liquid is reduced by half. Add mussels and all other ingredients and simmer gently for 2 minutes. Pour contents in a glass or ceramic dish, cover and refrigerate for 3 days before serving.

Gravlax (Salt and Sugar Cured Salmon)

For Eight to Ten

3 to 4 lbs. center cut
    of fresh salmon
½ cup sugar
½ cup coarse (kosher) salt

1¼ cups coarsely chopped
    fresh dill
1 tbsp. crushed white
    peppercorns

Scale the salmon, do not skin. Bone it or have it boned. There should be two equal size sections. Do *not* rinse the salmon, but wipe it well and pat dry. Mix salt, sugar and pepper and rub both sides of the fish with the mixture. Sprinkle some of the mixture and a little dill in a glass or stainless steel dish. Place one half of the salmon, skin side down, in the pan. Cover the cut side with dill, more of the salt-sugar mixture and place the second half of the fish on top. Sprinkle top with remaining salt and sugar, cover with aluminum foil and weigh down lightly. Store in refrigerator for 3 days. Pour off every day any liquid accumulated in bottom of the pan and turn the fish every day. Before serving, wipe dry and slice on a bias like smoked salmon.

Serve with a **Mustard Dill Sauce**

¼ cup oil
2 tbsp. white wine vinegar
1 tbsp. sugar

salt and pepper to taste
2 tbsp. Dijon mustard
3 tbsp. minced dill

Combine all ingredients and blend well.

Note: For added flavor, add to the salmon marinade a few crushed juniper berries.

Clams a la Bourguignonne

For Four

24 clams
⅔ cup butter
1 large clove garlic, crushed

4 tbsp. parsley, minced
salt and freshly ground
    pepper to taste

Shuck clams, reserve meat and 24 half shells. Rinse clams in a little dry white wine. (This is optional, but it does enhance the flavor of the clams.) Pat clams dry and place each on one half shell. Blend all other ingredients, cover clams with the butter mixture and bake at 400° for about 6 to 7 minutes, until hot and bubbly.

Note: Oysters and bay scallops can be prepared the same way.

Clams Casino

For Four

2 doz. clams
3 tbsp. butter
3 anchovy filets (mashed)
2 tbsp. green pepper, minced

2 tbsp. canned pimiento, chopped
pepper to taste
4 slices lean bacon
coarse or rock salt

Shuck clams, drain and reserve clams along with one half shell for each. Cream butter and blend with mashed anchovies. Put a small pat of anchovy butter in each of 24 half clam shells, place a shucked clam on top of each, sprinkle with a little green pepper and pimiento, season with pepper and cover with a small piece of lemon.

Cover the bottom of a shallow baking pan with coarse salt or rock salt, place clams on top and broil under a very hot preheated broiler, about 3 inches from the flame, for about 3 to 4 minutes.

Taramasalata

About One Cup

⅓ of an 8-oz. jar of tarama (mullet roe)
2 tbsp. grated onion
1 small clove garlic, crushed (opt.)

1½ cups olive oil (approx.)
juice of 2 lemons
4 slices of white bread, crust removed, moistened with water and squeezed dry

Blend tarama, onion and garlic. Add oil slowly while beating as if making a mayonnaise. Add alternating, while beating, pieces of bread, a little lemon juice and oil. Continue until tarama is cream colored and light. A tablespoon or two of water beaten in at the end will make the tarama fluffier. Serve as a dip with crackers or toast fingers.

Note: Smoked codfish roe can be used instead of mullet roe.

Kibbeh

For Eight to Ten
1 lb. lean lamb (leg or
    shoulder)
1 large onion

salt and pepper to taste
2 tbsp. ice water
1 cup fine bulgur
    (cracked, wheat)

This dish is best prepared in a food processor, combining lamb, onion, salt, pepper and ice water, and processing with the steel blade until the mixture is reduced to a fine paste. Then place bulgur in a strainer, rinse with cold water and squeeze out as much moisture as you can. Blend into the meat mixture, knead for a few minutes to blend well, then put in the processor again and blend until smooth.

Without a processor the preparation is a bit more time consuming. Put meat several times through a grinder, grate the onion and grind, mix with bulgur and grind again.

This is a raw meat appetizer, the Middle-East version of Beef Tartare.

Broiled Kibbeh
Use the same ingredients as for Kibbeh above, increase the amount of bulgur to 1½ cups, shape into small patties and broil until nicely browned.

Meat Salad

4 cups of lean cooked
    pork or beef, cut
    in julienne strips
1 onion, sliced paper thin
2 tbsp. capers, drained
    and chopped
2 tbsp. pimiento-stuffed
    green olives, sliced

¼ cup olive oil
3 tbsp. wine vinegar
1 tsp. oregano
1 tsp. Dijon mustard
1 anchovy filet, mashed
salt and pepper to taste
2 tbsp. chives, chopped

Arrange meat in a shallow serving bowl, top with the sliced onion, sprinkle with capers, olives and chives. Combine and blend all other ingredients, pour over the meat. Chill well before serving.

Chirashi Sushi   ⟡

Sushi is a Japanese specialty. They are rice rolls or patties, covered with a great variety of foods, slices of raw fish or octopus or squid, shrimp or lobster; others are covered with sheets of seaweed.

To properly roll and present the great variety of sushi rolls requires a considerable amount of dexterity. The easiest to prepare is a rather delightful dish — on the order of a mixed rice salad.

For Four to Six
3 cups sushi rice
4 dried Japanese mushrooms
1 tbsp. soy sauce
1 tsp. mirin*
1 cup cooked shrimp,
    shelled, deveined
½ cup finely sliced raw
    tuna or bass filet (opt.)
1 tbsp. oil

1 canned bamboo shoot,
    sliced
1 canned lotus root, sliced
½ cup cooked green peas
2 eggs, lightly beaten
1 tbsp. pickled seaweed
    (kombu), sliced*
1 tbsp. pickled red ginger,
    shredded
salt to taste

Soak mushrooms in scalding water for half an hour. Drain, discard stems and slice mushrooms thinly. Save half a cup of the water they soaked in. Place the half cup water in a saucepan, add soy sauce, mirin and the sliced mushrooms. Cook gently for 10 minutes. Drain. Cut shrimp in slices. Heat oil in a skillet, add eggs and make a thin omelette, do not let it brown. Cool the omelette and slice in narrow strips. Boil bamboo shoots and lotus root in water for about 5 to 6 minutes until cooked but still crisp.

Mix all ingredients carefully into the rice — decorate the top with a few slices of lotus root, shrimp and the pickled ginger.

Rice for Sushi

2½ cups medium-grain rice
2¾ cups water
2-inch piece dried
    kombu (opt.)*
2 tbsp. sugar

5 tbsp. rice vinegar
    (or mild white vinegar)
2 tsp. salt
2 tbsp. mirin*
¼ tsp. MSG (opt.)

Wash rice well under running cold water, drain and let stand for 30 minutes. Put in a saucepan with 2¾ cups water. Rinse the kombu well, add to rice. Bring quickly to a boil, cover pan, turn heat low and simmer for 15 minutes. Do not uncover. Remove from fire and let stand covered for 10 minutes. Put rice in a large bowl, discard the piece of kombu. Pour the combined remaining ingredients over the rice, mix quickly and thoroughly. Quickly cooked rice will acquire a beautiful glossy sheen.

*See Glossary

Smoked Salmon Mousse

For Eight to Ten

6 oz. smoked salmon
5 tbsp. butter
dash of Tabasco sauce
pinch of mace
1 tsp. dried dill leaves (weed)
¼ cup chicken broth

½ envelope unflavored gelatin
¼ cup clam juice
1 tbsp. lemon juice
1 tbsp. Cognac brandy
½ cup heavy cream, whipped

Place salmon, butter, Tabasco, mace and dill in a food processor and purée until well blended, or chop salmon and rub through a strainer and blend with above ingredients.

Soften gelatin in chicken broth, heat to dissolve and mix with clam juice; stir in lemon juice and Cognac. Cool, blend in processor or blender with the salmon mixture. Fold in whipped cream, spoon into a mold and chill until well set. Serve on toast fingers.

Crab Meat Ravigotte

For Six

1½ lbs. cooked crab meat
¾ cup mayonnaise
1 tbsp. lemon juice
1 tbsp. lime juice
2 tbsp. minced onion
2 tsp. minced shallots
2 tbsp. chopped sweet pickles
1 tbsp. minced parsley

1 tsp. dried tarragon leaves
salt and pepper to taste
pinch of cayenne pepper
2 tbsp. chopped green olives
1 tbsp. chopped pimiento
½ tsp. paprika
6 anchovy filets
sliced tomato
sliced hard-boiled eggs

Pick over crab meat, discard pieces of cartilage. Mix ½ cup mayonnaise with lemon juice, lime juice, onion, shallots, pickles, parsley, tarragon, salt, pepper and cayenne. Combine with crab meat, chill for an hour or two. Place crab meat mixture in a serving bowl. Combine remaining mayonnaise with chopped olives, pimiento and paprika, spread mixture over crab meat. Decorate with anchovy filets, garnish with tomato and egg slices.

Crab Meat Salad Delmonico

For Four to Six

1¼ cups mayonnaise
3 tbsp. ketchup
⅛ tsp. Tabasco sauce
1 tsp. minced shallots
1 tbsp. grated onion
1½ tbsp. minced parsley
1 tbsp. minced fresh tarragon (or 1 tsp. dry)
3 tbsp. oil
1 tbsp. wine vinegar

1 tsp. lemon juice
salt and pepper to taste
¼ cup heavy cream, whipped
1 tbsp. finely chopped green olives
1 tsp. drained capers
1 lb. cooked flaked crab meat
sliced tomatoes and sliced hard-boiled eggs

Combine mayonnaise, ketchup, Tabasco, shallots, onion, parsley, tarragon, oil, vinegar and lemon juice season with salt and pepper, blend well. Fold in whipped cream. Add chopped olives and capers, chill for an hour or two. Before serving place chilled crab meat in a serving bowl, spoon dressing over the crab meat, garnish with tomato and egg slices.

Chopped Herring

For Four

3 salt herrings
2 slices white bread
1 large red onion
1 medium carrot, peeled
1 large apple, peeled, cored, quartered
3 hard-boiled eggs

1 tsp. capers, chopped
small pinch of grated nutmeg
4 tbsp. white wine vinegar
small pinch powdered bay leaf
pepper to taste

Soak herrings overnight in cold water, drain and filet. Soak bread in water and squeeze dry. Grind herring filet, bread, onion, carrot, apple and eggs, mix well; add all other ingredients, blend and chill.

Escabeche

For Four
2 lbs. fish filets
¼ cup olive oil
1 tbsp. grated onion
2 scallions, minced
1 bay leaf, crumbled
1 small clove garlic,
   crushed

2 green chilis (canned)
   chopped
2 tbsp. pimiento, chopped
¼ cup wine vinegar
juice of 1 large orange
1 tbsp. lime juice
salt and pepper to taste

Sauté fish in olive oil until lightly browned on both sides. Remove fish to a serving dish, add all other ingredients to pan, blend and heat for a minute, then pour over fish. Chill well before serving. Garnish with olives, lettuce leaves, and strips of pimiento.

Fish Monte Carlo

For Six
2 cups mayonnaise,
1 tbsp. celery, white
   part, minced
1 tbsp. shallots, minced
3 anchovy filets, mashed
1 tbsp. capers, drained,
   chopped
1 tsp. Worcestershire sauce
2 dashes Tabasco sauce

1 tbsp. sour gherkins,
   chopped
½ tsp. dried tarragon
2 tbsp. parsley, minced
1½ tbsp. pimiento, chopped
salt and pepper to taste
2 cups cold cooked fish,
   flaked (cod, bass, halibut
   or other)

Blend all ingredients except fish and 1 tablespoon parsley. Arrange fish in large scallop shells. Cover completely with the blended mayonnaise, sprinkle with parsley. Chill well before serving.

Marinated Fish

For Six
1 lb. striped bass or
   flounder filet
¼ cup lemon juice
¼ cup lime juice
1 tsp. salt
½ green pepper, thinly
   sliced

4 scallions, sliced thin
1 large clove garlic, crushed
1 tsp. grated fresh ginger
½ tsp. crushed red pepper
   flakes (or 1 fresh chili
   pepper, thinly sliced)
2 tbsp. minced parsley

This is an Oriental version of the familiar South American Seviche.

   Cut fish in small dice, place in a bowl, add lemon and lime juice, and salt. Mix and let stand for 3 or 4 hours. Add all other ingredients, correct seasoning and let stand for one hour. Chill and sprinkle with parsley before serving.

Mussels Piquante

For Four to Six
2 quarts mussels
¼ cup dry white wine
1 tbsp. onion, minced
3 tbsp. parsley, chopped
1 cup mayonnaise
1 small clove garlic,
   crushed

1 tbsp. shallots, minced
1 tbsp. Dijon mustard
pinch of cayenne pepper
1 tsp. Worcestershire sauce
salt and pepper to taste
1 tsp. lemon juice
1 tbsp. paprika

Scrub mussels well, put in a saucepan, also wine, onion and 2 tablespoons parsley. Cover and cook until mussels open — about 5 minutes. Remove mussels from shells and reserve; discard any unopened shells. Combine all other ingredients except paprika and remaining parsley, blend with mussels. Line a bowl with lettuce leaves, mound mussels on the leaves, sprinkle with paprika and the remaining parsley. Chill before serving.

Sauerkraut Soup ◁

For Six

1 lb. sauerkraut
1 medium onion, sliced
6 cups beef broth
½ tbsp. paprika
salt and pepper to taste
½ lb. smoked sausage, sliced thin
2 tbsp. parsley, chopped
½ cup sour cream

Squeeze sauerkraut, dry, discard juice. Put sauerkraut in a saucepan, add onion, beef broth, paprika, bring to a boil, cover and cook for about 1 hour or until sauerkraut is tender. (Canned sauerkraut will take considerably less time but is not recommended.) Add sliced sausage, salt, pepper and parsley, simmer 15 minutes longer. Top each serving with a big spoonful of sour cream.

Noodle Broccoli Cheese Soup ▷

For Twelve

2 tbsp. oil or butter
¾ cup onion, chopped
6 cups chicken broth
8 oz. fine egg noodles
    (about 4 cups)
1 tsp. salt
2 packages frozen broccoli
1 clove garlic, crushed
6 cups milk
1 lb. (4 cups) American
    cheese, cubed
pepper to taste

In a large saucepan heat oil. Add onion and sauté over medium heat for 3 minutes. Add chicken broth, heat to boiling. Gradually add noodles and salt so that the broth continues to boil. Cook uncovered for 3 minutes, stirring occasionally. Stir in broccoli and garlic; cook 4 minutes more. Add milk, cheese and pepper and continue cooking until the cheese melts, stirring constantly.

Soups

45

Austrian Beef Soup

For Six
3 stalks celery
1 parsley root
2 medium carrots
1 small parsnip
1 small ripe tomato
1 turnip
1 onion
10 cups water

6 peppercorns
beef marrow bone and
    other beef bones
2 lbs. beef shin or chuck
small piece of beef liver,
    diced (about ½ cup)
1 tsp. parsley, minced
salt to taste
    (about 1 tbsp.)

Wash meat, peel vegetables. Put all ingredients except parsley in a large saucepan. All ingredients should be covered with water, add more water if necessary. Bring to a boil, cover and cook gently for 2½ to 3 hours. Strain soup, skim off fat, sprinkle soup with parsley and serve with any of the garnishes. The meat is usually served as the main course. If stress is laid on the taste of the meat, do not add meat until the water boils.

Beef Consomme

About Six Cups
3 qts. cold water (approx.)
1 lb. lean beef
    (shin or shoulder)
1 lb. veal shoulder, cubed
2 lbs. beef bones, cracked
1 lb. veal bones
1 tsp. salt

2 carrots, chopped
1 turnip, chopped
3 leeks, trimmed,
    washed, chopped
3 stalks celery, chopped
2 large onions, each
    stuck with 1 clove
bouquet garni*

Put water, meats and bones in a big kettle, bring slowly to a boil. Skim, season with salt and skim again. Add all the vegetables to the kettle, the bouquet garni and the onions stuck with cloves. Add more water if necessary — all the ingredients should be well covered.

Bring slowly to the boiling point, skim and simmer very slowly for 4 hours, skimming as necessary. The liquid should reduce to about 6 cups and be of a good, strong flavor.

At the end of the cooking time, correct the seasoning and strain through a fine sieve.

*See Glossary.

Black Bean Soup

For Eight to Ten
2 cups dried black beans
6 cups cold water (or half
    water, half beef broth)
2 tbsp. butter
⅓ cup chopped onions
¼ cup chopped celery tops
2 small leeks, trimmed,
    cut lengthwise in half,
    washed, chopped

1 carrot, scraped, chopped
salt and pepper to taste
1 small bay leaf
pinch of thyme
¼ lb. salt pork, or
    a hambone
¼ cup sherry wine
2 hard-boiled eggs,
    finely chopped
1 tsp. parsley

Wash beans and pick over carefully. Soak overnight in cold water to cover. Drain, put beans in a heavy pot or soup kettle, add water and beef broth, salt pork or hambone. Cover and bring slowly to a boil.

In the meantime, heat butter in a skillet, sauté onion, carrot, celery and leek over gentle heat until light golden brown. Add to beans, together with salt, pepper, bay leaf and thyme. Cover and simmer for about 3 hours or until beans are quite soft. Stir occasionally to prevent sticking. If soup gets too thick add a little more boiling water or broth. When beans are done, remove salt pork and reserve. Rub contents of pot through a foodmill (or purée in a food processor). Return to pot, heat through. Dice salt pork and add to soup. If soup is too thick, thin with scalded milk. Correct seasoning. When ready to serve, stir in sherry wine. Mix chopped egg and parsley and sprinkle on top. Serve with lemon slices.

Chicken Soup

For Eight

4 to 5 lb. fowl
3 cups water per lb.
  of chicken
2 carrots, peeled
  and sliced

1 large onion
2 stalks celery
1 parsley root
pinch of grated nutmeg
salt and pepper to taste

Wash and disjoint fowl. Put in a deep saucepan or kettle, together with gizzard, heart and neck. Add the water and let come to a boil. Skim carefully, cover and simmer for 2 hours. Then add all other ingredients and cook for one hour longer. Strain, skim off fat and correct seasoning.

The chicken meat can be used for croquettes or salads. For an extra rich soup, buy additional giblets and chicken feet, if available, and cook with the fowl.

Minestrone

For Six

¼ cup chopped salt pork
½ cup chopped onion
1 clove garlic, chopped
1 tbsp. parsley, minced
½ tsp. basil
3 stalks celery
2 medium carrots, peeled
  and sliced
2 medium potatoes, diced
2 cups cooked fava beans
1 cup green peas

1 green pepper, seeded
  and diced
1 cup shredded white
  cabbage
6 cups chicken broth
2 tbsp. tomato paste
1 cup pasta shells
  or macaroni
salt and pepper to taste
⅓ cup grated Parmesan
  cheese
2 zucchini, diced

Sauté salt pork, in a heavy saucepan until rendered, then add onion, garlic and parsley. Stir and sauté until onion is soft. Add all other ingredients except pasta shells and cheese, cover and cook gently for about one hour. Then add pasta and cook 10 minutes until pasta is done. Sprinkle with cheese before serving.

Clam Bisque

For Four

2 doz. clams
1 cup milk
½ cup dry white wine
3 tbsp. parsley, chopped
4 tbsp. butter
3 slices good white
  bread, trimmed, diced
1 tbsp. minced chives

1 large clove garlic,
  crushed
1½ tbsp. shallots, minced
pinch of basil
pepper to taste
pinch of cayenne pepper
½ cup additional clam
  juice

Wash and scrub clams, place them in a saucepan, add milk, wine and parsley. Cover and cook until the shells have opened. Heat butter in another pan, add diced bread, garlic, shallots and basil; sauté over gentle flame, stirring a few times, until bread is golden. Remove clams from shells and reserve. Strain broth into the bread cubes, add extra clam juice and simmer for 15 minutes. Then put clams and contents of the saucepan in a food processor or blender and process until smooth. Correct seasoning, add cayenne pepper and heat through. Sprinkle with chives when serving.

This bisque can be served hot or well chilled.

◁ Onion Soup

For Eight
6 medium sized onions, minced
2 tbsp. cooking oil
6 tbsp. butter
3 tbsp. flour
8 cups hot chicken broth
salt and pepper to taste
French bread, sliced and toasted
grated Swiss or Parmesan cheese
cayenne pepper to taste

Combine oil and butter and sauté onions gently until they turn golden. Sprinkle the flour over onions and cook them, stirring constantly until they are light brown. Stir in the hot broth and simmer 15 minutes; season to taste with salt and pepper. Put soup in serving bowls or plates, put a few slices of toast in each plate, sprinkle liberally with grated cheese, add cayenne if desired and brown quickly under the broiler.

Gazpacho Andaluz

For Six
4 cups day-old French or
    Italian bread or hard
    rolls, cubed
1½ cups pared and diced
    cucumber
1 medium green pepper,
    seeded and diced

chicken broth
2 cloves garlic
2 tsp. salt
½ cup olive oil
¼ cup wine vinegar
2 lbs. fresh ripe tomatoes,
    seeded and cubed
ice cubes

Accompaniments:
sliced stuffed Spanish olives
diced cucumber
chopped scallions
diced green pepper

crumbled crisp bacon
toasted slivered almonds
diced tomatoes
chopped hard-boiled eggs

Place bread cubes in a shallow dish and add broth 1 inch deep. Let bread soak, turning once.

Combine cucumber, green pepper, garlic, salt, oil and vinegar in an electric blender or in a food processor, blend smooth. Add half of the bread cubes and blend smooth again. Pour mixture into a bowl. Mix remaining bread and tomatoes and add to the bowl. Correct seasoning adding more salt and vinegar if desired. Chill well. When serving place one or two ice cubes in each soup bowl, serve with accompaniments.

Avgolemono Soup

For Eight

6 cups chicken broth
¾ cup raw rice
3 eggs

1 egg yolk
juice of 2 lemons
salt and pepper to taste

Bring broth to a boil, add rice and cook until rice is cooked but still firm (about 15 minutes). Remove soup from fire. Beat eggs and yolk until frothy, add lemon juice a little at a time and continue beating. Add a cup of hot broth, a spoonful at a time, while beating constantly. Then beat this mixture into the soup, season with salt and pepper and serve.

Pungent Soup

For Six

1 small chicken breast,
  boned, skinned and
  cut in strips
⅓ lb. lean pork, cut in
  thin strips
4 cups chicken broth
2 scallions, cut in 1-inch
  pieces

2 cups water
1 tsp. ginger, shredded
2 tbsp. sherry
⅓ cup vinegar
1 clove garlic, minced
½ tsp. hot red pepper
salt to taste
4 tbsp. water
3 tbsp. cornstarch

Combine broth and water and bring to boil in a saucepan. Add chicken and pork and simmer for 15 minutes. Add all other ingredients except cornstarch and water; simmer 5 minutes longer. Combine cornstarch and water, add to soup and stir until thickened.

Gazpacho

For Four to Six
1 cucumber, peeled, diced
1 red onion, minced
1 clove garlic, minced
2 large tomatoes, peeled,
    seeded, cut into chunks
2 cups tomato juice

1 green pepper, seeded
    and diced
1 cup chicken broth
¼ cup wine vinegar
1 tsp. oregano
salt and pepper to taste
pinch of cayenne pepper

Combine all ingredients, chill well for a few hours. When serving, put a cube of ice into each soup bowl.

Cream of Lettuce Soup

For Six
3 firm heads Boston
    lettuce
4 cups water
    (or 2 cups water,
    2 cups chicken broth)

2 tbsp. butter
salt and pepper to taste
½ cup heavy cream
pinch of grated nutmeg
1 tbsp. lemon juice

Wash and trim lettuce, cut in quarters, remove core. Put in boiling water and cook for about 10 minutes. Drain well and chop. Heat butter in a saucepan, add lettuce, cover tightly and cook gently for 5 minutes. Add water season with salt, pepper and nutmeg, bring to a boil, cover and simmer for 45 minutes. Put contents of pan in a blender or food processor and purée. Return to saucepan, blend in cream and lemon juice, correct seasoning. Heat through and serve with croutons or thin slices of fired French bread.

Turkish Wedding Soup

For Six
6 cups chicken broth
1 lb. lean lamb, diced
4 tbsp. flour
4 tbsp. butter
1 onion, peeled

salt and pepper to taste
2 tsp. paprika
pinch of cayenne pepper
3 egg yolks, lightly beaten
juice of 1 large lemon
pinch of cinnamon (opt.)

Heat butter in a saucepan. Sprinkle diced meat with flour and sauté while stirring until browned. Add broth, bring to a boil. Skim off scum. Add onion, salt, pepper, paprika and cayenne pepper. Cover and cook gently for 1½ hours. Remove onion and discard. Remove soup from fire. (Add lemon juice, while beating, a little at a time, to beaten egg yolks); beat in 1 cup of hot broth, a spoonful at a time, until smooth. Blend egg mixture into the soup, add cinnamon and serve.

Chinese Fishball Soup

For Six
½ lb. flounder filet,
    minced
¼ lb. lean pork,
    finely ground
2 tbsp. soy sauce
1 tbsp. sherry
2 scallions, white part,
    chopped

pinch of powdered ginger
pepper to taste
1 small clove garlic,
    crushed
1 egg, lightly beaten
2 tbsp. cornstarch
4 cups chicken broth
2 cups water

Mix all ingredients except broth and water. Blend well and form into small balls. Bring broth and water to a boil, drop the balls gently into the simmering liquid and cook covered for 15 minutes.

German Beer Soup

For Four

3 tbsp. butter	¼ tsp. ground cinnamon
3 tbsp. flour	2 egg yolks
4 cups light or dark beer	2 tbsp. dry white wine
pinch of grated nutmeg	1 tbsp. sugar
salt	grated rind of ½ lemon
1 tsp. ground ginger	8 to 10 slices of toast

Melt the butter in a casserole, stir in the flour, and cook for 2 minutes, stirring constantly. Cool the mixture. Stir in the beer. Mix well and season with the nutmeg, salt to taste, the ginger and the cinnamon. Return to high heat and cook for 15 minutes, stirring constantly.

Beat together the egg yolks, the wine, sugar and grated lemon rind. Stir a few spoonfuls of the hot soup into the *liaison*, beating vigorously. Then add the mixture to the soup in the casserole, which should be barely simmering. Stir over very low heat for 3 minutes, but do not allow to boil.

Serve the soup in a tureen, with the toast on the side.

Noodle Spinach Cheese Soup ⇨

For Eight to Ten

2 tbsp. salad oil
¾ cup chopped onion
1 large garlic clove, crushed
6 cups chicken broth
8 oz. fine egg noodles
1 tsp. salt
paprika
packaged croutons
6 cups milk
2 packages (10 oz. each)
   frozen chopped spinach,
   thawed and drained
½ lb. shredded Fontina cheese
   (about 2 cups)
½ lb. shredded Provolone cheese
   (about 2 cups)

In a large saucepan, heat oil. Add onion and garlic; sauté over medium heat, stirring occasionally, until onion is tender, about 5 minutes. Add chicken broth. Heat to a rapid boil. Gradually add noodles and salt. Cook uncovered, stirring occasionally, until tender, about 6 minutes. Stir in milk, spinach, and cheeses. Cook until heated through and cheeses melt, stirring constantly. Do not boil.

To serve, sprinkle each serving with paprika and croutons. Serve immediately.

Iced Cucumber Soup

For Four

2 cups peeled cucumber, minced or grated
1 tbsp. salt
1 clove garlic, minced
2 cups plain yoghurt

1 tsp. vinegar
1½ tbsp. fresh dill, chopped
3 tbsp. olive oil
pepper to taste
fresh mint leaves

Combine cucumber and salt, let stand for one hour. Put cucumbers in a sieve or colander, press out as much of the liquid as you can and discard the liquid. Whip yoghurt until smooth, blend with cucumber and all other ingredients except mint leaves. Chill for several hours. (If soup is too thick add a little cold chicken broth or ice water.)
Serve in cups and float one mint leaf in each cup.

Mushroom Barley Soup

For Six

½ cup pearl barley
6 cups beef broth
8 dried imported mushrooms
2 carrots, diced small

1 stalk celery, diced
salt and pepper to taste
1 tbsp. fat
1 onion, diced

Wash barley in cold water. Bring beef broth to a boil, add mushrooms and barley and simmer until barley is cooked. Add salt and pepper, carrots and celery and cook for 15 minutes until vegetables are soft. Brown onion in fat and add to soup. Simmer 10 more minutes before serving.

Dill Soup

For Four to Six

1½ tbsp. flour
2 tbsp. butter or margarine
½ cup sour cream
2 tbsp. dill, chopped

salt and pepper to taste
½ tsp. caraway seed, crushed
4 cups water
    (or 2 cups water and
    2 cups chicken broth)

Heat butter in a deep saucepan, stir in flour and cook while stirring, until light golden brown. Stir in ½ cup liquid, together with the dill and keep stirring until smooth. Add gradually the remaining 3½ cups liquid, salt, pepper and caraway seed, blend well and simmer for 15 to 20 minutes. Serve and top each serving with a spoonful of sour cream.

Chicken Sub Gum Soup

For Six

1 chicken breast, boned skinned and shredded
½ cup celery, white part, sliced
½ cup fresh mushrooms, sliced

1½ tsp. oil
7 cups chicken broth
4 water chestnuts, diced
½ cup bean sprouts, washed and drained
1 egg, lightly beaten
salt and pepper to taste

Heat oil in a heavy saucepan, stir-fry chicken for one minute, add celery and mushrooms, stir-fry one minute, add water chestnuts and stir-fry 30 seconds longer. Add broth, sprouts, salt and pepper, bring to a boil, cover and cook gently for 10 minutes. Add beaten egg, stir quickly and serve.

Italian Onion Soup

For Four
6 tbsp. butter
2 Bermuda onions,
   sliced thin
1 clove garlic, minced
2 tbsp. flour
6 cups hot chicken broth

salt and pepper to taste
3 egg yolks
½ cup grated Parmesan
   cheese
slices of toasted French
   bread
2 tbsp. minced parsley

Heat butter in a heavy saucepan, sauté onion and garlic until light golden brown. Add flour and cook stirring for a minute or two. Add chicken broth, salt and pepper, blend well and simmer covered for half an hour. Beat egg yolks lightly and blend in the grated cheese. Remove soup from fire, whisk in the egg yolk mixture. Put toasted bread in soup plates, ladle soup over the bread and sprinkle with parsley.

Highland Broth

For Eight
1½ lbs. lamb shoulder,
   cubed
lamb bones (about 1 lb.)
1 cup chopped onion
1 cup chopped celery

½ cup chopped leeks
1 cup diced carrots
½ cup diced white turnip
2½ qts. water
salt and pepper to taste
½ cup pearl barley

Rinse lamb bones, tie them in a piece of cheesecloth. Place cubed lamb, bones, vegetables in a saucepan, add water, bring to a boil. Skim off scum, season with salt and pepper, simmer for 1½ hours. Add barley, cover and cook until meat and barley are tender — about 45 minutes. Remove bones, correct seasoning and serve.

◁ Tortilla Soup

For Four
½ cup lean bacon, chopped
1 medium onion, chopped
1 clove garlic, minced
1 small green pepper,
  seeded and diced
1 small chili pepper, minced
4 tortillas, cut in strips
½ tsp. oregano
4 cups chicken broth
salt and pepper to taste
¼ cup grated Parmesan cheese
¼ cup grated cheddar cheese

Sauté bacon in a saucepan for a few minutes until lightly browned. Add onions, garlic and green pepper, sauté for 5 minutes, stirring occasionally. Add chili and tortilla strips and sauté 3 minutes longer. Add broth and seasonings, bring to a boil and simmer for a few minutes. Ladle soup into individual, ovenproof bowls, sprinkle combined cheeses on top and bake in a 475⁰ oven for about 5 minutes or until cheese topping is browned.

Chicken Soup a la Parisienne

For Six
1 small broiler fryer
  (about 2 lbs.)
6 cups water
4 chicken bouillon cubes
salt and pepper
⅓ cup uncooked rice
½ cup fresh or frozen
  green peas
¼ cup dry white wine

1 tbsp. snipped parsley
2 ribs celery, cut in
  1-inch slices
¾ cup sliced green onions
  with tops
½ tsp. thyme leaves
½ tsp. summer savory leaves
1 can (14½ oz.) all green
  asparagus cut
  spears and tips

Combine chicken, water, bouillon cubes, salt, and pepper. Simmer, covered, about 30 minutes or until chicken is tender. Cool. Remove chicken from broth. Add water to broth, if necessary, to make 6 cups. Remove skin and bone from chicken and discard. Cut chicken into 1-inch pieces. Add chicken, rice, peas, celery, onions, wine, thyme, and savory to broth. Bring to a boil. Stir, reduce heat, cover, and simmer 15 minutes. Add asparagus and parsley; cook 5 minutes longer. Adjust seasonings, if necessary.

Vichyssoise

For Eight

9 tbsp. sweet butter
½ lb. leeks, white part
   only, washed and chopped
1 cup thinly sliced white
   onion
6 cups chicken broth
2 large potatoes, peeled
   and diced

pinch of dried tarragon
small pinch of thyme
pinch of cayenne pepper
salt and white pepper
   to taste
2 cups heavy cream
4 tbsp. chives, chopped
   fine

Melt butter in a saucepan, add the leeks and onions, cover and simmer for 20 minutes. Add chicken broth, potatoes, tarragon, thyme, cayenne, salt and pepper and simmer covered for about one hour, until vegetables are very soft. Strain all through a fine sieve and rub vegetables through it, or use a food processor with the steel blade, or purée in a blender. Return to saucepan, and simmer again for 15 minutes. Add the cream, bring to a simmer, cool, correct seasoning and chill until ice cold. When serving sprinkle chives on top of soup.

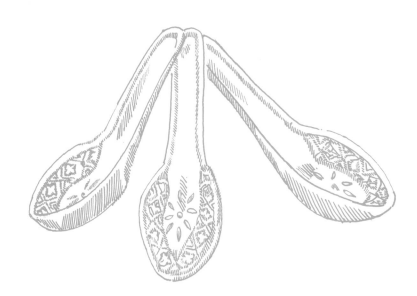

Beet Borscht

For Eight

6 medium beets
1 onion
1 clove garlic
8 cups water
3 tbsp. light brown sugar

salt and pepper to taste
¼ tsp. "sour salt"
   (citric acid) or
   juice of 1 lemon
2 egg yolks
1 cup sour cream

Wash and scrub beets, cut off tops. Put in saucepan with water, cover and boil until the beets are tender enough to be pierced with a toothpick (about 15 minutes). Strain the water the beets were boiled in and return to pot. Slip skin off beets, grate beets, onion and garlic into the strained beet water; add sugar, salt and pepper and cook gently for about 30 minutes or until vegetables are very soft. Add sour salt or lemon juice. Beat egg yolks in a bowl, add a little of the hot soup, return egg mixture to the soup, blend well and simmer for 5 minutes. Do not let boil. Add a spoonful of sour cream to each serving.

The borscht can also be served cold.

Mulligatawny

For Four
3 tbsp. butter
1 medium onion, chopped
1 carrot, peeled, diced
2 stalks celery, diced
1½ tbsp. flour
2 tsp. curry powder (or curry paste if available)
4 cups chicken broth

1 small green tart apple, peeled, cored, diced
½ cup boiled rice
¾ cup cooked chicken meat, diced
salt and pepper to taste
pinch of thyme
pinch of cayenne pepper
½ cup heavy cream

Heat butter in a saucepan, add onion, carrot and celery, sauté for a few minutes — do not let brown. Stir in flour and curry powder, sauté 3 minutes longer while stirring. Gradually add chicken broth and stir until smooth. Cover and simmer for 30 minutes. Add all other ingredients except cream and cook another 15 minutes. Heat cream, blend into soup and serve.

Potage St. Germain

For Eight
1 lb. green split peas
4 cups chicken broth
4 cups water
5 tbsp. butter
1 cup carrots, peeled, diced
1 cup celery, white part, diced

1 large onion, diced
2 or 3 sprigs parsley
1 small bay leaf
pinch of thyme
pinch of cayenne pepper
1 smoked pig's knuckle
1 cup light cream
salt and pepper to taste
2 tbsp. chopped chives

Soak peas overnight in cold water. Drain, put in a heavy saucepan. Add chicken broth and water and bring to a boil. Sauté onion, carrots and celery in butter until golden brown. Add to soup together with all other ingredients, except cream and chives. Cover and simmer slowly for 2 to 3 hours until peas are very soft. Remove pig's knuckle and purée contents of pan with a food mill or food processor; return to saucepan. Remove all meat off the knuckle, chop fine and add, together with light cream, to the soup. Correct seasoning, heat through. Sprinkle with chives when serving.

New England Clam Chowder

For Six
1 qt. shucked clams
¼ lb. salt pork, diced
1 large onion, minced
4 potatoes, peeled, diced

salt and pepper to taste
3 cups milk
1½ cups light cream
water crackers
2 tbsp. butter

Rinse clams in water to remove sand or grit. Chop or grind the clams coarsely. Strain and reserve ½ cup of juice. Sauté salt pork in a saucepan. When crisp, remove the pork bits and reserve. Add onions to fat, sauté until limp but not browned, add potatoes, sauté for 10 minutes, stirring often. Add clams, clam juice, barely cover with water, bring to a boil, then simmer for 15 minutes. Skim off any scum. Add milk, cream, season with salt and pepper, add split crackers, dried out pork bits, and butter. Simmer for 2 minutes. Then let stand for an hour or longer. Heat through before serving.

Note: Canned minced clams can be used instead of fresh clams. If canned clams are used, omit covering with water and boiling for 15 minutes.

Spanish Garlic Soup

For Eight

16 cloves of garlic
1 qt. boiling water
2 qts. chicken broth
¼ tsp. ground sage
¼ tsp. thyme
1 small bay leaf
4 sprigs parsley
2 whole cloves
3 tbsp. olive oil

3 cups diced raw potatoes
¼ tsp. Spanish saffron
salt and pepper to taste
¾ cup pimiento-stuffed
    Spanish olives, sliced
rounds of toasted French
    bread
1 cup grated Gruyere or
    Parmesan cheese

Drop unpeeled cloves of garlic into boiling water. Boil for a minute, drain and cool garlic under running water. Peel the cloves. In a large saucepan combine garlic, chicken broth, herbs, cloves and olive oil. Bring to a boil, cover and simmer for 30 minutes. Strain and return strained soup to saucepan; add saffron, potatoes, salt and pepper. Bring to a boil and simmer, covered, for 20 minutes or until potatoes are just soft. Add olives and heat through. Add toasted French bread to each bowl and sprinkle with grated cheese.

Matzo Balls ▷

For Four

2 matzos
3 tbsp. fat
1 small onion, minced
1 tsp. parsley, chopped
¼ cup matzo meal (approx.)
pinch of grated nutmeg
salt and pepper to taste
2 eggs, slightly beaten

Soak the matzos in cold water for a few minutes, then drain and squeeze dry. Heat the fat in a skillet, sauté the onion until golden brown. Add the matzos and cook while stirring until the mixture leaves the sides of the skillet. Add parsley, seasonings, eggs, and just enough matzo meal to make a soft dough. Remove from fire and let stand 2 or 3 hours. Roll into small balls. Test one by dropping it into the boiling soup; if it falls apart, add more matzo meal to the dough. Cook matzo balls for about half an hour in the boiling soup.

Hearty Spring Turkey and Vegetable Chowder ▷

For Eight

3 cups cooked turkey meat,
  cut into pieces
1 cup turkey stock or
  chicken bouillon
1 cup sliced green onions,
  including tops
1 cup finely diced celery
2 cups finely diced potatoes

¾ cup turkey fat or
  butter or margarine
¾ cup flour
1 qt. whole milk or
  Half and Half
1½ tsp. salt
few grains pepper
½ tsp. sugar

Pour turkey stock over vegetables in medium saucepan and simmer, covered, over medium heat until potatoes are tender — about 20 minutes. Do not drain.

In the meantime in large saucepan, melt turkey fat or butter, add flour and blend, cooking a minute or two. Add cream and cook and stir until smooth and thick, using a wire whisk to blend. Add undrained vegetables and turkey meat, and heat through. Season with salt, pepper, and sugar to taste. Garnish with chopped fresh tomato.

Note: 1 cup cooked peas and 1 cup cooked finely diced carrots may also be added, if desired.

Billi Bi (Cream of Mussel Soup)

For Four

1½ qts. mussels
1 medium onion, sliced
1 carrot, pared, sliced
1 stalk celery, cut
  in pieces
2 cups water
½ cup clam juice
½ cup dry white wine

8 tbsp. butter
¼ cup flour
salt and white pepper
  to taste
2 egg yolks
⅓ cup dry sherry
1 cup light cream
minced parsley and chives

Scrub the mussels under running water. Put them in a kettle, add onion, carrot and celery, water, clam juice and wine. Cover, bring to a boil and cook for about 5 minutes until the shells have opened. Shell the mussels, remove the beards. Strain the liquid through a cheesecloth and reserve along with mussels. Melt 6 tablespoons butter in a saucepan, stir in flour, blend and then add the strained mussel juice. Blend well again and bring to a boil over gentle heat. Season with salt and pepper. Force half the mussels through a coarse sieve or chop fine and add to the soup. Beat egg yolks with the sherry, then blend with the scalded light cream; add 2 tablespoons butter, dilute with some of the hot soup, mix and return the mixture to the soup. Stir well, add the mussels. Sprinkle with parsley and chives before serving. This soup is equally good hot or cold.

Fish Soup (Halászlé)

For Four

3 lbs. carp, pike, bass
  or any other fresh
  water fish
6 cups water
1 tsp. salt
3 medium onions, minced

1 large ripe tomato,
  peeled, seeded and cubed
1 tbsp. paprika
1 green pepper, seeded and
  sliced very thin
salt and pepper to taste

Have fish boned and skinned, and cut into thick chunks. Keep the trimmings, head and skin. Try to buy a fish that has roe or spawn and buy some extra roe if possible.

Put fish trimmings and head in 6 cups water, add 1 teaspoon of salt and boil for about 30 minutes. Strain through a fine sieve and return liquid to pan. Add onion and cook for 30 minutes, add tomato and cook 15 minutes longer. Strain and rub onion and tomato through the strainer into the broth. Put pieces of fish in the bottom of a saucepan, pour broth over it and add more water if needed to just cover the fish. Bring to a boil, reduce to a simmer, add salt and pepper to taste, paprika and green pepper, cover and simmer for 10 minutes. Add roe or spawn, if any, cook 5 minutes longer. Shake the pot a few times during cooking, but do not stir. Serve in soup plates.

Eggs and Cheese

Eggs are the most versatile of foods and can be prepared in countless ways — they can provide whole meals — breakfast, lunch or dinner; meals for festive occasions or the simplest ones. They are the base for many sauces; most baking without eggs is nearly impossible — in short they are an essential ingredient in our lives. Most methods of cooking eggs are simple.

Soft Boiled Eggs:
Put eggs in a saucepan, cover with cold water and bring to a boil. Reduce heat to simmering, cook for 2 or 3 minutes then remove egg.

Coddled Eggs:
Lower eggs carefully into rapidly boiling water, turn off the heat, cover the pan and let stand for 6 to 8 minutes, depending on the firmness of the eggs desired.

Hard Boiled Eggs:
Put eggs in a pan, cover with cold water, bring to a boil. Reduce heat and simmer for 10 minutes. Remove eggs, cool immediately in cold water. To peel the eggs, crack the shells and peel them under cold running water. When eggs are too fresh they are more difficult to shell.

Poached Eggs:
Choose very fresh eggs. Poach only a few at a time. Use a heavy, rather flat saucepan. Add water and vinegar — 1 part vinegar to 5 parts water. Bring to just below the boiling point. The water should just barely simmer. Stir water in a swirling motion, break the egg and drop it into the center of the swirling water. This method will produce a fairly rounded poached egg with few "streamers". Cook for 3 minutes, remove carefully with a skimmer or slotted spoon, trim streamers off the eggs. If eggs are to be used immediately, keep them in a pan with warm, salted water until all are done, then remove them, drain on a towel and serve.

Scrambled Eggs:
First method: Break eggs into a well buttered skillet, cook over low heat, stirring constantly. When eggs start to set, stir in a little heavy cream, remove from fire, stir in a little softened butter.

Second method: Beat the eggs lightly in a bowl. Pour them into the buttered top part of a double boiler, cook over simmering water, stirring constantly. When the eggs start to set, stir in a few small pats of butter, and if desired, a little heavy cream.

Omelettes:
There are a few basic rules. Omelettes take less than a minute to cook, so have all your utensils and ingredients ready. Have eggs at room temperature. Using cold eggs will often result in failure. Do not use too many eggs at a time. An omelette of three eggs is best. Never use an omelette pan for anything else but making an omelette. Never wash the pan with water. After a pan is seasoned, all it needs is to wipe it clean with a paper towel.

French omelette: Break three eggs in a bowl, season with salt and pepper. Blend with a fork but do not overbeat. Heat a tablespoon of butter in an omelette pan, pour the beaten eggs into the pan, stir the surface of the eggs with a fork, holding the fork parallel to the surface. At the same time, shake or tap the pan a few times to prevent eggs from sticking. Remove from fire. At this point put a filling on top of the omelette if desired. To fold the omelette, lift the pan at a 45 degree angle so that the still liquid part of the eggs runs to one side of the pan where it will solidify. At the same time slip the fork under the edge of the omelette near you and lift the edge. When the liquid egg is nearly solid, flip the edge over with the fork to make the correct fold.

To tilt the omelette out of the pan, hold a heated serving plate in your left hand. Hold the handle of the pan with your right hand, palm up, rest the edge of the pan on the edge of the plate. Now tilt both of them toward each other, in one motion flip the omelette into the serving plate.

To fill a cooked omelette, make it in the usual manner, slide it folded on a serving dish, shape it properly with a clean towel. Make a lengthwise cut in the center and push the sides apart slightly. Slide the stuffing into the omelette.

Egg Tips

Eggs should always be cooked slowly, whether scrambled, boiled or fried. Fast cooking toughens the egg white.

Don't beat whites in aluminum bowls or pans. Aluminum will darken them.

To remove a bit of yolk that slipped into the egg white, take a piece of egg shell and touch the yolk. It will adhere to the shell and can be lifted out easily.

When slicing hard boiled eggs, dip the knife blade in water, and the yolk won't crumble.

If you forget which eggs are hard boiled and which are raw, place them on a flat surface and spin them — raw eggs won't spin freely.

To prevent a cracked egg from bursting, add a little vinegar to the water the egg is to be boiled in.

Cold eggs crack often when put into boiling water. To prevent this, puncture the rounded end with a needle or pin.

When boiling eggs, bring them to room temperature after removing from refrigerator, or allow 2 extra minutes cooking time.

Fried Eggs Aumoniere

For Four

For the crépe batter:	For the dish:
¼ cup milk	4 slices of French bread
2 tbsp. butter	2 slices Swiss cheese
½ tsp. salt	2 slices cooked ham
½ cup flour	1 cup oil
2 eggs	2 tbsp. butter
¼ cup beer	4 eggs

Make the batter: Heat the milk to lukewarm. Melt butter, add salt. Put flour in a bowl, add eggs, milk and butter. Beat thoroughly and stir in beer. Let rest in the refrigerator for 2 hours.

Cut four 3-inch rounds from the bread, the cheese and the ham. Heat 2 tablespoons oil and all of the butter in a skillet and fry the bread rounds until golden on both sides. Remove bread, drain and keep warm. Fry the ham on both sides in the same skillet. Put a round of cheese on each round of fried bread, top with a piece of ham and keep hot.

In a very small skillet, heat the remaining oil. When it is very hot break an egg into it. Tilt the skillet so that the egg will be covered with oil on all sides, and with the help of a spatula push the white over the yolk. The egg, when fried, should be an oval the size of the bread rounds. Drain the egg on paper towels, quickly cook the rest of the eggs.

Make 4 crépes about 8 or 9 inches in diameter with the batter. Place them side by side on paper towel. Put in the center of each one of the bread rounds, top each with a fried egg. Tie up the crépes with string as if making a pouch. Put them in a buttered baking dish and brown them quickly under a broiler. Serve very hot.

Acapulco Omelette

For Two to Three	8 eggs
1 large avocado	1 tbsp. oil
salt and pepper	2 tbsp. butter

Peel the avocado, cut in half, and remove the pit. Dice one half and cut the other half with a melon baller into small balls.

Beat the eggs with salt and pepper to taste, add the diced avocado. Heat oil and butter in a skillet, add the eggs and make a flat omelette, turning it over with a large spatula when the eggs begin to set; finish cooking.

Place the omelette on a hot serving dish and garnish with avocado balls.

French Fried Eggs

Heat cooking oil in a deep skillet to about 375⁰. The oil should be about 3 inches deep. Drop raw eggs, one at a time, into the hot oil. Turn them often with a slotted spoon or spatula to brown them on all sides. Fry for about 3 minutes. Remove with a slotted spoon and drain on paper towel. Sprinkle with salt and pepper when serving.

Camembert Soufflé

For Three to Four
3 tbsp. butter
3 tbsp. flour
salt and pepper to taste
4 eggs, separated
2 egg whites

½ cup Camembert cheese
3 tbsp. grated Gruyere
   cheese
1 tsp. dry mustard
¾ cup milk
dash of Tabasco sauce

Butter soufflé dish (1-quart size) with 1 tablespoon butter, also a 3-inch paper collar to be tied around the dish. Melt remaining butter in a small saucepan. Remove from heat, blend in flour, salt, pepper and milk. Return to very low heat and cook while stirring until smooth and thickened. Rub Camembert through a strainer into the white sauce, stir until blended, then add, while stirring, Gruyere cheese, mustard and Tabasco. Add egg yolks, one by one and blend until smooth, remove from heat and fold in stiffly beaten egg whites. Spoon mixture into the soufflé dish. Put dish in a pan, half filled with hot water and cook in 375° oven for about 45 minutes, until well risen.

Chicken Liver Omelette Epicure

For Four
2 oz. fresh pork fat
4 tbsp. butter
⅓ lb. chicken livers
¼ tsp. dried thyme

1 bay leaf
salt and pepper to taste
1 tbsp. minced shallots
½ cup port wine
9 eggs

Cut the pork fat into small dice and sauté them in a skillet in 1 tablespoon butter for about 3 minutes. Add the whole chicken livers, thyme, bay leaf, salt and pepper and sauté the livers over high heat until nicely browned. Sprinkle them with shallots, reduce heat and sauté 3 minutes longer. Pour in a strainer, discard pan juices and discard bay leaf. Reserve the livers and what remains of the shallots. Marinate the livers in port wine for 1 hour. Drain livers and cut them into thin slices.

Make two omelettes in the usual manner using the livers as filling. Serve immediately.

Spanish Omelette

For Four
4 tbsp. butter
1 medium onion,
   sliced thin
½ cup canned pimientos,
   chopped
1 small green pepper,
   seeded, diced small

1 large clove garlic,
   minced
1 tbsp. green olives,
   chopped
6 tbsp. olive oil
6 eggs
salt and pepper to taste

Heat butter in a skillet, add onion, cook gently for 10 minutes. Do not let brown. Add garlic, pimiento, pepper and olives and simmer 2 minutes longer. Remove vegetables with a slotted spoon and keep warm. Beat eggs lightly, add salt, pepper, mix well. Heat oil in another skillet, and vegetables and sauté for a minute or two to heat through. Add eggs and stir constantly until they start to set. Then cook another minute without stirring, put a serving plate over the skillet and invert the flat omelette on the plate.

Onion and Tomato Frittata

For Four

3 large yellow onions,
    sliced thin
⅓ cup olive oil
1 cup canned plum
    tomatoes, drained,
    coarsely chopped
salt and pepper to taste

½ tbsp. anchovy paste
cayenne pepper to taste
3 tbsp. grated Parmesan
    cheese
4 tbsp. fresh basil, chopped
3 tbsp. butter
6 eggs

Heat oil in a skillet, sauté onion slices until very soft and golden brown. Stir occasionally. Add tomatoes, salt and pepper, cook over gentle heat for about 10 minutes. Stir a few times. Drain off pan juices; cool and reserve the onion and tomato mixture.

Beat eggs with anchovy paste, cayenne pepper; add tomatoes and onion, also cheese and basil. Blend well.

Heat butter in a large skillet, add eggs, turn heat very low. When the bottom of the eggs has set and the surface is barely runny (this will take about 10 to 15 minutes) put under the broiler for half a minute to cook the surface. Slide on a serving dish.

Eggs in Avocado Sauce

For Four

2 tbsp. minced onions
2 tbsp. butter
¼ cup milk
1 tbsp. cornstarch

2 ripe avocados
pinch of cayenne pepper
salt and pepper to taste
8 eggs
1 tbsp. chopped parsley

Sauté onions in butter until soft and transparent. Dissolve cornstarch in milk, add to onions and stir until smooth and thickened. Peel avocados, rub them through a sieve and add to the onion mixture. Blend well, simmer and stir for a few minutes until the sauce is hot and smooth. Season with cayenne, salt and pepper.

While preparing the sauce, boil the eggs for 10 minutes, shell them and keep hot. When the sauce is ready, cut the eggs in quarters, arrange them on a serving dish and coat with the avocado sauce. Sprinkle with parsley and serve.

Egg Foo Young ▽

For Four
5 eggs
1 ¼ tsp. salt
¼ tsp. pepper
½ cup onion, chopped
1 small clove garlic, minced
3 scallions, chopped

½ cup bean sprouts, washed
   and dried
½ cup celery, finely chopped
1 cup cooked pork or chicken,
   diced
2 tbsp. soy sauce
4 tbsp. oil

Lightly beat eggs with salt and pepper; mix meat with vegetables and soy sauce and blend well with eggs. Heat oil in a wok and using a ladle or ¼ cup measure, drop mixture, one portion at a time, into the oil. Fry each portion as you would a small omelette until browned on both sides. Remove each as it is cooked and keep warm.

Sauce
¾ cup chicken broth
salt to taste
1 tbsp. sherry
1 tbsp. soy sauce

1 tbsp. oyster sauce*
1 tiny pinch cayenne pepper
½ tsp. sugar
2 tbsp. cornstarch
1½ tbsp. water

Blend all ingredients except cornstarch and water. Simmer for a few minutes. Dilute cornstarch with water, blend into the sauce and stir to thicken.

*See Glossary

Eggs Benedict with Champagne Sauce
◁

For Six
½ cup butter
½ cup flour
1 cup champagne
3 cups Half and Half
1 cup (4 oz.) grated Gruyere cheese
salt and pepper to taste
6 English muffins, split and toasted
12 thin slices Canadian
   bacon, sautéed in butter
12 poached eggs

In a saucepan melt butter and stir in flour. Gradually stir in champagne and Half and Half. Stir constantly over low heat until sauce bubbles and thickens. Add cheese and stir until sauce is smooth. Season with salt and pepper, remove from heat. Place muffin halves on serving plates, top each with a slice of Canadian bacon and a poached egg. Spoon sauce over eggs and serve.

Camembert Omelette

For Two to Three

6 eggs
2 tbsp. cream or milk
salt and pepper to taste

2 tbsp. butter
½ cup Camembert cheese
1 tbsp. chopped chives

Let cheese stay at room temperature until quite soft, scrape off the rind and measure half a cup.

Beat eggs, cream, salt and pepper lightly. Heat butter in an omelette pan, pour in eggs and cook until the bottom starts to color. Lift edges to let liquid egg flow in the bottom. When the top is still moist, add cheese, distribute quickly with a spatula or the back of a spoon, sprinkle with chives, fold omelette over and serve.

Cheese Frittata

For Four

6 large eggs
salt and pepper to taste
1 tsp. paprika

¾ cup grated Parmesan
    cheese
4 tbsp. butter

Beat eggs until well blended, add salt, pepper, paprika and cheese and beat to blend well. Heat butter in a skillet until it starts to foam, but do not let brown. Add the eggs and turn the heat down to simmer. Cook for about 15 minutes or until the eggs have set but the surface is still slightly runny. Then either flip the frittata and finish cooking or put for about 15 seconds under the broiler until the surface is just set.

Swiss Custard

For Four

4 slices smoked bacon
2 eggs
½ cup ale
½ cup heavy cream
¼ cup minced cooked ham

1 tbsp. minced onion
¾ cup grated Gruyere
    or Swiss cheese
¼ cup grated Romano
    cheese
salt and pepper to taste

Fry bacon until well browned, drain on paper towel and crumble. Blend eggs, ale and cream, beat well; add crumbled bacon, ham, onion, both cheeses, season with salt and pepper. Pour mixture into individual custard cups, set them in a pan half filled with hot water, bake at 425° for about 15 to 20 minutes. When a knife inserted in the center comes out clean, the custard is done.

Eggs Mornay

For Four

4 slices buttered toast
1 tbsp. butter
4 thick slices boiled ham
4 poached eggs

Sauce Mornay (p. 314)
½ tsp. paprika
dash of Tabasco sauce
    (opt.)

Heat 1 tablespoon butter in a skillet, sauté ham gently, about 2 minutes on each side to heat through. Line broiler pan with aluminum foil, put toast in pan, cover each with a slice of ham and top carefully with a poached egg. Coat well with Sauce Mornay, broil for 1 or 2 minutes until nicely browned and very hot. Sprinkle with paprika and Tabasco and serve.

Singapore Omelette

For Four
2 tbsp. oil
1 small onion, minced
1 clove garlic, minced
2 chili peppers (fresh or
  canned), sliced thin

6 eggs
1 tbsp. sherry
1 tbsp. soy sauce
pinch of powdered ginger
1 tsp. brown sugar
½ tsp. lime juice

Heat oil in a skillet, add onion, garlic and chilis, sauté gently until soft, but do not let brown; stir occasionally.

Blend eggs with all remaining ingredients, beat with a wire whisk until light and foamy. Add to skillet, cook over moderate heat until nearly set and the bottom browned. Put under the broiler for a minute or so to cook and brown top.

Scrambled Eggs Acapulco

For Two
4 eggs
2 tbsp. heavy cream
1 tbsp. butter
1 sweet green pepper,
  seeded, minced
1 small ripe tomato,
  peeled, seeded, chopped

2 scallions, minced
2 tsp. chili powder
  (or to taste)
pinch of cayenne pepper
¼ tsp. lemon juice
salt to taste
1 tbsp. parsley, minced

Beat eggs and cream lightly and set aside. Sauté green pepper in butter until soft, add all other ingredients except eggs and parsley, simmer for 2 or 3 minutes. Add eggs and scramble over gentle heat while stirring. Add parsley just before serving. The eggs should be quite creamy.

Piperade

For Four
¼ cup butter
¼ cup oil
1 medium onion, sliced
  very thin
1 green pepper, cut
  into thin strips
salt and pepper to taste

1 red sweet pepper,
  cut into strips (or
    ½ cup canned pimiento)
1 cup tomatoes, peeled,
  seeded, diced
4 anchovy filets, chopped
6 large eggs

Heat butter and oil in a heavy skillet, add onion and peppers, sauté gently for about 15 minutes. Stir several times, do not let brown. Add tomatoes, cook 5 minutes more. Beat eggs lightly, mix in anchovies, season with salt and pepper, and pour eggs into the skillet. Mix with the sautéed vegetables, cook until firm but still moist. Turn out on a serving dish.

Stuffed Eggs au Gratin

For Six
6 hard-boiled eggs
2 slices white bread,
  crust trimmed off
¼ cup milk
2 anchovy filets
2 tbsp. sour cream
salt to taste

½ tsp. paprika
1 tbsp. butter
1 cup sour cream
¼ cup flour
1 tbsp. melted butter
2 tbsp. grated Parmesan
  cheese
2 tbsp. fine breadcrumbs

Cut eggs lengthwise in half. Remove yolks. Soak bread in milk, squeeze dry. Rub yolks, bread and anchovy through a strainer, blend with sour cream, season with salt and paprika. Stuff egg whites with the mixture. Butter a baking dish, place stuffed eggs in the dish. Blend sour cream and flour, spoon over eggs, sprinkle with melted butter, grated cheese and breadcrumbs. Bake at 450⁰ for 5 minutes.

Frittata with Peppers and Sausage   ⇨

For Four

2 tbsp. butter
½ cup sliced onion
¼ cup green peppers, chopped
1 large ripe tomato, peeled, seeded, chopped
2 anchovy filets, mashed
1 tbsp. green olives, chopped

2 tbsp. pimiento, chopped
1 tsp. basil
salt and pepper to taste
6 large eggs
3 tbsp. Parmesan cheese, grated
3 tbsp. butter
6 sweet Italian sausages, fried and fully cooked

Frittatas (Italian omelettes) have nothing in common with French omelettes, but the use of eggs. A frittata is never folded, it is perfectly flat and round, prepared over low heat and must be cooked on both sides. Unless one attempts to flip the frittata with a toss of the skillet, it is best to turn it over on a plate and slide it back into the pan, or to put the pan for a few seconds under a medium hot broiler to brown the top without having to turn the omelette. A frittata should never be deep brown, just golden in color.

Heat 2 tablespoons butter in a skillet, add onion and sauté until soft and light golden. Add green pepper, tomato, anchovy filets, olives and pimiento, basil, salt and pepper; blend well and simmer for 10 to 15 minutes, stirring occasionally. Remove from fire. Remove vegetables from pan with a slotted spoon and put in a bowl to cool. Beat eggs until well blended, add Parmesan, beat again and then blend in the vegetable mixture. Heat 3 tablespoons butter in a skillet and proceed to cook as above. Garnish with sausages.

Cheddar Rarebit

For Four

2 cups sharp cheddar cheese, diced
1 cup stale ale or beer
1 tsp. Worcestershire sauce
1 dash Tabasco sauce
2 anchovy filets, mashed (opt.)
1 tbsp. grated onion
1 tsp. lemon juice
4 egg yolks, lightly beaten

Place cheese, ale, Worcestershire sauce, Tabasco, anchovy, onion and lemon juice in the top of a double boiler or chafing dish. Cook over simmering water, while stirring constantly, until the cheese is melted and mixture well blended and smooth. Add egg yolks and continue stirring and cooking until the mixture has thickened. Serve piping hot on buttered toast.

Omelette Soufflé with Peppers

For Four

6 large red or green
    sweet peppers
4 tbsp. olive oil

2 tbsp. butter
5 eggs, separated
2 whole eggs
salt and pepper to taste

Brush the peppers with 2 tablespoons oil, put them in a pre-heated 500° oven. Take them out when they are well scorched, rub off the scorched outer skin under running cold water. It will come off quite easily. Cut them lengthwise in half, remove seeds and membrane. Cut 2-inch diamonds out of each pepper half and cut the remaining parts into thin strips.

Heat butter and remaining oil in a skillet. Sauté the diamond-shaped pepper pieces until they are barely golden. Keep them flat by pressing them down with the back of a spoon. Take them out with a slotted spoon and reserve. Cook the thin pepper strips in the same skillet and reserve them separately.

Lightly beat together the 5 egg yolks and the 2 whole eggs. Beat the egg whites until stiff, fold them carefully into the beaten yolks, so that the mixture will be light and airy. Fold the pepper strips into the mixture. Reheat oil and butter in the skillet, adding a little more if necessary, pour the egg mixture into it. Cook the eggs on one side, turn them over with a wide spatula and let cook until golden on the other side, shaping them into the usual omelette shape.

Put the omelette on a hot serving dish, decorate with the diamond-shaped pieces of pepper, pour the pan juices over it and serve.

Soy Eggs

For Four

4 eggs
½ cup Chinese soy sauce
½ cup chicken broth

6 tbsp. sugar
1 tbsp. grated onion
1 tbsp. sherry

Put eggs in a saucepan, cover with water and boil gently for 10 minutes. Remove from pan and cool under cold running water for 5 minutes. Shell carefully. Place eggs in a small saucepan, add all other ingredients and bring to a boil. Cover pan and simmer for 1 hour, turning the eggs several times during cooking so that they will color evenly. After one hour, remove pan from heat and cool eggs in their liquid for 30 minutes. Drain, quarter eggs, serve on a bed of lettuce leaves.

Whitstable Rarebit

For Four

1 pint shucked oysters
2 tbsp. butter
1 tsp. flour
¼ lb. Swiss cheese,
    shredded

pepper to taste
dash of Tabasco sauce
light cream
2 eggs, lightly beaten
2 tbsp. sherry

Simmer oysters in their liquor until edges curl and the oysters plump up. Drain, reserve oysters and the liquor.

Put butter and flour in the top of a double boiler and cook over simmering water until butter is melted and blended with the flour. Add cheese and cook while stirring until cheese is melted. Blend in pepper and Tabasco sauce. Add oyster liquor, stir and blend. Add some cream if the sauce is too thick. Blend in beaten eggs, stir for a minute; add oysters, sherry and salt if needed. Heat through and serve.

Eggs in Aspic

For Six

1½ cups clear chicken
   broth or consommé
1 tbsp. (envelope)
   gelatin soaked in
   ¼ cup cold water

6 eggs
salt to taste
½ tsp. lemon juice
3 tbsp. Madeira wine
6 slices cooked ham
2 sprigs parsley

Boil eggs about 6 minutes, cool under cold running water and shell carefully, since the yolks are still somewhat soft. Heat chicken broth, add softened gelatin and stir until gelatin is completely dissolved. Add salt, lemon juice and Madeira, blend well and cool until the mixture is just starting to thicken. Use small ramekins or individual molds, pour aspic about ¼ deep into the ramekins and chill until almost set. Put a small piece of parsley in each ramekin, place one egg in each, spoon aspic on top to nearly fill the mold. Then cover with a slice of ham trimmed to the size of the ramekins, spoon a little more aspic over it and chill until well jelled. To unmold, dip each ramekin for just a second in hot water and then reverse onto a serving platter or dish.

Greek Cheese Pie

For Six

3 eggs, well beaten
1 lb. feta cheese
pepper to taste
3 tbsp. softened butter

2 tbsp. parsley, chopped
2 tbsp. dill, chopped
½ lb. phyllo pastry sheets
melted butter

Note: Phyllo pastry sheets can be bought in all stores selling Greek or Mid-Eastern foods. They are also carried by many supermarkets.

Crumble cheese and mash with a fork. Blend with eggs, pepper and softened butter. Mix in parsley and dill. Place a sheet of phyllo pastry in a pan about the size of the sheet, butter the sheet, place another sheet on top, butter again and continue for a total of 8 sheets. Spread the cheese mixture on top and cover with 8 more buttered phyllo sheets. Bake in 350° oven for about 30 minutes until golden brown. Cut into squares and serve warm.

Raclette

For Four

Raclette is a traditional Swiss cheese dish— not dunked like a Fondue, but prepared in front of a fireplace. A big piece of Valais, a semi-soft cheese, is put on a wooden board or platter, set in front and close to the fire, and each person scrapes off the melted cheese onto his plate. Served with the Raclette are boiled potatoes, onions, pickles and usually a white Valais wine.

The following is an approximation — a substitute Raclette:

4 slices Muenster or caraway cheese, cut in half
12 new potatoes, boiled in their jackets
12 sour gherkins or pickles

On each of 4 ovenproof plates, overlap 2 halves of cheese, place in 400⁰ oven for 5 minutes or until cheese bubbles. Arrange potatoes and pickles on plates with cheese. Serve immediately.

Note: If desired, sprinkle cheese with freshly ground pepper before baking.

Asparagus Frittata ▷

For Four to Six

1 package (10 oz.) frozen
  chopped asparagus*
8 eggs
1 tbsp. grated onion
¾ tsp. salt
⅛ tsp. nutmeg
⅛ tsp. pepper
1 cup (4 oz.) shredded Swiss cheese
2 tbsp. butter

Cook asparagus according to package directions. Drain well. Beat together eggs and seasonings until well blended. Reserve ¼ cup cheese for topping, then stir remaining cheese and drained asparagus into egg mixture. Melt butter in large (10-12-inch) ovenproof skillet over medium heat. Pour in egg mixture. Cook until eggs are set, about 5 to 7 minutes. Sprinkle with reserved cheese. Broil about 6 inches from heat 2 to 3 minutes or until eggs are set. Loosen edges with spatula. Slide onto warm serving platter. Cut in wedges to serve.

*Substitute ½ pound fresh asparagus spears, chopped, if desired. Cook, covered in small amount of boiling salted water until tender, about 8 to 10 minutes. Drain well.

Eggs Capri

For Three to Four

3 tbsp. olive oil
½ cup pitted, pimiento-
  stuffed olives, cut
  in half
1 small green pepper,
  seeded, diced
1 small clove garlic,
  minced
2 tbsp. grated onion

4 oz. ricotta cheese
6 eggs
3 tbsp. light cream
salt and pepper to taste
small pinch of oregano
small pinch of crushed
  rosemary
½ cup grated Romano or
  Parmesan cheese

Heat oil in flameproof casserole or small baking dish, sauté olives, pepper, garlic and onion over gentle flame for 3 or 4 minutes until peppers are soft, add crumbled ricotta and cook, stirring constantly for 2 minutes. Beat eggs lightly with cream, salt, pepper, oregano and rosemary, add to casserole and mix well. Cook over very low heat while stirring gently with a fork until the eggs start to set and are nearly done. Remove from fire, sprinkle with grated cheese and put under the broiler for 2 minutes until the cheese has melted and browned.

Quiche on Toast

For Four

¼ lb. Gruyere (or
  Swiss cheese) grated
1 tbsp. butter
1 cup hot chicken broth
3 tbsp. grated onion

2 tbsp. chopped chives
2 tbsp. sherry wine
salt and pepper to taste
4 eggs, lightly beaten
paprika
buttered toast

Put cheese and butter in top of a double boiler over simmering water, stir until melted. Add all other ingredients except eggs and paprika, blend well and stir for a minute. Add eggs, blend and stir until the mixture is quite firm. Spoon on buttered toast, sprinkle with paprika and serve.

Cooked Cheese

For Four to Six
1 lb. farmer cheese
1 tsp. crushed caraway
   seeds

salt to taste
1 tsp. paprika
1 cup butter
2 egg yolks, lightly beaten

Put a layer of cheese in a glass dish, sprinkle with some salt, caraway and paprika; add several more layers of cheese sprinkled with salt, caraway and paprika. Cover the dish and let stand in a cool place — not refrigerated — for 2 or 3 days. By that time the cheese will be slightly runny.

Melt butter in a saucepan, add cheese and stir constantly over low heat until well blended and the cheese has melted. Add egg yolks, blend for another minute. Pour mixture in a crock or bowl and chill well. For serving, unmold and slice.

Curried Devilled Eggs

For Four to Five
12 hard-boiled eggs
   (the smaller the better)
1 tsp. curry powder (or,
   if available, curry paste)

⅓ cup mayonnaise
1 tsp. Dijon mustard
salt and pepper to taste
1 tsp. paprika
2 tbsp. minced parsley

Shell eggs and cut lengthwise in half. Remove yolks and rub through a strainer, then blend with all other ingredients. Fill the egg halves. The best and easiest way to fill them is using a pastry bag with a star tube. Garnish each egg half with a sprinkle of parsley and paprika.

Eggs Meuniere

For Two
4 eggs
6 tbsp. butter
2 tbsp. capers, well drained

½ tsp. lemon juice
3 tbsp. dry white wine
salt and pepper to taste

Poach the eggs to taste, drain well, trim and place on a hot serving dish. Melt butter in a small saucepan over medium heat until browned, while stirring constantly, whisk in capers, lemon juice, wine, salt and pepper. Pour piping hot over the eggs and serve.

Eggs Boulangère

For Four
5 tbsp. butter
4 small baking potatoes
¼ cup grated Swiss
   cheese
¼ cup grated Parmesan
   cheese

2 tbsp. butter
8 eggs
salt and pepper to taste
pinch of grated nutmeg
⅓ cup light cream
   (approx.)
½ tsp. paprika

Peel potatoes, slice thinly, sauté in 5 tablespoons butter until soft and golden brown — turning them occasionally while sautéing.

Butter a baking dish with 2 tablespoons butter, cover the bottom with sautéed potatoes, sprinkle with grated cheese. Break eggs carefully over the cheese, season with salt, pepper and nutmeg. Spoon cream over eggs, sprinkle with paprika and bake at 350° for 10 to 12 minutes until eggs are set.

Spanish Picnic Omelette   ⇨

For Six
¼ cup finely chopped
   Spanish stuffed
   green olives
10 tbsp. butter
1 large round loaf
   unsliced French or Italian
   bread (about 10 inches
   in diameter)

½ cup chopped onions
¼ lb. mushrooms, finely
   chopped
¼ lb. boiled ham, chopped
1 large cooked potato,
   peeled, diced
½ cup sliced stuffed
   green olives
12 eggs, well beaten

Combine chopped olives and 2 tablespoons softened butter until well mixed. With sharp knife cut bread horizontally in half. With a spoon scoop out soft center of the bottom half of the bread leaving a 1-inch thick shell. (Save crumbs for another use.) Spread the scooped out surface of the shell and the cut surface of the upper half with the olive-butter mixture. Reassemble loaf, wrap in heavy duty aluminum foil and keep warm in a 300⁰ oven while preparing the omelette.

In a medium saucepan melt 2 tablespoons butter. Add onion and mushrooms, sauté until tender, 2 or 3 minutes. Stir in ham, potato and sliced olives. Cook, stirring occasionally, for 3 minutes.

Meanwhile, in a 10-inch skillet, melt 4 tablespoons butter. Pour in half the beaten eggs. Quickly add mushroom-ham mixture to cover eggs evenly. Pour in remaining eggs. As the edges begin to set, push egg mixture to center and shake pan vigorously to allow uncooked egg mixture to flow underneath. Cook omelette until top is just set but still moist — about 5 minutes, shaking pan constantly to keep omelette from sticking.

◁ Swiss Fondue

For Four
1 garlic clove
½ lb. Gruyere cheese,
   shredded or diced
½ lb. Swiss cheese, shredded
3 tbsp. flour or 1½ tbsp. cornstarch
2 cups dry white wine
1 tsp. lemon juice
pinch of cayenne pepper
ground white pepper to taste
3 tbsp. Kirsch brandy

Rub the inside of a casserole or chafing dish with garlic. Put the cheeses into the chafing dish, mix with flour or cornstarch. Add wine and lemon juice, season with cayenne and white pepper. Simmer over low heat, stirring, until the cheeses have melted. Stir in the Kirsch. Transfer the chafing dish to the burner of the dish or of a fondue set, and keep bubbling.

Regulate the heat so that the fondue keeps hot without boiling, or the cheese will become stringy. Serve with Italian or French bread cut into bite-sized cubes.

To eat, spear a piece of bread with a long-handled fondue fork, (or a skewer), dip into the fondue with a stirring motion until it is thoroughly coated with cheese. Serve with the same wine used in the fondue.

Ranchero Eggs

For Four
3 tbsp. oil
4 tortillas
1 tbsp. onion, minced
1 small clove garlic,
    minced
½ tsp. basil
½ tsp. marjoram

canned pimiento
1 tbsp. parsley, minced
½ tsp. ground coriander
salt and pepper to taste
1 cup canned tomato
    sauce
8 eggs, poached or fried
1 small avocado, sliced

Fry tortillas in oil, set aside and keep hot. Add onion and garlic to the same oil, sauté for a minute or so, add all other ingredients except eggs, avocado and pimiento. Blend and simmer for 2 minutes. Then place two cooked eggs on each tortilla, cover the eggs with sauce and top with slices of avocado and pimiento.

Note: Tortillas can be found in most markets in the section for Mexican foods.

Baked Eggs Italian Style

For Four
8 eggs
2 tbsp. butter
1½ cups tomato, peeled,
    seeded, chopped
2 tbsp. parsley, minced
1 tbsp. chives, chopped

salt and pepper to taste
4 Italian sausages (sweet
    or hot, according
    to taste)
3 tbsp. grated Romano
    cheese
paprika

Simmer sausages for a few minutes in water, then drain and fry until browned. Butter a shallow baking dish, cover the bottom with chopped tomatoes, sprinkle with parsley and chives, season with salt and pepper. Break eggs carefully on top of tomatoes, slice sausages lengthwise in half and arrange around eggs. Sprinkle with cheese and paprika, bake in preheated 375° oven for about 5 minutes until eggs are well set.

Deep Fried Stuffed Eggs

For Four
4 hard-boiled eggs
1 cup ricotta cheese
2 tbsp. Parmesan cheese,
    grated
2 anchovy filets, mashed

1 tsp. grated onion
salt and pepper to taste
flour
2 eggs, lightly beaten
fine dry breadcrumbs
oil for deep frying

Cut eggs lengthwise in half, remove yolks. Rub yolks through a strainer, blend with ricotta and Parmesan, anchovy, onion, salt and pepper. Fill the egg halves with this mixture and mound the mixture on each half to look like a whole egg. Roll each half in flour, dip in beaten egg and coat with breadcrumbs. Fry in deep oil until golden brown.

Cheese Chili

For Four
½ cup minced onion
½ small clove garlic,
    minced
½ tbsp. oil
1 cup canned tomatoes,
    drained

½ cup light cream
salt and pepper to taste
2 tsp. chili powder
pinch of cayenne pepper
1 cup grated sharp
    cheddar cheese
3 eggs, lightly beaten

Sauté onions in oil until limp and lightly browned, add garlic, tomatoes, cream, salt, pepper, chili powder and cayenne, cover and simmer very gently for 15 minutes. Stir in the cheese, cook while stirring until melted, then stir in the eggs. Cook while stirring constantly until the mixture has thickened. Do not let boil.

Steamed Eggs and Ham

For Four
1 cup chicken broth
½ cup minced lean cooked
  or smoked ham
2 scallions, minced
½ small clove garlic,
  minced

1 tbsp. sherry
¼ tsp. sugar
salt and pepper to taste
1 tsp. oil
5 eggs
1 tbsp. soy or oyster sauce

Heat broth until hot, not boiling. Blend ham, scallions, garlic, sherry, sugar, salt and pepper and oil. Beat eggs very lightly and blend gently with the meat mixture. Oil a shallow heatproof baking dish, pour in the egg mixture, and steam over boiling water for about 20 minutes until eggs have a custard-like consistency. After 15 minutes check with a toothpick or the point of a knife. If it comes out clean, the eggs are done. Sprinkle with soy or oyster sauce before serving.

Egg and Gruyère Casserole

For Four
3 cups grated Gruyere
  cheese
3 tbsp. butter
1¼ cup dry white wine
1 tsp. chives, chopped

1 tsp. parsley, minced
1 scallion minced
1 tsp. minced shallots
salt and pepper to taste
dash of Tabasco sauce
6 eggs, separated

Put all ingredients except eggs in a fireproof casserole, mix well and cook over a gentle flame, while stirring constantly, until the mixture is smooth and bubbly and all the cheese has melted. Whisk in the egg yolks until well blended, then blend in the stiffly beaten egg whites and cook while stirring, over the lowest possible flame until the mixture is well scrambled. Serve on hot toast triangles.

Grilled Eggs

For Two
4 slices firm white bread
3 tbsp. butter
4 eggs

salt to taste
cayenne pepper to taste
½ cup grated Gruyere
  cheese

With a cookie cutter cut out 4 rounds of bread, 2½ inches in diameter. Fry the rounds in butter until light golden brown on both sides. Keep warm. Poach eggs, trim them neatly, place on bread rounds, season with salt and cayenne pepper, cover thickly with grated cheese. Put under hot broiler, brown the surface quickly.

Scotch Woodcock

For Two
6 toast triangles or
  strips
butter
anchovy paste or
  6 anchovy filets

4 egg yolks
½ cup light cream
salt and pepper to taste
pinch of cayenne pepper
2 tbsp. minced parsley

Butter the toast and spread with anchovy paste or put an anchovy filet on each. Keep warm.

Beat egg yolks lightly, blend with cream and put in top of a double boiler over simmering water. Add salt, pepper, cayenne and parsley. Stir the mixture until thick and creamy. Spoon over pieces of toast, broil for a minute until top is browned.

Eggs Meurette ⇩

For Four

½ cup butter
½ lb. bacon, cut into
    narrow strips
1 medium onion, chopped
1 clove garlic, minced
2 whole cloves
2 cups dry red wine
½ cup chicken broth

½ tsp. sugar
salt and pepper to taste
bouquet garni (parsley,
    thyme, bay leaf)*
4 slices of firm white bread,
    crusts trimmed off
8 eggs
2 tbsp. beurre manié*

*See Glossary

Heat 3 tablespoons of the butter in a casserole, add the bacon, onion and garlic. Sauté until they are golden. Add cloves, wine, broth and sugar, salt and pepper and the bouquet garni. Simmer covered for about half an hour.

Fry the bread slices on both sides in the remaining butter until they are golden and keep warm on a hot serving dish.

Strain the sauce into a skillet, reserve the bacon strips. Bring the sauce to the boiling point and poach the eggs in it, pushing the whites gently over the yolks with a spatula. Remove eggs with a slotted spoon, drain and place two on each slice of fried bread. Quickly thicken the sauce with the beurre manié, pour over eggs and top with the bacon strips.

◁ Cheese Soufflé

For Four

4 tbsp. butter
3 tbsp. flour
1 cup milk
salt to taste
pinch of cayenne pepper
pinch of grated nutmeg
4 egg yolks
2 tbsp. heavy cream
½ lb. Swiss cheese, grated
6 egg whites, beaten stiff

Melt butter in a saucepan, add the flour and stir constantly over medium heat for 2 or 3 minutes. Then add the milk. Season with salt, cayenne and nutmeg, stir with a whisk until the mixture is smooth and thick. Remove from heat and cool slightly.

Combine the egg yolks with the cream, beat them into the other mixture, then stir in grated cheese. Finally fold in the beaten egg whites. Butter and flour the bottom and sides of a soufflé dish, pour the mixture into it. Bake in 375° oven for about 30 minutes. Serve immediately.

Seafood

Moules Marinière

For Four

4 doz. mussels
1 cup dry white wine
Beurre Manie (2 tbsp. butter creamed with 2 tbsp. flour)

2 tbsp. minced shallots
1 tbsp. parsley, minced
2 tsp. minced chives
1 tbsp. butter
salt and pepper to taste

Scrub mussels and wash them well. Put them in a deep saucepan or kettle, add wine and shallots. Cover tightly and cook for about 10 minutes until shells are open. Remove mussels from pan. Discard unopened mussels, remove and discard a half shell from each of the others. Leave mussels in the other half. Remove the black "beard" which can be just lifted off. Put mussels in a serving bowl and keep warm. Reduce liquid in pan quickly by half, stir in Beurre Manie, 1 tablespoon butter, parsley, chives, salt and pepper. Stir and simmer for 2 or 3 minutes. Put mussels in serving plates, pour juice over them.

Lobster Fra Diavolo

For Four

4 lobsters, 1¼ lbs. each
⅓ cup olive oil
2 cloves garlic, minced
4 tbsp. onion, minced
½ cup dry white wine
2 cups canned Italian tomatoes

1 tbsp. vinegar
1 tsp. dry basil
¼ tsp. thyme
1 tsp. marjoram
½ tsp. crushed red pepper (or to taste)
salt and pepper to taste
½ cup clam juice

Have lobsters split, the tails cut in two or three pieces, the carcass cut in half again, the claws cracked. Remove the sack near the eyes, reserve tomalley and coral, if any.

Heat oil in a saucepan, add lobster pieces, season with salt and pepper and sauté, stirring frequently, until all pieces are bright red. Sprinkle with onion and garlic, add wine, stir and cook rapidly until most of the wine has evaporated. Add all other ingredients, stir, cover and simmer for about 15 minutes. Add more clam juice if lobster looks too dry.

Mussel Stew

For Four
4 doz. large mussels
3 tbsp. olive oil
1 large onion, minced
1 large carrot, peeled, minced
2 small potatoes, peeled, diced
1 cup minced heart of celery (white part)

2 large cloves garlic, crushed
2 tomatoes, peeled, seeded, chopped
1 tsp. lemon juice
1 tsp. sugar
a few threads of saffron
pepper to taste
2 tbsp. parsley, minced

Wash mussels and scrub with a stiff brush. Place mussels with ¼ cup water in a saucepan, cover and cook over high heat for 3 or 4 minutes until shells open. Remove from fire, discard unopened mussels. Take mussels out of shells and reserve. Strain juice through several layers of cheese cloth and reserve.

Heat oil in a skillet. Sauté onion until light golden, add carrots, potatoes, celery, sauté 2 minutes longer. Add garlic, tomatoes, lemon juice, sugar, saffron and pepper; mix well. Add 1 cup of mussel juice, cover and simmer for 25 minutes. Stir occasionally, add more mussel juice if too dry. Add mussels, salt if needed, heat through, sprinkle with parsley and serve.

Oysters Charente

For Six
3 doz. oysters
5 tbsp. butter
1½ cups firm mushrooms
1 tbsp. minced shallots

1 tbsp. minced parsley
1½ tbsp. flour
½ cup dry white wine
salt and pepper to taste

Shuck the oysters, reserve the deep half of the shells. Poach oysters in their juice until edges curl. Drain, reserve oysters and the juice. Sauté shallots in butter until soft but not browned, add chopped mushrooms and parsley. Sauté for 3 minutes, add flour and cook for 2 minutes, stirring constantly, do not let brown. Add 4 tablespoons of the oyster liquid, wine, salt and pepper, blend well and simmer while stirring until quite thick. Put 2 oysters in each half shell, cover with the mushroom sauce, top with a pat of butter. Bake at 400° for about 5 minutes until sizzling hot and slightly browned.

Filet of Sole Vin Blanc

For Two
2 large filets of sole (or flounder)
salt and pepper to taste
6 tbsp. butter

2 tbsp. shallots, minced
1 cup dry white wine
¼ cup heavy cream
¼ lb. cooked small shrimp, shelled and deveined

Put the filets in an oblong or oval baking dish, season with salt and pepper. Dot with 2 tablespoons butter and sprinkle with shallots. Add wine, cover very tightly, cook in preheated 350° oven or simmer on top of stove for 15 minutes. Remove pan juices but leave fish in pan. Reduce pan juices over high heat to about ½ cup. Stir in heavy cream and bring to the boiling point, beating with a wire whisk. Correct the seasoning. Remove from heat and stir in the remaining butter, bit by bit, swirling the pan to melt the pieces as they are added. Garnish the fish with the shrimp, coat with sauce and serve.

Seafood Rice ◁ Casserole

For Eight to Ten
2 cups cooked rice
½ cup chopped green pepper
1 cup chopped celery
½ cup finely chopped onion
1 can (4½ oz.) water chestnuts
  drained and diced
½ lb. medium shrimp, cooked,
  peeled, deveined
½ lb. crabmeat
1 cup mayonnaise
1 cup tomato juice
salt to taste
pepper to taste
½ cup sliced almonds
1 tbsp. butter or margarine,
  melted
1 cup shredded cheddar cheese
paprika

Combine rice, green pepper, celery, onion, water chestnuts, seafood, mayonnaise, tomato juice, and salt and pepper. Mix well. Pour into a buttered 2½ quart casserole. Toast almonds in butter. Sprinkle casserole mixture with nuts, cheese and paprika. Bake at 350⁰ for 25 minutes.

Stir-fried Striped Bass

For Four
1½ lbs. bass filet, skinned
1 tbsp. cornstarch
1 tbsp. soy sauce
1 tbsp. sherry
½ tsp. salt
pinch of cayenne pepper
1 clove garlic, crushed
1 scallion, minced
½ cup chicken broth

½ tsp. fresh ginger, minced
½ cup fresh mushrooms,
  sliced
¼ cup bamboo shoots,
  sliced thin
¼ cup celery, sliced thin
1 tsp. vinegar
½ tsp. sugar
4 tbsp. oil

Cut filets against grain in ¼ inch thick strips. Combine cornstarch, soy sauce, sherry, salt, cayenne and garlic, pour over fish filets and coat them. Heat 2 tablespoons oil in a wok, add scallion and ginger, stir for a few seconds, add vegetables, stir-fry for one minute. Then add broth, vinegar and sugar, cover and simmer for 2 or 3 minutes. Remove vegetables and their liquid from pan and keep warm. Add remaining oil to wok, add fish and stir-fry for about 2 or 3 minutes. Be careful not to break the fish. Return vegetables and liquid to pan, stir, heat through and serve.

Codfish a la Portuguaise

For Four

4 codfish steaks, 1½ inches
   thick (about 2 lbs.)
2 tbsp. butter
2 tbsp. olive oil
1 large clove garlic,
   crushed
1½ cups drained canned
   tomatoes, chopped

2 tbsp. minced onion
¾ cup dry white wine
1 carrot, peeled, chopped
1 bay leaf
pinch dried thyme
1 tbsp. parsley, chopped
pinch dried marjoram
dash of Tabasco sauce
salt and pepper to taste

Heat butter and oil in a saucepan, sauté onion and garlic until light golden brown. Add all other ingredients except codfish, bring to a boil, cover and simmer for 15 minutes. Add fish, cover again and simmer for 15 to 20 minutes or until fish is cooked and flaky. Remove fish carefully and keep warm. Reduce sauce quickly until thickened, strain and rub through a sieve, pour over fish and serve.

Note: Haddock or any other delicate flaky fish can be prepared the same way.

Shrimp ▷ with Dill Sauce

For Four

2 tbsp. butter
1 tbsp. cornstarch
½ tsp. dried dill weed
¼ tsp. salt
⅛ tsp. pepper
1 cup milk
¼ cup dry sherry
1 tbsp. lemon juice
1 lb. shrimp cleaned,
   deveined and cooked
cooked rice

In medium saucepan melt butter over low heat. Stir in cornstarch, dill, salt and pepper until smooth. Remove from heat. Gradually stir in milk until smooth. Bring to a boil over medium heat, stirring constantly, and boil 1 minute. Stir in sherry, lemon juice and shrimp. Reduce heat. Simmer 3 minutes or until heated through. Serve over rice.

Tempura

For Six
12 large shrimp
6 small fish filets (smelts,
   small flounder, blowfish)
6 firm mushroom caps
2 green peppers
1 sweet potato
salt
6 scallions
1 onion

Shell, devein, butterfly shrimp, leaving tail intact. Cut fish in slices about 3 inches long and 1½ inches wide. Remove seeds and membranes from peppers and cut in slices 1 inch wide. Trim scallions to uniform length and slice onion into ¼ inch thick slices. Arrange all ingredients on a platter, salt them lightly.

To Fry Tempura

Heat a mixture of ¾ vegetable oil (such as peanut or corn oil) and ¼ sesame oil to a temperature of 340°. The oil should be about 2 to 3 inches deep. If you have no frying thermometer, test the temperature by dropping a little batter in the oil. If the batter stays on the surface and bubbles, the oil is too hot. If the batter sinks to the bottom and stays there without bubbling for a second or two, the oil is too cold. At the proper temperature the batter will sink to the bottom, then immediately rise and splutter.

Dip pieces of food in the batter, then put them gently, a few at a time, into the hot oil and fry until they are golden brown. Remove and drain the pieces, as soon as they are cooked, on a wire rack or on paper and serve immediately. Serve each guest a bowl of Tempura Sauce.

Tempura Batter

1 egg
pinch of baking
   soda
¾ cup unsifted
   unbleached flour
1 cup ice water

Make the batter just before using. Beat the egg, add ice water and beat until frothy. Add baking soda and flour and beat quickly and lightly. Do not overbeat. The batter should not be too smooth and have a few lumps. It should not be sticky and heavy — but rather on the thin side. Add a little more water if too thick.

Tempura Sauce

1½ cups dashi*
4 tbsp. soy sauce
4 tbsp. sake or sherry
1 tbsp. scallions, minced
¼ cup Japanese white radish
   (daikon), grated (opt.)

Mix liquids, add scallions and daikon just before serving.

Note: There are a number of ready-made Tempura batter mixes on the market, some of them quite acceptable.

*See Glossary

Halibut Genovese

For Four
2½ lbs. halibut
3 tbsp. olive oil
1 medium onion, minced
2 cloves garlic, crushed
3 large tomatoes, peeled,
   seeded, chopped
1 tbsp. lemon juice
1 large green pepper,
   seeded, chopped
1 tbsp. parsley, minced
1 tbsp. fresh basil (or
   1 tsp. dried), chopped
salt and pepper to taste

Heat oil in a heavy saucepan, add onion and garlic and sauté until soft, do not brown. Add all other ingredients except fish, cover and simmer for 25 minutes. Add fish, cover and simmer for about 15 minutes or until fish is done. Move fish carefully to a serving dish and pour sauce over it.

Tuna Pie

For Six

2½ cups cooked rice
1 egg
1 cup shredded Swiss cheese
1 6½-oz. can tuna, drained,
  flaked
1 tbsp. finely chopped onion

1 10-oz. package frozen
  peas and carrots,
  cooked, drained
2 eggs, beaten
¾ cup milk
salt and pepper to taste
1 tsp. butter, melted

Combine rice and egg: mix well. Press into bottom and sides of buttered 9-inch pie plate, building ridge on rim. Layer ¾ cup cheese, tuna and vegetables in pie plate. Pour combined eggs, milk and seasonings over vegetables. Brush rim of crust with butter. Bake in a preheated oven at 350° for 50 to 55 minutes or until set. Sprinkle with remaining cheese.

Coquille St. Jacques Provencale

For Four

2 medium tomatoes,
  peeled, seeded, chopped
2 large cloves garlic,
  crushed
1 shallot, minced
2 tbsp. parsley, minced

1 tbsp. chives, chopped
2 tbsp. dry vermouth
1 tbsp. butter
salt and pepper to taste
1 lb. bay scallops
¼ cup flour
4 tbsp. butter

Sauté garlic and shallot for 2 minutes in 1 tablespoon butter. Do not let brown. Add tomatoes, parsley, chives, salt, pepper and vermouth. Blend and simmer 10 minutes. Dredge scallops with flour. Using another skillet sauté scallops in 4 tablespoons butter over fairly high heat for about 3 minutes until scallops have browned. Add tomato mixture, stir well and simmer 2 more minutes. Serve in scallop shells or ramekins and spoon sauce over them.

Bay Scallops en Coquille

For Four

1 lb. scallops
1½ cups firm mushrooms,
  finely chopped
1 small clove garlic,
  crushed

1 tbsp. minced shallots
1 tbsp. minced parsley
salt and pepper to taste
1 tbsp. dry vermouth
4 tbsp. butter
dry white breadcrumbs

Sauté shallots and garlic in butter for a couple of minutes. Remove scallops and reserve. Add mushrooms and sauté until mushrooms are cooked (about 3 minutes). Add vermouth, parsley, salt and pepper, sauté quickly until most of the liquid is absorbed. Put scallops into 4 buttered shells or ramekins, cover with the mushroom mixture, sprinkle with breadcrumbs and top with a pat of butter. Bake at 425° for about 6 to 8 minutes, until sizzling and browned.

Bayou Shrimp

For Four

2 tbsp. butter
1 large onion, chopped
1 large green pepper,
  seeded, chopped
2 cloves garlic, chopped
1½ cups stewed tomatoes
  (canned, drained)
1 package frozen okra

1 tsp. paprika
1 tsp. basil
cayenne pepper to taste
  (the sauce should be
  rather hot)
salt and pepper to taste
1½ lbs. fresh shrimp,
  shelled, deveined

Sauté onion in butter until soft but not browned. Add all other ingredients except shrimp, cover and simmer until okra is cooked, about 20 minutes. Add shrimp, simmer for 6 to 8 minutes longer, correct seasoning and serve on a bed of rice.

Creole Gumbo

For Six to Eight

2 lbs. unshelled shrimp
12 live blue fin crabs *or*
    4 cups crab meat, fresh
3 slices bacon
4 large onions, minced fine
4 cloves garlic, crushed
2 bay leaves
2 tbsp. finely chopped
    green pepper
pinch of thyme
1½ tsp. sugar
salt and pepper to taste

⅓ cup chopped parsley
2 lbs. fresh okra (or three
    10 oz. frozen packages)
1 large ham bone
½ lb. chicken wings or any
    leftover chicken
1 lb. boneless stewing veal
1 heaping tbsp. lard
1 large can (24 oz.) tomatoes
    or 4 large tomatoes, peeled
juice of ½ lemon
1 pint shelled fresh oysters
4 dashes Tabasco sauce

Remove shells from shrimp. Cover with water in a saucepan and bring to a boil. Drop the crabs into boiling water, cooking 5 minutes only. Strain shrimp shells, but reserve liquid, while discarding shrimp shells.

Clean the crab. Remove the shells, keeping intact. Discard "dead fingers" or lungs and entrails in center. Twist off the fins. Scrape out the shells, catching meat, juices and fat particles. Reserve this and the claws.

Fry the bacon in a large pot until crisp, remove and set aside.

Fry the onions until golden, add the garlic and fry until brown. Then add the bay leaves, green pepper, thyme sugar, salt and pepper. Cook slowly until the green pepper is limp. Add the fresh okra (if frozen, add later), cook until okra loses its gummy texture. In another pot, fry the ham bone with the lard, chicken and veal until brown. Pour off half the excess fat from the meat mixture and onion mixture. Combine the two mixtures.

Add the chopped parsley, tomatoes, Tabasco sauce and lemon juice. Add the crab meat with the juice. Then add the claws, shells, shrimp, oysters and bacon. Fill the pot with water, including reserved shrimp liquid, covering everything completely. At least 2 quarts of liquid are needed.

Simmer for 2 hours, stirring occasionally. Remove ham bone and chicken bones before serving with piping hot rice in soup plates.

Stuffed Striped Bass

For Six

5 to 6 lb. striped bass
4 tbsp. melted butter

½ cup dry vermouth
salt to taste

Stuffing:

3 tbsp. minced shallots
1 small clove garlic, minced
1 tbsp. parsley, minced
2 tsp. paprika
1 tsp. rosemary, crushed
4 tbsp. butter

2 cups chopped mushrooms
1 cup cooked lobster or
    crabmeat, diced or flaked
2½ cups soft white
    breadcrumbs
1 cup dry white wine
salt and pepper to taste

Have fish scaled, completely boned, but leaving the skin intact. Prepare the stuffing: Sauté shallots in butter until soft but not browned. Add all other ingredients except breadcrumbs and wine, blend well and sauté over gentle flame 3 or 4 minutes longer. Stir often. Remove from fire, mix with breadcrumbs and add enough wine to moisten mixture.

Spread fish open. Salt lightly inside and out. Fill with stuffing, fold fish back to its natural shape, push skewers or toothpicks through skin and close opening by lacing with string. (The skin is quite tough. It is easier to push the toothpicks through, starting from the inside.) Brush fish liberally with melted butter, sprinkle with paprika. Place in a roasting pan, add ⅓ cup vermouth and bake at 350° for about 45 minutes until cooked and fish is flaky. Baste and add more vermouth if needed. Remove to serving dish, remove skewers and string, garnish with fresh parsley, serve with melted butter and lemon juice mixed.

Note: Instead of a whole bass, you may use filets (not skinned). Place stuffing on one filet, top with the other and close openings with toothpicks.

◊ Zarzuela

For Six
1 lb. fresh codfish
1 lb. striped bass
¾ lb. eel, skinned
6 large shrimp, cooked
1 lb. mussels
4 small squid (opt.)
6 tbsp. olive oil
2 tbsp. butter
2 onions, thinly sliced
¾ cup tomato purée
4 cups dry white wine
1 tbsp. rum
salt and pepper to taste
1 clove garlic, minced
½ cup fresh white breadcrumbs
⅛ tsp. Spanish saffron
½ cup minced parsley
12 blanched almonds

Cut the codfish, bass and eel into thick pieces. Shell the cooked shrimp. Scrub the mussels and cook over high heat until the shells open. Remove from shells, discard any that have not opened. Add mussels to shrimp. Strain and reserve all the mussel juice. Wash squid and cut them in pieces.

Heat half the oil and all the butter in a large skillet, sauté the onions until they are soft. Add the eel, squid, tomato purée, wine and rum. Bring to a boil, cook over high heat for 10 minutes. Pour the contents of the skillet into a casserole, add half of the mussel liquid, mix well.

Add remaining oil to the skillet and cook the pieces of codfish and bass in it for about 3 minutes or until the flesh begins to firm. Season with salt and pepper and add fish to casserole. Simmer covered for 20 minutes but do not let boil.

Mix garlic, breadcrumbs, saffron and half the parsley. Add the remaining mussel liquid and mix until smooth. Add this mixture and almonds to casserole. Blend carefully. Finally add the mussels and shrimp, cook for 2 minutes. Sprinkle with remaining parsley, decorate with bread triangles and serve directly from the casserole.

Shrimp Ajillo ▽

For Four to Six
10 garlic cloves, peeled
¼ cup olive oil
2 lbs. medium shrimp, peeled and deveined
2 bay leaves
¼ cup dry sherry
½ tsp. salt
½ tsp. celery salt
pinch of cayenne pepper
alli-o-li (p. 313)

In a large skillet brown garlic cloves in oil. Add shrimp and bay leaves. Sauté over high heat until shrimp are cooked — about 3 to 4 minutes — stirring and shaking the pan. Stir in sherry, salt, celery salt and cayenne pepper. Remove from heat, stir in Alli-o-li by the large spoonfuls and serve immediately.

Shrimp and Chicken Salad

For Four

¾ lb. medium shrimp, cooked, shelled, diced
1½ cups diced cooked chicken meat
1 tbsp. grated onion
2 cloves garlic, minced
3 scallions, minced

2 tbsp. lemon juice
1 tbsp. lime juice
1 tbsp. white vinegar
½ tsp. grated lemon peel
pinch of cayenne pepper
2 tsp. sugar
½ tsp. ground coriander
2 tbsp. parsley, minced

Place chicken and shrimp in a serving bowl. Combine and blend all other ingredients except parsley and mix with shrimp and chicken. Let stand for 1 hour. Sprinkle with parsley when serving.

Baked Swordfish Marmara

For Four

2 lbs. swordfish steak, cut about 1 inch thick
salt and pepper to taste
1 tbsp. butter
4 tbsp. olive oil
4 scallions, chopped

1 clove garlic, crushed
¼ cup chopped dill
¼ cup chopped parsley
¼ cup tomato puree
¼ cup dry white wine
2 tbsp. lemon juice

Place fish in a buttered baking dish, season with salt and pepper and spread oil on top of fish. Mix scallions, garlic, dill and parsley, sprinkle over fish; mix tomato puree, white wine and lemon juice and spread on top. Bake at 350° for about 20 to 25 minutes until fish is done. Baste once or twice with pan juices.

Oysters Mornay

For Four

24 large oysters
1 cup dry white wine
1 cup very thick Mornay Sauce (p. 314)

½ lb. fresh mushrooms, minced
3 tbsp. butter
½ cup grated Swiss cheese

Shuck the oysters and reserve their liquid. Strain the oyster liquid and combine it with the wine in an enamel sauce-pan, add the oysters and heat them through without boiling, for about 5 minutes. Drain the oysters and strain the liquid again through a very fine sieve into another sauce-pan. Reduce over high heat to about 1 cup and stir in the Sauce Mornay. Remove from heat and reserve.

Clean and wash the deep halves of the oyster shells. Heat the butter and sauté the mushrooms until they are soft. Line the bottom of the oyster shells with a little of the sautéed mushrooms, cover with some of the sauce, place an oyster on top of each shell and cover with the remaining sauce. Sprinkle with cheese and run briefly under a broiler until the tops are bubbling and lightly browned.

Sautéed Codfish Lyonnaise

For Four

1 lb. salted dried cod
1 large onion, sliced thin
2 potatoes, peeled, sliced ⅛-inch thick
6 tbsp. butter

4 tbsp. oil
2 cloves garlic, minced
1 tsp. chervil
salt and pepper to taste
4 tbsp. wine vinegar
2 tbsp. minced parsley

Soak fish overnight in cold water, change water a couple of times. Next day, drain fish, rinse under cold running water and drain again. Put fish in a saucepan, cover with water, bring to a boil, simmer for about 20 minutes. Drain, put cooked fish in a colander to drain more, let stand half an hour. Remove bones from fish. Heat butter and oil in a heavy skillet, add onions and potatoes and sauté for about 10 to 15 minutes until potatoes are nearly cooked. Add fish, garlic, chervil, sauté over medium fire until fish, potatoes and onions are golden brown. Season with salt and pepper, sprinkle with vinegar and parsley and serve.

Frog Legs Meuniere

For Four

16 pair frog legs
2 cups milk or stale beer
flour
3 tbsp. butter

3 tbsp. oil
juice of 1 lemon
2 tbsp. minced parsley
salt and pepper to taste

Soak the frog legs in milk or beer to cover for 2 hours. Drain and pat dry. Coat the legs with flour, shake off excess flour. Heat butter and oil in a skillet, sauté the legs, a few at a time, until golden brown, then turn and sauté the other side. Transfer the legs to a hot platter and sauté the remaining legs. When cooked, sprinkle with fresh lemon juice and a little parsley, season with salt and pepper and serve.

Clam Patties

For Four to Six

2 cups finely chopped clams
2 eggs, well beaten
2 tbsp. parsley, minced
1 tbsp. onion, grated
pinch of thyme

1 tbsp. lemon juice
salt and pepper to taste
1 cup cracker crumbs
   (approx.)
5 tbsp. butter

Blend clams, eggs, parsley, onion, thyme, lemon juice, salt and pepper. Add enough cracker crumbs to make a fairly stiff mixture. Shape into patties and fry in butter until golden brown on both sides, turning them only once while frying. Add more butter if needed. Serve with lemon wedges.

Seafood Casserole

For Four

½ lb. bay scallops (or sea
   scallops cut in 3 pieces)
½ lb. raw shrimp, shelled
2 tbsp. butter
1½ tbsp. shallots, minced
1 small clove garlic, minced
¼ cup clam juice
¼ cup dry sherry wine

1 tbsp. lemon juice
dash of Tabasco sauce
salt and pepper to taste
1 tsp. dry mustard
½ lb. cooked lobster meat
2 egg yolks
3 tbsp. heavy cream
4 tbsp. mayonnaise
1 tbsp. cornstarch

Melt butter in a skillet, add scallops, shrimp, shallots, garlic, sherry, clam juice, lemon juice, Tabasco, salt, pepper and dry mustard. Mix well, sauté for about 4 minutes while stirring. Remove scallops and shrimp with a slotted spoon and arrange together with lobster meat in a buttered baking dish. Dissolve cornstarch in 2 tablespoons water, add to juices in the skillet, blend well. Beat egg yolks until creamy, blend with cream and mayonnaise, mix with sauce in skillet. Pour the sauce over the shellfish, bake at 400° for 8 to 10 minutes until top is golden brown.

Filet of Flounder Ile de Ré

For Four

8 medium flounder filets
¾ cup crabmeat or
   shrimp, chopped
6 tbsp. butter
2 tbsp. shallots, minced
1 small clove garlic, minced
1 tbsp. parsley, minced

⅓ cup mushrooms, chopped
2 tsp. paprika
pinch of cayenne pepper
salt to taste
1½ cups soft breadcrumbs
2 tbsp. Cognac
dry white wine or
   dry vermouth

Sauté shallots and garlic in 3 tablespoons butter until soft. Add mushrooms, sauté 2 more minutes, then add crabmeat or shrimp, parsley, paprika, cayenne and salt; sauté, stirring, another 2 minutes then blend in Cognac and remove from fire. Salt to taste. Mix with breadcrumbs and add enough wine or vermouth to make the stuffing slightly moist. Trim filets to uniform size, spread stuffing on 4 filets, top with the other four. Brush liberally with melted butter, sprinkle a few breadcrumbs on top. Put in buttered baking dish and bake at 375° for 15 to 20 minutes. Baste once or twice with butter and a little wine.

Lobster Cantonese ▽

For Four

2 lobsters (1½ lbs. each)
½ lb. lean pork, ground
3 tbsp. oil
½ cup chicken broth
1½ tbsp. cornstarch
2 tbsp. soy sauce
2 tbsp. sherry

1 tsp. salt
1 clove garlic, minced
1½ tsp. fresh ginger root, minced
2 scallions, minced
2 eggs, beaten
3 tbsp. water

Have the lobsters split and cleaned. Chop each in 1½ inch pieces and the claws in three pieces. Heat oil in a wok, add garlic and ginger, stir-fry a few seconds; add pork and scallions and fry 3 minutes until all traces of pink have disappeared. Add lobster, stir-fry 1 minute, stir in broth and salt, cover and cook gently for 3 minutes. Blend cornstarch with soy sauce and sherry, add to wok and stir to thicken. Beat eggs lightly and combine with water. Remove wok from heat and add eggs, stir until well mixed and serve.

Poached Haddock ◁ with Mussels

For Six

2 lbs. cod or haddock filets
4 dozen mussels
1 cup dry white wine
1 cup water
1 small onion, sliced
salt to taste
½ cup heavy cream
¼ cup butter
pepper to taste
pinch of nutmeg
2 tbsp. chopped parsley

For garnish:
parslied potatoes
julienne cut* carrots, celery and
    zucchini, sautéed in butter

Cut fish in serving size portions. Scrub mussels under cold running water. Combine wine, water and onion in a large saucepan and bring to a simmer. Add mussels, cover and steam for about 5 minutes or until shells open. Remove mussels from shells and reserve. Strain cooking liquid into a large skillet. Add fish and salt, cover and simmer for 8 to 10 minutes or until fish flakes easily when tested with a fork. Transfer fish carefully to a serving platter and keep warm. Reduce cooking liquid quickly to about ½ cup. Add mussels and parsley, heat through. Spoon the mixture over the fish, garnish with potatoes and vegetables and serve.

*See Glossary

Baked Clams Caruso

2 doz. clams
1 cup soft white
   breadcrumbs
1 large clove garlic, minced
1 tsp. oregano
1 tbsp. parsley, minced

½ tsp. basil
pepper to taste
1 tbsp. tomato paste
3 tbsp. grated Parmesan
   cheese
⅓ cup olive oil

Scrub clams, open and discard one half shell each. Drain juice off clams. Mix all other ingredients except oil. Cover each of the clams with some of the mixture, sprinkle with oil, bake in preheated 400° oven for 7 to 8 minutes until golden brown.

Steamed Sea Bass

For Four
2½ - 3 lb. sea bass
1 tsp. salt
1 clove garlic, crushed
2 thin slices fresh
   ginger root, minced

½ tsp. salt
2 scallions, minced
3 tbsp. soy sauce
1½ tbsp. sherry
1 tsp. sugar
1 tbsp. oil

Leave head and tail on cleaned and scaled fish. Score both sides of fish with three diagonal cuts. Sprinkle with one teaspoon salt. Mash garlic with ½ teaspoon salt to a paste. Combine with all other ingredients, blend well. Put fish on a shallow serving dish, spread mixed sauce over the fish. Place dish in a steamer and steam for about 30 minutes until fish is done.

Fried Shrimp

For Three
12 jumbo shrimp
1 large clove garlic
½ tsp. salt
1 tbsp. grated ginger root
1 cup flour, sifted
4½ tsp. baking powder

2 tbsp. cornstarch
6 tbsp. oil
1 cup water (approx.)
oil for deep frying
scallions, cut lengthwise
   in thin strips

Shell shrimp but leave the tail segment of the shell, butterfly shrimp and devein. Crush garlic with salt to a paste and rub into shrimp, sprinkle with a little ginger root.

Blend flour, baking powder, cornstarch; add oil gradually while stirring. Stir until mixture forms a ball. Add water, a little at a time, while stirring until the mixture has the consistency of pancake batter.

Heat oil, dip each shrimp into the batter and fry, two or three at a time, until golden brown. Drain before serving. Garnish with scallion strips.

Marinated Shrimp

For Six
1½ lbs. medium shrimps,
   cooked and deveined
1 medium ripe tomato,
   peeled, seeded, minced
2 tbsp. Dijon mustard
2 tsp. prepared horseradish

2 tbsp. lime juice
¾ cup olive oil
1 tsp. chili powder
pinch of cayenne pepper
salt and pepper to taste
¾ cup white wine vinegar

Combine all ingredients, pour over shrimp, blend well and marinate for several hours before serving.

Filet of Flounder Amandine

For Four

milk or beer
flour
4 large flounder filets
3 tbsp. oil
4 tbsp. butter

¼ cup slivered blanched
   almonds
2 tbsp. parsley, minced
1 tbsp. lemon juice
1 peeled lemon, sliced

Dip filets in milk or beer, then coat them with flour. Heat oil and butter in a skillet, sauté the filets quickly until golden brown on both sides. Do not overcook. Transfer filets carefully to a hot serving dish. Add almonds and lemon juice to skillet, cook stirring constantly until almond slivers turn brown. Pour almonds and pan juices over the filets, sprinkle with parsley, garnish with lemon slices and serve.

Cod Filets a la Turque

For Four

2 lbs. cod filets
salt and pepper to taste
flour
2 eggs, beaten with
   2 tbsp. milk
4 tbsp. butter

¼ cup cooking oil
1½ cups sour cream
1 tbsp. fresh dill, chopped
   (or 1½ tsp. dried dill
   leaves)
1 tsp. paprika

Trim filets and cut into serving pieces, season with salt and pepper, dredge with flour, shake off excess flour. Dip fish in beaten egg. Heat butter and oil in a skillet, fry fish until golden brown on both sides. Place fish in a baking dish, dot with a few pats of butter. Combine sour cream and dill, pour over fish, sprinkle with paprika. Bake in 350° oven for 15 minutes.

Crabmeat Casserole

◁

For Six to Eight
1 lb. crabmeat
1 bunch broccoli
4 tbsp. butter
4 tbsp. flour
salt and pepper to taste
2½ cups milk
1 cup light cream
⅓ cup thinly sliced scallions
2 tbsp. chopped pimiento
3 tbsp. slivered almonds

Trim broccoli, cut off florets and cut stems into bite-sized pieces. Heat butter in a small saucepan, stir in flour and salt, sauté while stirring for a minute or two. Gradually add milk and cream, stir constantly and cook over gentle heat until the sauce is smooth and has thickened. In the meantime cook broccoli in water until just tender, drain.

Fold crabmeat, scallions and pimiento into the white sauce, season with pepper and more salt if needed. Arrange broccoli florettes around edge of a shallow baking dish. Fill center with remaining broccoli pieces and spoon crabmeat and sauce over broccoli in the center of the dish. Bake at 375° for about 20 minutes or until hot and bubbly.

Maryland Crab Cakes ▷

4 slices bread
½ cup olive oil
¼ tsp. mustard
½ tsp. salt
1 dash paprika
1 tsp. Worcestershire sauce
2 eggs
1 tsp. chopped parsley
1 lb. crab flakes
     (backfin lump)

Trim crusts from bread. Lay on flat tin or platter. Pour olive oil over them. Let stand 1 hour. Pull bread apart with two forks. To the small bits of bread add seasonings, yolks of egg and crab meat; mix lightly with fork, fold in stiffly beaten egg whites and shape into cakes. Brown in hot skillet just brushed with fat. Cakes will be light, fluffy.

Crab Loaf ▷

Take a whole loaf, cut off the top and scrape out all the crumb. Have the crabs picked and dress with pepper, salt, a few celery seed and a good deal of mustard. Mix some of the crumb with a little sweet cream with the crabs. Fill the loaf, put the top on, and put in the oven to crisp. Wrap in foil, take along on picnic. Can be garnished with sliced tomatoes, sliced eggs.

Lobster Tails Bordelaise

For Four
4 tbsp. butter
2 medium carrots, diced
1 small onion, minced
4 frozen lobster tails
    (about 4 oz. each)
1 tbsp. olive oil

2 tbsp. Cognac
½ clove garlic, minced
½ cup dry white wine
3 tbsp. tomato paste
¼ cup chicken broth
salt and pepper to taste
pinch of cayenne pepper

Heat 2 tablespoons butter in a small saucepan, add carrots and onion, cover and cook over low heat for 30 minutes. Stir a few times. Cut lobster tails in 2-inch pieces, remove thin under-shell using scissors. Heat 1 tablespoon butter and olive oil in a skillet, add lobster pieces, meat side down, add garlic and sauté until lobster is lightly browned. Add Cognac to pan, ignite. When flame dies down, add carrots, onion and all other ingredients except 1 tablespoon butter. Stir well, cover, simmer 10 minutes. Remove lobster to hot serving dish, rub sauce through a sieve, return to pan and reduce quickly to half its volume. Stir in remaining butter, pour over lobster and serve.

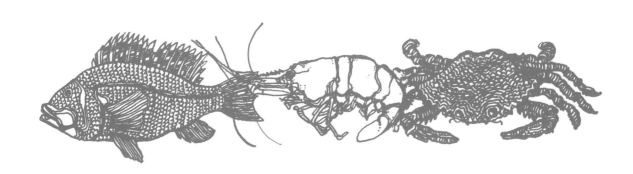

Braised Carp

For Six
1 carp (4 to 5 lbs.), cleaned
    and cut into large pieces
¾ cup peeled and diced
    carrots
¾ cup celery, white part
    only, diced
1 parsley root,
    peeled and diced

2 tbsp. butter or margarine
1½ cups chopped onion
3 cups water
1 bay leaf
¼ tsp. peppercorns
1 small pinch allspice
1 tbsp. vinegar
salt to taste
1 small white turnip, diced

Melt butter in a saucepan, spread vegetables on top and simmer covered for about 5 minutes. Add all other ingredients except fish, cover and cook for about 10 minutes or until vegetables are nearly cooked. Place fish on top of vegetables, cover and cook gently for another 15 to 20 minutes. Serve pieces of fish with the vegetables and broth.

Jellied Carp
Proceed as above, use 4 cups of water instead of 3, add 1 tablespoon of sugar to the vegetables. When fish is cooked, spread the cooked vegetables in a serving dish, place fish on top, cover with the cooking liquid and chill until jelled.

Sole Bonne Femme

For Four to Six

2 tbsp. butter
2 lbs. filet of sole
　or flounder
¾ cup sherry, medium dry
1½ tbsp. lemon juice

2 tbsp. minced white onion
½ lb. mushrooms, minced
1 tbsp. parsley, minced
salt and pepper to taste
2 cups white sauce*

Grease a shallow oblong baking dish with 1 tablespoon butter, place filets in dish, mix sherry and lemon juice and add to the dish. Spread mushrooms on fish, sprinkle with onion and parsley, season with salt and pepper.

Cover baking dish, bake in 325⁰ oven for about 15 minutes until fish is tender and flaky. Pour white sauce over fish, dot with remaining butter, put under the broiler and broil for about 2 minutes until well browned.

*See Glossary

Skate with Brown Butter

For Four

2 lbs. skate, cut in
　serving pieces
3 tbsp. vinegar
1 medium onion, sliced
1 bay leaf

3 sprigs parsley
1 clove garlic, peeled
pinch of thyme
½ tsp. peppercorns
1 tbsp. salt

Rinse fish with cold water. Put in a saucepan, pour boiling water over fish and let stand 10 seconds. Drain. Cover fish with cold water, add all other ingredients, bring to a boil and simmer gently for 15 minutes. Remove fish from liquid, slip off skins, put on a serving platter.

Brown Butter

⅓ cup butter
1 tbsp. parsley, chopped

1½ tbsp. capers, drained
½ tsp. lemon juice
1 dash Tabasco sauce (opt.)

Melt butter until it foams, and starts to turn light brown. Add all other ingredients, blend and pour over fish before serving.

Matelote Marinière

For Eight

2 eels, cleaned, skinned,
　cut in 2-inch pieces
　(about 1½ lbs.)
1 lb. blackfish or striped
　bass filet, cut in
　1-inch pieces
1 lb. halibut, anglerfish or
　other firm fish, cut in
　1-inch pieces
1 medium onion, sliced thin
1 small carrot, peeled,
　cut in thin rounds

1 sprig thyme
4 sprigs parsley
1 tbsp. butter
dry red wine
salt and pepper to taste
2 tbsp. Cognac (opt.)
16 small white onions,
　peeled, cooked
2 tbsp. butter
2 tbsp. flour
2 cloves garlic, minced
1 bay leaf

Melt 1 tablespoon butter in a heavy saucepan, add onion, garlic, carrot, also thyme, bay leaf and parsley tied together with a string. Place pieces of eel and fish on top, season with salt and pepper, barely cover with red wine. Bring to a boil, add Cognac and ignite. When the flame has died down, cover pan and simmer for 15 to 20 minutes. In the meantime, cream 2 tablespoons butter and flour. When fish is done, remove carefully with a slotted spoon to a serving dish and keep hot. Add the flour mixture to the sauce, simmer while stirring until dissolved and has thickened. Simmer 2 or 3 minutes longer. Correct seasoning, strain sauce over fish, garnish with hot onions and serve.

Lobster a l'Armoricaine

For Four
2 live 2-lb. lobsters
3 tbsp. oil
½ cup minced onion
4 shallots, minced
salt and pepper to taste
2 cups tomato sauce
¼ cup Cognac
2 tbsp. Madeira wine
2 tbsp. butter

Put the lobsters in boiling water and cook for 8 minutes after water returns to a boil. Drain lobsters and cool slightly. Cut the tails, shell and all, into thick slices, split the upper bodies lengthwise in half, discard the sac behind the head, reserve tomalley and coral, if any. Sever the claws from the bodies and crack them.

Heat oil in a casserole, sauté onions and shallots until they are soft. Add all the lobster pieces, season with salt and pepper and sauté them for 4 minutes. Add tomato sauce, cook 5 minutes longer, add Cognac. Flambe; when the flames die down, simmer over low heat for 10 minutes. Transfer lobster pieces to a hot serving dish. Strain the sauce and return it to the casserole. Rub tomalley and coral through a sieve into the sauce, add Madeira. Reduce sauce quickly by one third, correct seasoning. Swirl in 2 tablespoons cold butter, cut into small pieces, return lobster to sauce and heat through. Serve with plain boiled rice.

Rice Seafood Filets

For Six
1½ lbs. fish filets (flounder, sole, or other white fish)
1 tsp. lemon juice
salt, pepper, and paprika
1 egg, beaten
⅔ cup tomato juice
2½ cups cooked rice
1 tbsp. minced onions
⅔ cup soft bread crumbs
1 can (5 ozs.) small shrimp
2 tbsp. snipped parsley
1 tsp. celery salt
¼ tsp. pepper
6 slices bacon
lemon juice

Cut fish into 6 long thin strips. Sprinkle with lemon juice and season with salt, pepper, and paprika. Set aside. Combine remaining ingredients except bacon and lemon juice. Mix thoroughly. Form into 6 rolls and wrap each with a fish filet and a strip of bacon. Secure with wooden picks or metal skewers. Place in greased baking pan. Bake at 350° for 25 to 30 minutes or until fish flakes easily. Remove from oven and brush with lemon juice.

Stuffed Mackerel

For Four
4 small mackerel
10 tbsp. oil
1 large onion, minced
1/3 cup ground walnuts
2 tbsp. pine nuts
1/3 cup soft white
  breadcrumbs

1/4 cup currants
salt and pepper to taste
2 tbsp. parsley, chopped
1 tbsp. fresh dill, chopped
2 eggs, lightly beaten
dry breadcrumbs
sliced lemon

Clean mackerel, wash and pat dry. Heat 2 tablespoons oil in a skillet, add onion, sauté until light golden brown, add nuts, currants, soft breadcrumbs, salt, pepper, parsley and dill. Blend and cook gently for another 3 or 4 minutes while stirring. Remove from fire, let cool. Stuff mackerel with the mixture, close openings with toothpicks. Dip mackerel in beaten egg, roll in breadcrumbs. Heat remaining oil in a skillet, fry fish for about 3 minutes on each side until done and nicely browned, drain on paper towel, garnish with lemon slices and serve.

Paupiette of Sole

For Six
1 cup firm mushrooms,
  minced
3 tbsp. butter
1/3 cup shallots, chopped
1/3 cup parsley, chopped
1 cup chives, chopped
1 small clove garlic, minced
6 filets of sole
  (or flounder)
2 eggs

salt and pepper to taste
1/2 cup milk
fritter batter
dry white breadcrumbs
5 tbsp. butter
3 tbsp. flour
1 cup dry white wine
1 cup heavy cream
pinch of cayenne pepper
1/4 cup grated Parmesan
  cheese

Sauté mushrooms in butter for 3 minutes, add shallots, parsley, chives and garlic, sauté until the shallots are soft. Season filets with salt and pepper, spread some of the mushroom mixture on each, roll them up and fasten with toothpicks. Beat eggs and milk, dip fishrolls in the egg mixture then roll in breadcrumbs and finally dip in the batter. Let them rest for 15 minutes before cooking.

Melt 5 tablespoons butter in a heavy skillet, brown the fishrolls gently on all sides, then remove carefully and keep warm. Stir flour into the skillet, blend with the butter used in frying, then add wine. Stir until sauce is smooth and has thickened. Add the cream and cayenne, blend well and heat through. Spoon the sauce over the fish, sprinkle with cheese and put under the broiler until golden brown.

Fritter Batter
2 egg yolks
2 egg whites beaten stiff
7 tbsp. flour

1/2 cup milk
1 scant tsp. baking powder
salt and pepper to taste

Blend egg yolks, flour, milk, baking powder, salt and pepper. Fold in egg whites. Coat shrimp or clams or pieces of fish with the batter, fry a few pieces at a time in hot fat.

Bacala (Salt Codfish)

For Four
1 lb. salt codfish
flour
1/3 cup olive oil
1 large onion, minced
2 cloves garlic, minced
1 bay leaf

salt and pepper to taste
3 ripe tomatoes, peeled,
  seeded, chopped
1/2 tsp. basil
3 tbsp. pimiento, chopped
a few threads of saffron
2 tbsp. parsley, chopped

Soak cod for 8 hours in cold water. Change water two or three times. Drain fish, dry with paper towels, cut fish in strips, dust with flour and sauté in oil until golden brown. Remove from pan and reserve. Add onion to pan and sauté until soft, do not let brown. Return fish to pan, add all other ingredients, blend and simmer on top of stove for about 45 minutes or until fish is cooked; or cover and cook in 350° oven for about the same length of time.

Broiled Shrimp (Sate Udang)

For Four
16 jumbo shrimp
  (approx. 1½ lbs.)
3 tbsp. fresh lemon juice
½ cup coconut cream*
pinch of cayenne pepper
½ tsp. ground coriander

1 tbsp. dark soy sauce
1 large clove garlic,
  crushed
2 tsp. grated lemon peel
1 tsp. sugar
salt to taste
3 tbsp. oil

Peel and devein shrimp. Combine all other ingredients except oil, marinate shrimp in the mixture for an hour or more. Thread shrimp on small skewers, brush with oil and broil quickly turning them once, until lightly browned. Do not overcook. Serve remaining marinade as a sauce to go with the shrimp.

*See Glossary

Braised Soy Fish

For Three
2 lbs. fish (large whiting,
  sea bass, weakfish)
1 tsp. salt
flour
1½ tsp. fresh ginger root,
  minced
2 scallions, minced

1 small clove garlic,
  minced
5 tbsp. oil
1 cup chicken broth
2 tbsp. soy sauce
2 tbsp. oyster sauce
2 tbsp. sherry
pinch of cayenne pepper

Have fish cleaned and carefully scaled, but left whole. Wipe and dry fish with paper towels, inside and out. With a sharp knife score both sides of fish with 2 diagonal cuts. Sprinkle with salt and let stand 15 minutes. Then dust lightly with flour.

Combine scallions, ginger, garlic, chicken broth, soy sauce, oyster sauce, sherry and cayenne pepper. Heat and keep warm.

Heat oil in a heavy saucepan until quite hot. Put fish into the pan, fry quickly for one minute, turn it over carefully with a spatula; fry the other side one minute, reduce heat, turn again very carefully and fry each side 2 minutes more. Baste fish with oil while frying. Pour the broth mixture over fish, bring to a boil, cover and cook gently about 15 minutes, until fish is done.

Bluefish Provencale

For Four
4 tbsp. butter
3 tbsp. minced onion
1½ cups firm mushrooms,
  chopped
¼ cup cooked ham, minced
½ cup tomato puree
1 tbsp. parsley, minced
1 large clove garlic, minced

1 tbsp. pimiento, chopped
½ tsp. tarragon
pinch of cayenne pepper
½ cup dry white wine
salt and pepper to taste
4 medium bluefish filets
soft white breadcrumbs
butter

Sauté onions and mushrooms in 4 tablespoons butter for about 5 minutes. Do not let brown. When onions are soft, add all other ingredients except fish and breadcrumbs. Mix well and simmer for 10 minutes. Arrange filets in well-buttered baking dish, spread the sauce over the filets, top with breadcrumbs, dot with a few pats of butter. Bake at 375° for about 15 minutes, then brown for a minute or two under the broiler.

Shrimp Tarragon with Pimiento Rice

For Four
2 tbsp. butter, melted
3 tbsp. flour
1 can (10 oz.) frozen cream
   of shrimp soup, thawed
½ cup chicken broth
½ cup Sauterne wine

2 tbsp. lemon juice
½ tsp. *each* tarragon,
   seasoned pepper, salt,
   and onion powder
1½ lbs. shrimp, peeled,
   deveined*
pimiento rice

Blend butter and flour until smooth. Slowly add soup, broth, Sauterne, lemon juice, and seasonings. Cook, stirring constantly, until thickened. Add shrimp and cook 5 to 10 minutes longer. Serve over pimiento rice. Sprinkle with fresh parsley.

Pimiento Rice
1 cup chopped onions
2 tbsp. butter

3 cups cooked rice
¼ cup diced pimiento

Sauté onions in butter until tender. Add rice and pimiento, and cook until thoroughly heated.

*Substitute 2 to 3 cups cooked crab meat or lobster meat for the shrimp, if desired.

⇦ Shrimp Sauce on Corn Bread

For Six
1 package (10 oz.) cornbread mix
½ cup sharp cheddar cheese,
   shredded
1 egg, beaten
¼ cup milk
1 cup creamed corn

Combine cornbread mix and cheese, toss lightly with a fork. Add egg, milk and corn, stir until just blended. Spread in a greased 8 x 8 pan, bake at 400⁰ about 25 minutes until done and lightly browned.

Shrimp Sauce
¾ lb. medium shrimp, cooked,
   shelled, deveined
½ cup chopped onion
½ cup green pepper, chopped
2 tbsp. butter
dash of Tabasco sauce
2 tbsp. flour
1 lb. canned tomato wedges
2 tbsp. tomato paste
1 tbsp. Worcestershire sauce
¼ cup chicken broth
salt and pepper to taste

Heat butter in a saucepan, sauté onion and pepper until soft, do not brown. Stir in flour and sauté for a minute. Add tomato wedges and all other ingredients, blend well and simmer until sauce has thickened. Stir often. To serve, spoon sauce over cornbread.

Baked Halibut

For Four
2 lbs. halibut
¾ cup chopped onion
1 clove garlic, chopped
2 tbsp. olive oil
¼ cup dry white wine
¼ cup water
salt and pepper to taste
1½ cups canned tomatoes,
    drained, chopped

¼ tsp. thyme
1½ tbsp. flour
3 tbsp. coarsely chopped
    green olives
3 tbsp. coarsely chopped
    ripe black olives
2 tbsp. capers, drained
2 tbsp. parsley, chopped
⅓ cup celery, white part,
    minced

Heat oil in a saucepan, add onion and garlic and sauté until golden brown. Add wine, water, salt, pepper, tomatoes, thyme, cover and simmer for half an hour. Dilute flour with a little water, stir into the simmering sauce and cook for another 2 or 3 minutes. Add olives, capers, parsley and celery, blend well. Put halibut in a buttered baking dish, pour the sauce over it and bake at 350⁰ for half an hour. Baste a few times.

Stuffed Pike or Whitefish

For Four
fish, 3 to 4 lbs.
8 anchovy filets
1 tbsp. butter or margarine
1 roll, moistened with milk
2 egg yolks
1 tbsp. parsley, minced

1 tsp. paprika
salt and pepper to taste
2 egg whites, beaten stiff
¼ cup melted butter
    or margarine
1½ cups sour cream
1 tbsp. flour

Wash cleaned fish and pat dry. Mash 4 anchovy filets, cream with 1 tablespoon butter. Squeeze moistened roll dry and mash, combine with anchovy butter, beaten egg yolks, parsley, paprika, salt and pepper, blend well. Fold in beaten egg whites and stuff the fish cavity with this mixture. Sew up the cavity with thread. Use a little of the melted butter to grease the bottom of a baking dish, place the fish in the dish, brush the fish with melted butter and put remaining 4 anchovy filets on the fish. Bake in 350⁰ oven for about 45 minutes. When fish begins to brown, baste with butter. About 15 minutes before fish is cooked, blend flour into the sour cream and spread the cream over the fish. Baste occasionally and continue cooking until well browned.

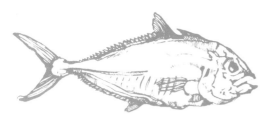

Fried Fish

For Four
1 whole large porgy
    (or red snapper),
    about 2½ lbs.
5 tbsp. oil
2 large cloves garlic,
    chopped
3 tbsp. light soy sauce
2 tbsp. fish sauce*

1½ tbsp. lime juice
1 tbsp. dark brown sugar
2 tsp. grated fresh ginger
½ tsp. ground coriander
¼ tsp. cayenne pepper
    (or to taste)
3 scallions, chopped
salt to taste

Have fish cleaned and scaled, rinse and dry well inside and out. Heat oil in a deep skillet, fry fish quickly until browned on one side, turn carefully and brown the other side. Do not over cook. Remove fish to a serving platter, keep warm.

   Pour off most of the oil in the skillet, add garlic and sauté until garlic is lightly browned. Add soy sauce, fish sauce, lime juice and sugar; mix and bring to a simmer. Add ginger, cayenne, scallions and simmer 2 or 3 minutes longer. Season with salt, cover fish with the sauce and serve.

*Available at most Oriental food stores.

Whiting a la Bretonne

For Four
8 whiting filets
6 tbsp. butter
1½ tbsp. shallots, minced
1 tsp. capers, drained,
    minced

1 tbsp. parsley, minced
¼ cup dry white wine
1 tsp. Dijon mustard
salt and pepper to taste
½ tsp. lemon juice

Put filets in a well-buttered shallow baking dish. Sprinkle shallots, parsley and capers on the filets, stir mustard into the wine and pour over the filets. Dot with pieces of butter, season with salt and pepper and simmer on top of the stove over gentle heat for 10 minutes. Drain off the cooking liquid and reduce it quickly to about half a cup. Add to it 1½ tablespoons melted butter, lemon juice, blend well, correct seasoning. Pour the sauce over the fish and brown quickly under a hot broiler.

Scalloped Clams

For Four
1 medium onion, minced
3 tbsp. butter
1 doz. large clams, chopped
⅓ cup firm mushrooms,
    chopped

3 tbsp. thick white sauce
2 egg yolks, lightly beaten
1 tbsp. parsley, minced
salt and pepper to taste
cracker meal
melted butter

Sauté onions in 3 tablespoons butter until soft. Add chopped clams and mushrooms, let simmer for about 3 minutes. Blend in white sauce, egg yolks, parsley, season with salt and pepper. Fill large clam shells or scallop shells with the mixture, dust with cracker meal, sprinkle with

melted butter. Bake in 400° oven about 8 minutes until nicely browned.

Thick White Sauce
1 tbsp. butter

1 tbsp. flour
¼ cup milk

Heat butter, stir in flour and cook over gentle heat while stirring for a minute. Do not let brown. Add milk, stir until smooth and thickened.

Note: Canned minced clams can be used in above recipe.

Fish Salad

For Six
1½ lbs. flounder filet
1 red onion, sliced
    paper thin
1 green pepper, seeded,
    diced
1 sweet red (ripe) pepper,
    seeded, diced
3 ripe tomatoes, peeled,
    seeded, diced

½ cup lemon juice
1 tsp. salt
2 tbsp. chopped chives
½ cup coconut cream*
1 tsp. grated fresh ginger
1 clove garlic, minced
¼ tsp. ground coriander
¼ tsp. turmeric
pinch of cayenne pepper

Cut filets into 2-inch long strips, place in a glass dish, add lemon juice, onion and salt, mix gently and let refrigerate for 4 to 6 hours. Place coconut cream, garlic, ginger, coriander, turmeric and cayenne in a blender or food processor and blend well. Chill this and all the vegetables. Drain the lemon juice from the fish strips, add coconut cream dressing and blend gently. Add all other ingredients, mix and serve.

*See Glossary

Regal Tuna Casserole

For Six

2 medium size cans tunafish
½ cup chopped onion
2 tbsp. butter
1 package frozen peas,
  thawed
1 can condensed cream
  of celery soup
¼ cup tomato purée

½ cup sliced fresh
  mushrooms
1 tbsp. Worcestershire sauce
salt and pepper to taste
1 cup shredded cheddar
  cheese
2 tbsp. chopped pimiento
½ lemon, thinly sliced
  and quartered

Drain and flake tuna. Heat butter in a saucepan, sauté onion and mushrooms until soft, but do not brown. Add peas, soup, tomato purée. Worcestershire sauce, salt and pepper, stir. Heat until the mixture is hot and bubbling. Fold in tuna, cheese, pimiento and lemon. Spoon the mixture into a shallow 2-quart baking dish. Cover with aluminum foil, crimping it securely to the edge of the dish. Bake at 400⁰ for 15 minutes, then uncover and bake 15 minutes longer. Garnish with pieces of pimiento.

Baked Cod Filets ▷

For Four

2 lbs. fresh cod filets, cut
  in four serving pieces
oil
salt and pepper to taste
4 scallions, green and
  white part, chopped
¾ cup tomato purée
2 tbsp. grated onion
1 small clove garlic, minced
1 small bay leaf
1 small lemon, sliced thin
½ cup parsley, chopped
½ cup dry white wine

Place filets in a well oiled baking dish. Season with salt and pepper, sprinkle with chopped scallions. Mix tomato purée, grated onion and garlic; spread over fish. Place lemon slices on top of fish, sprinkle with parsley and add bay leaf to dish. Bake at 350⁰ for about 20 minutes until fish is cooked and flaky. Add wine to dish and bake 5 minutes longer.

Baked Haddock

For Four

4 medium size haddock filets
6 rashers bacon
⅔ cup soft white
    breadcrumbs
2 tbsp. minced onion

1 small clove garlic, minced
½ tsp. anchovy paste
1 tbsp. parsley, minced
5 tbsp. dry vermouth
salt and pepper to taste
butter

Place filets in a well buttered, shallow baking dish. Mince 2 rashers of bacon, combine with other ingredients and blend well. Spread the mixture over the filets and top each with a rasher of the remaining bacon. Bake in 425° oven for about 8 to 10 minutes until well browned. Serve with lemon wedges.

Fish Filets in Caper Sauce

For Four

4 filets (sole, flounder, sea
    bass, whiting or other),
    about 1½ lbs.
salt and pepper to taste
1 tbsp. lemon juice
¼ cup flour

½ cup butter
1½ tbsp. capers, drained
1½ tsp. Dijon mustard
½ cup dry white wine
¼ cup heavy cream
2 tsp. cornstarch

Season fish with salt and pepper, sprinkle with lemon juice, dredge in flour. Shake off excess flour. Heat butter in a skillet, sauté fish and brown on both sides. Remove fish from skillet to a serving dish and keep warm. Add capers, mustard and wine to the skillet, bring to a boil, blend well and let simmer for 2 or 3 minutes. Blend in cream and cornstarch dissolved in 1 tablespoon water. Simmer for 2 minutes longer, pour over fish and serve.

Shrimp in Cream Sauce

For Four
4 tbsp. butter
1 ½ lbs. shrimp, shelled,
   deveined
salt and pepper to taste

2 tsp. paprika
pinch of cayenne pepper
⅓ cup Madeira wine
¼ cup dry white wine
1 cup heavy cream

Heat butter in a skillet, sauté shrimp over fairly high heat for about 3 minutes until cooked — do not overcook. Remove shrimp to serving platter and keep hot. Add Madeira and white wine to skillet, reduce quickly to about 4 or 5 tablespoons, season sauce with salt, pepper, paprika and cayenne. Add cream, cook while stirring until well blended. Pour sauce over shrimp and serve.

Swordfish Kebabs

For Four to Six
1 swordfish steak,
   2 inches thick
⅓ cup olive oil

1 ½ tbsp. lemon juice
1 large clove garlic, crushed
1 bay leaf, crumbled
salt and pepper to taste

Cut swordfish into cubes, mix all other ingredients and combine with fish cubes. Mix well and marinate for 1 hour. Thread cubes on oiled skewers, alternating with bay leaves. Broil over hot coals for about 4 to 5 minutes, turning the skewers frequently. Do not over cook — swordfish gets dry when cooked too long.

Fish Balls

For Four
1 ½ lbs. cod or haddock
   filets, poached
2 slices white bread,
   crust removed
2 eggs
3 scallions, including
   green tops, chopped
2 tbsp. fresh dill, chopped

2 tbsp. parsley, chopped
2 tbsp. currants
½ tsp. cumin
2 tbsp. pine nuts (opt.)
salt and pepper to taste
1 tbsp. water
½ cup cornstarch
oil for frying

Put all ingredients except cornstarch and oil in an electric blender or food processor, blend until smooth. Shape the mixture into a dozen balls, roll the balls in cornstarch and fry in hot oil until golden brown. Shake the pan a few times to prevent scorching. Serve hot or cold.

Fish in Orange Juice

For Four
4 fish filets
salt and pepper to taste
¼ cup lime juice
4 tbsp. olive oil
2 scallions, minced
1 small clove garlic, crushed
½ cup orange juice

1 large, very ripe tomato,
   peeled, seeded and
   chopped
2 tbsp. pimiento (canned),
   diced
2 tbsp. capers, drained
   and chopped
2 tbsp. dry sherry

Put fish in a shallow dish, sprinkle with salt, pepper and lime juice on both sides and let stand for 15 minutes. Grease a shallow baking dish with some of the oil, place fish on top, combine scallions, garlic, tomato, pimiento and capers and spread the mixture on top of fish filets. Sprinkle with remaining oil and bake in 350° oven for 10 minutes. Then pour orange juice and sherry over fish and bake another 10 to 15 minutes or until fish is done.

Tuna Croquettes

For Six

½ cup finely chopped onions
3 tbsp. butter or margarine
3 tbsp. flour
½ cup milk
2 tsp. salt
¼ tsp. pepper
1 tsp. dry mustard
1 can (6 to 7 ozs.) tuna,
   drained and flaked
2 cups cooked rice
2 tsp. lemon juice
2 tbsp. water
1 egg, slightly beaten
fine bread crumbs

Sauté onions in butter until soft but not brown. Blend in flour; add milk and seasonings. Cook until thickened; remove from heat. Add tuna, rice, and lemon juice. Chill. Form into balls. Mix water and egg. Dip tuna balls into egg mixture. Roll in crumbs. Chill about 15 minutes to dry. Fry in deep fat (375°) for 3 to 4 minutes. Serve with a sharp mustard sauce.

Poached Salmon with Egg and Parsley Sauce

For Six to Eight

¼ cup chopped scallions,
   or onions
1 shallot, diced

1 4 to 6 lb. whole salmon
salt
freshly ground pepper
white wine

Grease two sheets of heavy-duty aluminum foil. Scatter center with scallions and shallots. Place the foil in a large shallow pan. (The foil should be large enough to envelope fish.) Sprinkle salt and pepper over the fish. Pour in enough white wine to cover the fish after placing in a pan large enough to avoid spilling juices.

Bake salmon covered, in a 325° oven 35 to 45 minutes or until fish flakes, when tested with a fork. Make the following sauce while the fish is poaching.

Approx. Four Cups

3 tbsp. butter
4 tbsp. flour
1 cup fish broth
1 cup heavy cream
2 tbsp. tomato ketchup

salt and pepper to taste
2 raw egg yolks
½ cup sliced hard-boiled
   eggs
¼ cup chopped parsley

Melt butter in a skillet. Blend with flour and cook for 2 to 3 minutes. Add broth and stir until sauce thickens. Season to taste. Mix the cream and egg yolks together and stir into the sauce with tomato ketchup. (DO NOT BOIL). Fold in the hard-boiled eggs and parsley.

Baked Fish in Cream Sauce

For Four

1 bass, codfish, whitefish or other, about 3½ to 4 lbs.	4 tbsp. melted butter
1½ tbsp. lemon juice	4 medium potatoes, cooked, peeled and sliced ½ inch thick
1 tbsp. paprika	¾ cup heavy cream
1 tbsp. salt	1 tbsp. dill, chopped
pepper to taste	1 tbsp. parsley, minced

Have fish cleaned and scaled. Rinse fish, pat dry, make 3 diagonal incisions on one side of the fish. Rub in paprika, salt and pepper, sprinkle with lemon juice.

Put fish in a buttered baking dish, brush with remaining melted butter and bake in 375⁰ oven for about 10 minutes until fish is half done. Arrange cooked sliced potatoes around the fish, baste with pan juices and bake another 10 minutes or so until fish is cooked and flaky.

Blend dill into cream, pour over fish, bake another 2 minutes, sprinkle with parsley and serve.

Fish Teriyaki

For Four

4 portion-size pieces of mackerel, bluefish or other	4 tbsp. soy sauce
	4 tbsp. dry sherry
	4 tbsp. mirin*
	1 clove garlic, crushed

Mix all ingredients except fish, put in a saucepan, bring to a boil and simmer for one minute. Remove from fire, marinate fish in this mixture for half an hour. Broil fish under moderate heat for 5 to 8 minutes on each side — depending on thickness of fish. Baste a few times with the marinade while broiling.

Note: If mirin is not available, increase sherry to 6 tablespoons and add 1½ tablespoons sugar to the marinade.

*See Glossary

Gefilte Fish

For Six

4 lbs. fish of several varieties (carp, pike and whitefish or other)	4 cups water
	4 stalks celery with green tops
2 tsp. salt	1 cup celery, white part only, chopped
pepper to taste	2 thick slices white bread
4 carrots	2 eggs, lightly beaten
3 onions (about ½ lb.)	1 tbsp. sugar

Skin and bone fish. Put heads, skin and bones in a saucepan, along with 1 teaspoon salt, pepper, 2 peeled carrots, 2 sliced onions, 4 celery stalks with green tops and 3 cups water. Cook gently for 1 hour. Soak bread in a little water and squeeze dry. Put boned fish, 1 peeled carrot, 1 small onion, the white part of the celery and bread through a meat grinder. Grind two or three times. (A food processor will simplify the procedure very much.) Add 1 cup water, the beaten eggs, 1 teaspoon salt, sugar and pepper to taste. Blend well and shape with wet hands into large egg-shaped balls. Strain the fish broth into another pan, bring to a simmer, put fish balls in it, cover and cook gently for 1½ hours. Uncover and cook for another 30 minutes. Remove pan from fire. When cool, remove fish carefully with a slotted spoon, slice the remaining carrot into thin rounds and garnish the fish balls with it. Pour the cooking liquid over the fish and chill well before serving.

Leghorn Fish Stew

For Six to Eight
½ cup olive oil
½ cup onion, chopped
1 large clove garlic, minced
2 tbsp. parsley, minced
½ tsp. sage
¾ lb. raw shrimp, shelled,
   cut in pieces
¾ cup dry white wine
3 tbsp. tomato paste

6 cups water
salt and pepper to taste
2 dashes Tabasco sauce
½ lb. squid, cleaned, cut
   in strips (opt.)
1 lb. cod filet, cut in pieces
1 lb. haddock (or whiting)
   filet, cut in pieces
½ lb. sea scallops,
   cut in half

Heat oil in a deep saucepan, sauté onion and garlic until light golden brown. Add shrimp, cover and simmer for 3 minutes. Add wine and cook uncovered until wine is reduced by half. Add tomato paste, water, salt, pepper, parsley, sage and Tabasco. Blend well and simmer 5 minutes. Add squid, fish and scallops, cover and simmer 10 to 15 minutes until fish is flaky. Correct seasoning before serving.

While cooking, toast slices of Italian bread, rub each slice with garlic. Put one slice into each serving bowl and ladle the stew over it.

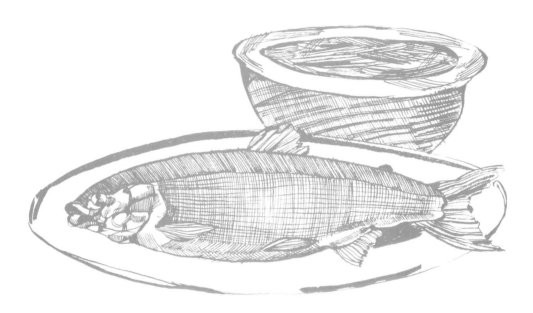

Paprika Fish

For Four
3 tbsp. butter
1 cup chopped onions
1 clove garlic, minced
¼ cup water
1 large green pepper,
   seeded, chopped

1 tbsp. paprika
salt and pepper to taste
1 ripe tomato, peeled,
   seeded, chopped
1 fish, about 3½ to 4 lbs.
   (pike, carp, bass),
   cleaned, scaled, rinsed

Sauté onion in butter until light golden brown. Add garlic, sprinkle with paprika, add water and simmer for about 1 minute. Add chopped green pepper and tomato, cover, simmer for 20 minutes. Add a little more water if mixture gets too dry. Place fish on top of mixture, season with salt and pepper, spoon sauce over fish. Cover and simmer for 10 to 15 minutes until fish is done.

Note: This fish can be left whole or cut into portion size pieces. Although this dish is usually prepared with freshwater fish, any delicate saltwater fish, such as cod, haddock, whiting, etc. can be used.

Grilled Fish

For Four

4 small whole fish (mullet, trout, whiting or other)
salt and pepper to taste
8 bay leaves
⅓ cup olive oil
1 lemon, sliced thin

3 tomatoes, peeled, seeded and chopped
1 large onion, sliced thin
3 tbsp. oil
pinch of thyme
salt and pepper to taste

Scale and gut fish, make 2 or 3 diagonal incisions on both sides of the fish. Season with salt and pepper, cover with bay leaves, sprinkle with olive oil and let marinate in a cool place for one hour.

Sauté onion in 3 tablespoons oil until very soft, add tomatoes, thyme, salt and pepper, cover and simmer for 1 hour.

When ready to broil fish, remove the bay leaves and lay the fish on the grill. Broil over hot charcoal or under a very hot broiler for 2 minutes, turn and broil the other side for 2 minutes. Turn over carefully, sprinkle with a little marinade and broil again 2 minutes on each side. Put the stewed tomatoes in a serving dish, place the broiled fish on top and garnish with lemon slices.

Fried Fish with Garlic Sauce ▷

About Two Cups

3 cloves garlic
½ tsp. salt
¼ cup pine nuts
2 cups boiled potatoes, mashed
¼ cup lemon juice
2 cups olive oil
1 small egg
¼ cup warm water

Mash garlic with salt in a mortar until smooth. Add pine nuts, pound until crushed and blended. Put potatoes in a bowl, add crushed garlic and nuts. Add lemon juice. Beat with a rotary or electric beater and gradually add oil while beating until all oil is absorbed and the mixture smooth. Beat in the egg and warm water.

Serve with fried or broiled seafood, boiled meats or vegetables.

Broiled Bluefish

For Four
1 bluefish, about 4 lbs.
1 clove garlic, mashed

1 cup olive oil
salt and pepper to taste
½ tsp. paprika

Have fish cleaned and scaled, leave on head and tail. Blend garlic, oil, salt, pepper and paprika and let stand for an hour or so before using. Wash fish, dry well and coat with the oil and garlic dressing. Place fish on a grill and broil over charcoal until done. Brush on more garlic oil as needed. Serve fish with:

Lemon Onion Sauce
1 large onion, sliced
    paper thin

1½ tbsp. salt
¼ cup lemon juice
⅓ cup parsley, chopped

Put onion slices in a bowl, mix well with salt and let stand for 1 hour. Then rinse onion under cold water, squeeze out as much liquid as you can, mix with other ingredients.

Lobster Thermidor

For Four
4 boiled lobsters,
    1¼ lbs. each
6 mushrooms, minced
1 medium green pepper,
    seeded, minced
3 tbsp. canned pimiento,
    chopped

6 tbsp. butter
melted butter
3 cups white sauce*
1¼ cups sherry wine
salt and pepper to taste
1 tsp. paprika
fine dry breadcrumbs
⅔ cup grated Parmesan

Split lobsters, remove meat from tail and claws, also tomalley and coral, if any. Keep the lobster shells for stuffing. Dice lobster meat. Heat butter, sauté mushrooms, pepper and pimiento for 2 minutes. Add the white sauce, paprika and sherry, blend well and simmer gently for 10 minutes or so until slightly reduced. Fold in lobster meat, tomalley and coral, mix well and heat through. Season with salt and pepper. Fill the lobster shells with the mixture, cover lightly with breadcrumbs, sprinkle with grated cheese, melted butter and a little paprika. Bake at 400° for about 10 minutes until lightly browned.

*See Glossary

Savory Mackerel

For Six
2 mackerel, about
    1½ lbs. each
4 tbsp. olive oil
3 onions, sliced thin
2 carrots, peeled and
    sliced thin
1 large clove garlic, crushed
1 green pepper, seeded and
    cut into strips

3 tbsp. parsley, chopped
2 large tomatoes, peeled,
    seeded and chopped
1 tbsp. dill, chopped
1 tsp. lemon juice
1 tsp. paprika
pinch of cayenne pepper
salt and pepper to taste
½ cup water or fish stock

Clean and wash mackerel. Pat dry and make 2 diagonal incisions on both sides of the fish. Heat oil in a skillet, sauté fish quickly and brown both sides. Remove fish from skillet and reserve. Add onions to skillet, sauté until limp and very light golden. Add garlic, carrots, green pepper and sauté 2 or 3 minutes longer. Add tomatoes, parsley, dill, lemon juice, cayenne, salt, pepper, paprika and water, cover and simmer for 20 minutes — stir once or twice. Return fish to the skillet, spoon sauce over fish, simmer for another 10 minutes.

Remove mackerel to a serving dish, cover with sauce, cool and chill before serving. Garnish with lemon slices.

Tournedos Chasseur

For Four
4 slices beef filet, about
   ¼ lb. each
6 tbsp. butter
3 tbsp. cooking oil
4 shallots, minced
¼ lb. firm mushrooms,
   minced

1 cup dry white wine
¾ cup beef broth
1 tsp. beef extract (Bovril
   or other)
1 tbsp. tomato paste
1½ tbsp. beurre manié*
salt and pepper
2 tbsp. minced parsley

Heat half the butter and all the oil in a casserole and sauté the meat over high heat quickly until well browned on both sides and done to taste. Remove to a serving dish and keep hot. Add remaining butter to the pan juices, together with the shallots and mushrooms. Sauté for about 5 minutes or until golden. Add the wine, bring to a boil and reduce quickly by two thirds. Then add the beef broth, beef extract and tomato paste. Stir in the beurre manié. Simmer sauce for 5 more minutes. Season with salt and pepper. Return tournedos to casserole and turn them in the sauce to coat them, but do not let them cook any further. Return them to serving dish, coat with the sauce and sprinkle with parsley.

*See Glossary

Green Peppersteak

For Three
¾ lb. flank steak
1 tsp. cornstarch
1 tsp. soy sauce
2 tsp. sherry
½ tsp. oil
½ tsp. sugar
2 green peppers
1 large clove garlic, minced
1 tbsp. fermented black
   beans (opt.)

1 slice fresh ginger root,
   minced
1 medium onion
1 tbsp. soy sauce
2 tbsp. cornstarch
1 pinch sugar
⅛ tsp. black pepper
1 dash Tabasco sauce
salt to taste
3 tbsp. oil

Slice trimmed steak across the grain into ¼ inch slices, 2 inches long. Blend sherry, soy sauce, 1 tablespoon cornstarch, ½ teaspoon sugar and ½ teaspoon oil. Coat the sliced meat with this mixture and marinate for 15 minutes. Cut peppers in half, remove membranes and seeds and cut into ¼ inch wide strips. Slice onion ¼ inch thick and then into 1 inch strips. Mix soy sauce, cornstarch, pinch of sugar, pepper, Tabasco and salt. Heat 1½ tablespoons oil in a wok. Stir-fry beef over high heat for one minute. Remove beef and reserve. Clean wok. Heat the other 1½ tablespoons oil. Add garlic, ginger root and the mashed black beans, stir-fry one minute, add green pepper and onion, stir-fry for 2 minutes. Return beef to wok, add the cornstarch mixture and cook, stirring for another minute until the sauce thickens.

Hot Monterrey Salad ▷

For Eight
1 lb. lean ground beef
1 clove garlic, minced
2 tsp. salt
¼ tsp. Tabasco sauce
1 tbsp. lemon juice
1 cup mayonnaise
3 cups cooked rice
2 cups sliced celery
1 cup chopped green peppers
1 cup chopped onions
3 medium tomatoes,
    cut into wedges
1 cup corn chips,
    crumbled or crushed

Cook meat and garlic in a lightly greased skillet for 10 minutes or until meat is done. Stir, while cooking, to crumble meat. Add salt, Tabasco, and lemon juice to mayonnaise. Stir into meat mixture with remaining ingredients except corn chips. Turn into a 2-quart casserole. Top with corn chips. Bake at 375⁰ for 25 to 30 minutes.

⬆ Bife a Portuguesa

For Six
2 lbs. flank steak*
½ lb. sliced Canadian bacon*
1 tbsp. olive or salad oil
1 clove garlic, crushed
1½ cups dry red wine
1 tbsp. cornstarch
1 tbsp. cider vinegar
2 tsp. lemon juice
1 beef bouillon cube

½ tsp. salt
¼ tsp. coarsely ground
    black pepper
¾ cup sliced Spanish
    stuffed green olives
pan fried potatoes
    (about 2 lbs. potatoes,
    peeled and sliced)
3 tbsp. chopped parsley
thin lemon wedges

Lay steak flat and wrap in a piece of aluminum foil. Place in freezer for 45 minutes or until slightly firm; cut steak on the diagonal into slices ½-inch thick. Set aside.

Brown bacon on both sides in large skillet over medium heat; remove and keep warm. Add oil and garlic to skillet; sauté just until garlic starts to brown. Add steak slices, a few at a time. Brown on each side; remove and keep warm. Steak slices should be slightly pink inside. Blend together wine, cornstarch, vinegar and lemon juice. Stir wine mixture, bouillon cube, salt and pepper into pan drippings. Add olives. Simmer stirring occasionally, for 2 minutes.

Alternate bacon and steak slices on warm serving platter. Pour sauce over meat. Surround with fried potatoes. Garnish platter with parsley and lemon wedges.

*To prepare this recipe the classic way, use 2 pounds tenderloin steak (cut in ½-inch slices) instead of flank steak and ¼ pound thinly sliced prosciutto ham instead of bacon.

Stuffed Flank Steak

For Four

4 sweet Italian sausages	1 flank steak, about 2½ lbs.
1 small onion, minced	1 clove garlic, crushed
¼ cup green olives, chopped	1 tsp. salt
1 tbsp. chili powder	flour
¼ cup minced parsley	3 tbsp. oil
1 egg, beaten	½ cup beef broth
½ cup breadcrumbs	1 cup tomato sauce (canned)
salt to taste	½ cup dry red wine
½ tsp. oregano	1 small bay leaf

Remove the sausage meat from casings, break up the meat and mix with onion, olives, chili powder, parsley, egg, breadcrumbs, salt to taste, and oregano.

Flatten flank steak with a mallet or ask your butcher to do it. Combine garlic and 1 teaspoon salt and rub both sides of the steak with this mixture. Spread the sausage mixture on one side of the steak, roll it up and fasten it with string or skewers. Dredge with flour and sauté in oil in a heavy saucepan until browned on all sides. Pour off the oil, mix all other ingredients and add to pan. Cover and cook in 350° oven for 1½ hours or until meat is soft.

Braised Steak

For Six

4 slices sirloin or rib steak, ½ inch thick	½ tsp. marjoram
3 tbsp. flour	1½ cups beef broth (or water)
salt and pepper to taste	2 tsp. paprika
4 tbsp. butter	4 medium potatoes, peeled and diced
1 large onion, chopped	1 green pepper, seeded and diced
1 large clove garlic, chopped	1 large tomato, peeled, seeded and diced
½ tsp. caraway seed	
1 tbsp. parsley, chopped	

Pound the steaks to flatten, score the edges. Season with salt and pepper and dust with flour. Heat butter in a saucepan and brown meat quickly on both sides. Remove steaks and reserve. Add onion to pan, lower heat and sauté until onion is very soft and just pale golden. Add garlic, caraway, marjoram, paprika and beef broth, and stir well. Place steaks on top, cover and cook over gentle heat for about 20 minutes or until steaks just start to soften. Add more water if gravy thickens too much.

Add potatoes, pepper and tomato and enough broth to barely cover the vegetables. Cover and cook gently until potatoes are done. Correct seasoning, sprinkle with parsley before serving.

Budapest Tenderloin

For Eight

3 lbs. beef tenderloin	1 stalk celery, minced
2 oz. salt pork, cut in strips	1 small carrot, minced
salt and freshly ground pepper to taste	1 tbsp. vinegar
	1½ tbsp. flour
3 tbsp. lard or butter	1 cup beef broth or water
2 oz. smoked bacon, diced	¼ cup tomato puree
1 medium onion, minced	1 cup sour cream
2 tsp. paprika	1 tbsp. flour
	1 tbsp. chopped dill

Pare the tenderloin, remove all fat and thin skin. Chill salt pork, cut in strips and lard the meat using a larding needle. Season with salt and pepper. Heat lard in a roasting pan, sear meat quickly on all sides and roast in a preheated 400° oven for 10 minutes. Remove from oven, remove meat, pour all fat off the roasting pan. Add diced bacon and onion and sauté on top of the stove while stirring until onions are golden yellow. Stir in paprika, add celery, carrot and vinegar, stir in flour, add broth and tomato puree. Blend well, let come to a simmer, place meat on top. Cover and cook gently for about 1 hour until meat is tender. Blend sour cream, 1 tablespoon flour and dill, pour over meat, cover and simmer 15 minutes longer.

Roast Brisket of Beef

For Eight

2 large onions, sliced thin
2 carrots, peeled, sliced
⅔ cup celery, white part, sliced
1 bay leaf

4 lbs. brisket of beef
2 tbsp. flour
1 tsp. paprika
salt and pepper to taste
1 cup beef broth

Cover the bottom of a roasting pan with the vegetables, add bay leaf. Blend flour and paprika, sprinkle it on meat and pat it into the meat. Season the roast with salt and pepper. Place roast on top of vegetables, add ½ cup of beef broth and roast in a pre-heated 350⁰ oven for 15 to 25 minutes per pound, depending on the degree of doneness desired. Baste occasionally and add more broth if needed. When done, remove roast to a hot serving platter, pour fat off the roasting pan, add more broth and stir to mix it with the vegetables and deglaze the pan. Let the gravy come to a boil, simmer for a few minutes, strain and serve with the meat.

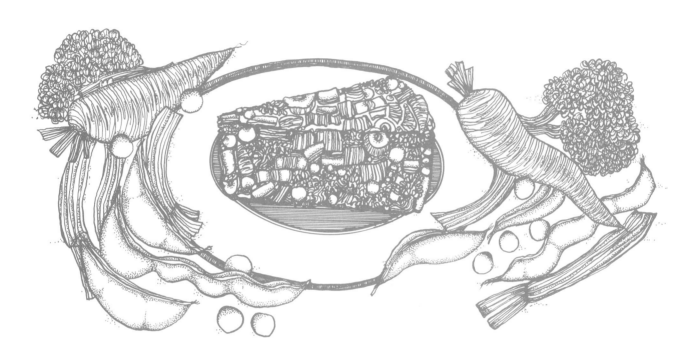

Sauerbraten

For Eight

5 lbs. beef chuck or brisket
1½ tsp. salt
1 onion, sliced
1 cup cider vinegar
¾ cup water
1 tsp. peppercorns
3 bay leaves

1 clove garlic, minced
1 onion, sliced thin
¼ cup raisins
4 to 6 ginger snaps
1 tsp. paprika
1 clove garlic, chopped
salt to taste
⅓ cup brown sugar (or to taste)

Rub salt into the meat. Place meat in a deep ceramic bowl or enameled pot. Heat vinegar and water and pour hot over meat. Add peppercorns, bay leaves, onion, sugar, salt and chopped garlic. Mix and cover. Place in refrigerator and marinate for 2 to 3 days, turning meat occasionally.

Remove meat from marinade, pat dry and sear in a heavy saucepan or dutch oven. Add garlic, onion, raisins, crumbled ginger snaps, paprika and about ¾ cup of the strained marinade; cover tightly, bring to a boil and then simmer over gentle heat for 3 to 4 hours until meat is soft. Turn once in a while. Add a little more marinade if needed. When cooked, remove meat from pot, skim fat off the sauce and serve.

Pot Roast Provencal ▽

For Six to Eight

5 lbs. eye round of beef, tied
12 to 14 whole Spanish stuffed green olives
3 to 4 large cloves garlic, slivered
1 medium onion, sliced
1 rib celery, cut into chunks
1 large bay leaf
4 whole cloves
¼ tsp. *each;* summer savory peppercorns, salt

1 tbsp. sugar
½ cup sliced Spanish stuffed green olives
1½ cups dry red wine
2 tbsp. olive or salad oil
1½ lbs. pared new potatoes
4 carrots, cut into 2-inch sticks
1 cup diced tomatoes
water
1 tbsp. flour
2 tbsp. cold water

Working with the fat side up, make small but deep incisions over the top of the beef. Insert 1 olive and a slice or two of garlic in each cut. Place in large bowl; add onion, celery, bay leaf, cloves, sugar, savory, peppercorns, salt, any remaining garlic and the sliced olives. Pour wine over all; marinate overnight; turning occasionally. Remove beef and reserve marinade. In Dutch oven, brown meat slowly in oil; pour off any excess fat. Add reserved marinating ingredients to beef. Cover tightly and simmer 3 to 3½ hours. Add potatoes, carrots and tomatoes the last 30 minutes; cover and continue simmering until meat and vegetables are tender. Remove meat to serving platter. Using a slotted spoon, place vegetables and olives around pot roast. Strain gravy and measure; add enough water to make 2 cups. Return to Dutch oven; bring to boil. Blend flour with 2 tablespoons water and quickly stir into boiling gravy; boil 1 minute, stirring constantly. Serve with beef.

Oven ◁ Beef Stew

For Eight

2 lbs. beef for stew, cut in 1½-inch pieces
2 medium onions, cut in eighths
3 stalks celery, cut in diagonal pieces
4 medium carrots, cut in half crosswise and lengthwise
1 cup tomato juice
⅓ cup quick-cooking tapioca
1 tbsp. sugar
1 tbsp. salt
¼ tsp. pepper
½ tsp. basil
2 medium-size red potatoes, cut in slices ¼ inch thick

Combine meat, onions, celery, carrots, tomato juice, tapioca, sugar, salt, pepper and basil in a 2½-quart casserole. Cover tightly and cook in a slow oven (300°F.) for 2½ hours. Stir potatoes into stew and continue cooking, covered, 1 hour or until meat and vegetables are done, stirring occasionally.

Beefsteak Pizzaiola

For Two
1 porterhouse steak,
  about 2 inches thick
2 tbsp. olive oil
salt and pepper to taste
2 cloves garlic, minced

1 cup canned tomatoes,
  drained and chopped
½ tsp. rosemary
1 tsp. oregano
¼ cup dry red wine

Trim the steak. Heat oil in a heavy skillet, fry steak to taste. Sprinkle with salt and pepper. Remove from skillet and keep warm. Pour off all fat but 1 tablespoon. Add garlic to skillet, sauté for one minute, add tomatoes, herbs and wine, blend well and cook over high heat for about 2 minutes until slightly reduced. Pour sauce over steak when serving.

Viennese Beef Goulash

For Six
5 tbsp. lard
1½ lbs. onions, sliced
3 lbs. beef shin or chuck,
  cut in 2-inch cubes
1 tbsp. paprika

½ cup beef broth (or water)
1 tsp. tomato paste
½ tsp. caraway seed
½ tbsp. vinegar
salt and pepper to taste

Heat lard in a heavy saucepan, add onion and sauté until onions are pale yellow. Stir in paprika, add beef, mix well, add all other ingredients, cover and cook gently for about 2½ hours until meat is done.
  Serve with boiled potatoes.

Znaimer Goulash
Prepare as Viennese Beef Goulash above. During last 10 minutes of cooking add 2 or 3 finely chopped sour pickles.

Braised Steak with Anchovies

For Four
4 sirloin or rib steaks,
  ½ inch thick
salt and pepper
¼ cup flour
3 tbsp. butter
1 small onion, minced

1 tbsp. flour
1½ cups beef broth
  (or water)
5 anchovy filets, chopped
1½ tsp. capers, drained
¼ tsp. grated lemon rind

Pound steaks, season with salt and pepper, dust with flour. Heat butter in a saucepan, brown steaks quickly on both sides. Remove steaks from pan. Add onion, sauté until light brown, stir in 1 tablespoon flour and gradually add beef broth while stirring. When smooth, return steaks to pan, bring to a boil, stir in capers, anchovies and lemon rind. Cover and simmer for about 45 minutes or until steaks are done. Skim fat off sauce before serving.

Swiss Steak

For Four
2 lbs. round steak
1 clove garlic, mashed
flour
¼ cup butter or bacon
  drippings
½ cup onion, minced

⅓ cup carrots, minced
⅓ cup celery, minced
⅓ cup green pepper,
  minced
1 ripe tomato, peeled,
  seeded, chopped
1 cup beef broth

Score the edges of the meat. Rub meat with mashed garlic. Roll in flour and pound in as much flour as meat will hold. Heat fat in a heavy saucepan, brown meat on one side, turn it over. Add vegetables, beef broth, salt and pepper, cover and cook in 325° oven for 2 hours or longer until meat is tender. Remove meat to a hot platter. Rub the liquid and vegetables through a sieve, skim off fat, return steak to pan and heat through before serving.

Picnic Beef Roll ▽

For Eight

1 flank steak, about
   2½ lbs.
prepared mustard
seasoned salt and pepper
6 dill pickles, quartered
   lengthwise
4 carrots, quartered
   lengthwise
6 scallions (or green onions)
solid all-vegetable
   shortening
2 cups water

1 beef bouillon cube
¼ cup vinegar
1 cup dry red wine (or
   additional 1 cup water)
1 tsp. whole black
   peppercorns
2 bay leaves
4 sprigs parsley
2 stalks celery, cut in
   2-inch pieces
8 seeded rolls, split
butter, softened
mustard and/or mayonnaise

Spread steak with mustard and sprinkle with seasoned salt and pepper. Starting at narrow side alternate rows of pickles, carrots and scallions on top of steak; roll up in jelly-roll fashion and tie securely with string at 1-inch intervals. Brown steak on all sides in hot shortening in Dutch oven; pour off drippings. Add water, bouillon cube, vinegar, wine, peppercorns, bay leaves, parsley and celery. Cover and cook about 2½ to 3 hours, or until meat is tender. Allow meat to cool in liquid; then cover and chill overnight.

To serve, take meat from liquid and remove strings. Place on serving platter and cut diagonally into slices about one inch thick. Spread rolls with butter and mustard; fill with meat to make sandwiches.

◁ Grilled Dill Steak

For Eight

¾ cup olive oil
¾ cup dill pickle liquid
⅓ cup sliced dill pickles
1 clove garlic, minced
salt and pepper
3-lb. piece London Broil
   beef (about 1½ to
   2-inches thick from top
   of round)

Combine oil, pickle liquid, sliced pickles and garlic in large shallow dish; add meat and turn until coated. Cover and marinate overnight, turning meat once. Remove meat to grill or broiler rack, reserving marinade. Cook steak 6 inches from source of heat for about 14 to 17 minutes per side for medium doneness. Brush meat with additional marinade during grilling and sprinkle each side with salt and pepper after grilling. (When done in the broiler, catch pan juices and pour over meat before serving.) Cut meat diagonally across grain into thin slices.

Hunter's Pot Roast

For Six

1 tbsp. butter
1 medium carrot, sliced thin
½ parsley root, pared and sliced thin
1 small celeriac (or 3 stalks of celery, white part only) sliced thin
3 lbs. beef brisket, blade chuck or round

1 small onion, sliced thin
3 thin slices smoked bacon
1 small bay leaf
½ tsp. black peppercorns
pinch of thyme
pinch of grated nutmeg
2 cup beef broth
2 tbsp. flour
⅔ cup sour cream
salt and pepper to taste

Melt butter in a skillet, sauté onion, carrot, parsley root and celery while stirring, for 3 or 4 minutes. Place in a roasting pan, place meat on top. Put bacon slices on top of meat, season with salt and pepper, add bay leaf, peppercorns, thyme, nutmeg and 1½ cups beef broth. Cover and cook in 375⁰ oven for 2 hours. Baste frequently and add more broth if needed. Remove the meat when nearly tender, stir flour and remaining broth into the gravy, blend well, return meat, lower heat to 350⁰ and cook uncovered until meat is tender, about one hour. Baste occasionally. When cooked, remove meat to heated platter, strain gravy and rub vegetables through the strainer. Degrease, blend gravy with sour cream, heat to simmering point and serve with meat.

Braised Short Ribs

For Four

3 lbs. lean, meaty short ribs of beef
¼ cup flour
3 tbsp. fat
1 medium onion, chopped
2 cloves garlic, chopped

1 cup celery, diced
1 large carrot, peeled and diced
1 cup canned tomato sauce
½ cup beef broth
½ tsp. caraway seed
salt and pepper to taste

Have butcher crack the rib bones. Dredge ribs in flour and brown on all sides in hot fat. Remove meat, add onion, sauté for 2 minutes, add garlic, carrot and celery, mix and sauté 2 minutes longer. Place meat on top of vegetables, add caraway, broth, season with salt and pepper, cover tightly and simmer for half an hour. Then add tomato sauce, cover and cook gently for one hour longer or until meat is cooked and soft. Remove meat to a serving platter, skim fat off gravy, correct seasoning and pour over meat.

Viennese Pot Roast

For Six

4 tbsp. butter
1 carrot, peeled and sliced
1 small parsley root, peeled and sliced
2 stalks celery, white part, sliced
½ parsnip, peeled and sliced
1 small onion, sliced

3½ lbs. beef (blade chuck, round or brisket)
1 small bay leaf
pinch of thyme
pinch of grated nutmeg
salt and pepper to taste
2½ cups beef broth
¾ cup sour cream
1½ tbsp. flour
1 clove garlic, minced

Heat 2 tablespoons butter in a skillet, sauté carrot, parsley root, celery, parsnip, onion and garlic until lightly browned. Heat remaining butter in a dutch oven or roasting pan, brown meat on all sides. Pour off fat. Add sautéed vegetables to meat, also all other ingredients except sour cream and flour. Cover pan and cook in 375⁰ oven for 1½ hours. Baste frequently.

Remove meat, skim off most of the fat. Stir flour into the pan juices. Return meat to pan and cook uncovered at 350⁰ for another hour or until meat is tender. Remove meat to hot serving platter. Rub gravy and vegetables through a strainer, add sour cream, heat through and serve with the meat.

Boeuf Bourguignon

For Four

3 tbsp. cooking oil
2 lbs. beef (chuck, sirloin, or "chicken steak") cut in 1½ inch cubes
1 tbsp. flour
3 cloves garlic, minced
3 cups red Burgundy wine
1 cup water

1 bouquet garni (thyme, bay leaf, parsley)*
salt and pepper to taste
pinch of grated nutmeg
½ lb. lean salt pork, rinsed and diced
24 small white onions, peeled

Heat oil in heavy saucepan, brown the meat cubes over high heat. Then drain off oil, dust with flour, blend with spoon and sauté until flour is browned, being careful not to burn it. Then add wine, water, garlic, bouquet garni, salt and pepper. Cover and simmer for about 1½ to 2 hours or until meat is tender. You can also cook it in a 350⁰ oven. Sauté the salt pork cubes in a skillet until lightly browned, then add peeled onions and sauté, stirring occasionally until onions are also lightly browned. Skim fat off the simmering stew, remove the bouquet garni, drain the fat off the skillet and add onions and pork bits to the stew. Heat through, skim fat off again, correct seasoning and serve. Small peeled carrots, cooked separately, also sautéed mushroom caps can be added just before serving.

*See Glossary

Braised Beef and Vegetables

For Six

2 lbs. round or shoulder beef
1 clove garlic, minced
2 scallions, minced
1 slice fresh ginger root, minced
¼ tsp. allspice
4 tbsp. soy sauce
3 tbsp. sherry

1 tbsp. vinegar
salt and pepper to taste
3 tbsp. oil
2 cups beef broth
1 cup shelled green peas
½ cup bamboo shoots, diced
2 stalks celery, white part, sliced thin

Heat oil in a heavy saucepan, stir in garlic, add beef and brown quickly on all sides. Blend scallions, ginger, allspice, soy sauce, sherry, vinegar, salt and pepper, add to meat, stir and turn the meat in the combined ingredients. Heat gently. In the meantime bring beef broth to a boil, pour over beef, bring to a boil again, cover the pan and simmer for about 1½ hours or until beef is tender. Fifteen minutes before the beef is done, add the vegetables, cover again and continue cooking.

Stuffed Beef Rolls (Bracioli)

For Four

4 thin slices of round steak
4 slices prosciutto ham
½ cup fresh white breadcrumbs
⅓ cup grated Romano
1 cup beef broth
2 cloves garlic, minced

salt and pepper to taste
4 tbsp. olive oil
2 cups canned Italian tomatoes, drained and chopped
2 tbsp. tomato paste
½ cup dry red wine
½ tsp. oregano
4 tbsp. parsley, minced

Have butcher pound the slices of steak; they should be quite thin. Blend breadcrumbs, cheese, garlic, parsley, oregano, and season with salt and pepper. Place a slice of prosciutto on top of each steak, then spread one fourth of the breadcrumb mixture in the center of each slice, roll it up, tuck in the ends and tie with thread.

Heat olive oil in a heavy casserole, brown the meat rolls on all sides. Add tomatoes, tomato paste, wine and half a cup of broth, bring to a boil, cover and simmer for about 1½ hours. Add more broth if necessary. When meat is tender, season sauce with salt and pepper and serve.

Steak Magnifico

For Eight

¼ lb. mushrooms, finely chopped	¾ tsp. thyme
2 tbsp. chopped scallions	salt and pepper
1 tbsp. butter	2½ lbs. round steak (about 1-inch thick)
½ cup chopped prosciutto (about 2 oz.) *or* 1 cup chopped boiled ham (about 4 oz.)	2 tbsp. salad oil
	⅔ cup dry red wine
	1 carrot, quartered
2 tbsp. fresh bread crumbs	1 large onion, quartered
1 tbsp. chopped parsley	4½ tsp. flour
	¼ cup water

In large skillet, sauté mushrooms and scallions in butter 2 minutes. Add prosciutto, bread crumbs, parsley, thyme, ½ teaspoon salt and ¼ teaspoon pepper; mix well. Turn steak on side and cut almost all the way through. Fill steak with mushroom stuffing. Secure with cord or toothpicks so that stuffing is well sealed. Heat oil in skillet; brown steak on all sides. Remove steak to shallow baking pan. Add wine, carrot and onion. Sprinkle salt and pepper over steak; cover with foil and bake in 350⁰ oven 45 minutes or until tender. (Turn steak over after 30 minutes.) Place steak on serving plate; cover and keep warm. Strain pan liquid and skim off fat. Blend together flour and water in small saucepan; add pan liquid. Cook over medium heat, stirring constantly, until gravy boils 1 minute; add salt to taste. Serve with steak.

Peppersteak ▷

For One

1 well-trimmed sirloin or
    porterhouse steak, about ¾ lb.
salt to taste
1 tbsp. green peppercorns
    coarsely crushed
2 tbsp. oil
2 tbsp. butter
¼ cup Armagnac brandy or Cognac
½ cup crème fraîche* or heavy cream

Season the steak with salt and rub in the green peppercorns. Heat oil and butter in a deep skillet, sauté the steak on both sides until done to taste. Transfer it to a hot serving dish and keep warm. Pour off the pan juices, add the brandy to the skillet and scrape off all the brown bits on the bottom of the skillet. Heat and ignite the brandy. Stir in the crème fraîche, bring to a simmering point and reduce by half. Do not let it boil fast or the sauce might curdle. Coat the steak with the sauce and serve.

Note: Green peppercorns are available in most markets in jars or cans, packed either in vinegar or water. Drain before crushing.

*See Glossary

Braised Steak Supreme

For Six

6 slices sirloin or round
steak ½ inch thick,
about ½ lb. each
salt and pepper to taste
6 tbsp. lard or butter
1 large onion, chopped
2 carrots, peeled, cut in
strips

1 tbsp. paprika
3 tbsp. flour
2 cups hot beef broth
½ tsp. grated lemon rind
1 cup sour cream
2 tbsp. parsley, chopped
2 stalks celery, white part
only, cut in strips

Pound steaks, season with salt and pepper. Heat lard in a skillet, sauté steaks quickly to brown on both sides. Remove from skillet and keep warm. Add onion, carrots and celery to skillet and sauté while stirring for 5 minutes. Then stir in paprika and flour, blend well and add gradually hot beef broth. Stir constantly until smooth. Add lemon rind. Cover and simmer for 10 minutes. Put steaks in a saucepan, pour sauce and vegetables over them, cover and simmer until meat is done — about one hour, depending on the cut used. Remove meat, rub sauce and vegetables through a strainer, return to pan. Blend in sour cream, return steaks to pan and heat through. Do not let boil. Garnish with parsley when serving.

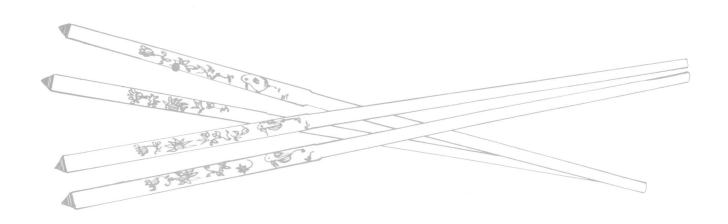

Dutch Oxtail Stew

For Four

1 meaty oxtail (about
2 lbs.), cut into pieces
½ tsp. juniper berries,
crushed
2 cloves
1 small bay leaf
small pinch thyme
salt and pepper to taste
2 cups water

1 cup beef broth (or water)
1 cup ale
4 carrots, peeled, sliced
1 cup shredded white
cabbage
½ lb. lean smoked bacon,
in one piece
3 large potatoes, peeled,
cubed

Blanch oxtail for 5 minutes in boiling water, drain. Tie juniper berries, cloves, bay leaf and thyme in a piece of cheesecloth. Put water, broth and ale in a heavy saucepan, add oxtail and cheesecloth bag, season with salt and pepper. Bring to a boil, cover and simmer for about 2 hours. Add carrots, cabbage, and bacon; simmer another hour. Add potatoes, cook half an hour longer until potatoes are done. Remove oxtail, vegetables and bacon with a slotted spoon. Discard cheesecloth bag. Slice the bacon. Serve with gravy.

Beef Brisket and Sauerkraut

For Six
3 lbs. brisket
1 onion, sliced
1 carrot, peeled
1 parsnip, peeled
6 peppercorns
1 tsp. salt

2 lbs. sauerkraut
2 tbsp. flour
1 apple, peeled, cored
  and cubed
2 tsp. caraway seed
1 tbsp. margarine or
  chicken fat

Place meat in a large pot, cover with water, add onion, carrot, parsnip, salt and peppercorns, bring to a boil, skim and cover. Cook gently for about 2 hours or until meat is tender.

When using fresh sauerkraut, rinse quickly with cold water, squeeze dry, put in a large saucepan, stir in flour, add apple, caraway and fat, cover and simmer for about the same length of time as the meat. Stir once in a while to prevent scorching and add a little water or broth if necessary. When using canned sauerkraut, strain off and discard some of the liquid, put kraut in a pan, add flour, apple, caraway and fat and bring to a simmer about half an hour before meat is done.

When meat is cooked, remove from pot, add to the sauerkraut with about ¼ of its cooking liquid, cover and simmer 15 minutes longer. Put meat on a serving platter, surround with drained sauerkraut and serve the broth separately as a soup.

Hungarian Goulash

For Six
1 large onion, chopped
2 tbsp. lard
3 lbs. beef chuck or
  heavy shin, cubed
1 large clove garlic,
  crushed
½ tsp. caraway seeds,
  crushed

salt and pepper to taste
1 tbsp. paprika
¼ tsp. marjoram
8 cups warm water
1 tomato, peeled, seeded
  and chopped
1 green pepper, seeded
  and diced
1 tbsp. vinegar

Heat lard in a kettle or dutch oven, add onion and sauté over low heat until onion is soft and just starts to color. Add beef and sauté, stirring often, for 10 minutes. Add garlic, caraway, salt, pepper, paprika and marjoram, blend very thoroughly; then add 8 cups water, cover and cook slowly for an hour. Add tomato, pepper and vinegar, cover and cook for another 30 minutes to an hour until meat is done. The length of cooking depends on the cut and the quality of the meat.

Serve with boiled potatoes or flour dumplings and plenty of gravy in deep bowls.

Beef Teriyaki

For Four
4 small sirloin steaks,
  well trimmed - or
  4 filets 1-inch thick
1 clove garlic, crushed

1 tsp. sugar
¼ cup mirin*
¼ cup soy sauce
2 tbsp. oil
1 tsp. grated fresh ginger

Trim meat well and remove all fat. Blend garlic, sugar, mirin, soy sauce and ginger. Coat steaks with the mixture and marinate for half an hour.

Heat oil in a heavy skillet, sauté steaks quickly until well browned on both sides. Spoon remaining marinade over steaks, sauté another 5 minutes or until steaks are done and look nicely glazed. Slice and reassemble the steaks to their original shape and size.

*See Glossary

◁ Stir-fried Beef and Beans

For Four
¾ lb. flank steak
1 tbsp. cornstarch
1 tbsp. sherry
2 tbsp. soy sauce
¾ tsp. sugar
½ tsp. salt
¾ lb. string beans, trimmed,
   cut in long strips
1 small clove garlic, minced
4 tbsp. oil
½ cup beef broth

Slice beef across the grain in thin slices. Mix cornstarch, sherry, soy sauce, and sugar, add to beef and toss to coat the slices. Parboil string beans for a minute, drain and cool. Heat 2 tablespoons oil in a wok, add garlic, stir-fry a few seconds, add beef and stir-fry a couple of minutes until lightly browned. Remove beef from pan and reserve. Add remaining oil to wok, add salt, heat and add string beans. Fry a minute, add broth, heat to a boil, return beef, cover and simmer for 2 minutes.

Farm Stew

For Four

2 lbs. beef (round or chuck), cut in 1½ inch cubes	½ cup beef broth
salt and pepper to taste	1 bay leaf
flour	1 tbsp. juniper berries, crushed
3 tbsp. butter	¼ tsp. black peppercorns, crushed
1 large onion, minced	pinch of grated nutmeg
1 large baking apple, peeled, cored, finely diced	3 large potatoes, boiled, peeled, mashed
½ cup dry red wine	3 tbsp. melted butter

Season beef with salt and pepper, dredge with flour. Heat butter in a heavy saucepan, add beef and sauté quickly, while stirring, until browned. Add onion and apple, cook while stirring 2 minutes longer. Add wine and broth, stir well to deglaze the pan. Tie juniper berries, bay leaf, peppercorns in a piece of cheesecloth, add to pan along with the grated nutmeg. Cover and cook very gently for 1½ hours. Remove cheesecloth bag. Remove meat and vegetables with a slotted spoon and place in a shallow baking dish. Strain the sauce over it. Cover with a smooth layer of mashed potatoes, sprinkle with melted butter. Bake in 425° oven for about 15 minutes until nicely browned.

Fiery Beef (Bulgoki)

For Six

2 lbs. lean filet or
   sirloin of beef
4 tbsp. light soy sauce
2 tbsp. water
2 tbsp. minced scallions
1 clove garlic, minced
½ tsp. grated fresh ginger

1½ tsp. sugar
1 tbsp. toasted sesame
   seed*
1 tbsp. oil
ample Tabasco sauce
   (to taste)
salt to taste

Cut beef in very thin slices and pound to flatten them out. Cut into medium size squares. Combine all other ingredients. The marinade — as the name of the dish implies — should be quite fiery. Mix meat with marinade and let stand for 4 to 5 hours or longer if refrigerated. Broil very quickly over hot charcoal, dip in Bulgoki Sauce (below) and serve immediately with white rice.

Note: This dish can also be prepared by frying the marinated beef slices in hot peanut oil for just a few minutes.

*See Glossary

Bulgoki Sauce

3 tbsp. dark soy sauce
1 tbsp. sesame oil
1 tsp. Chinese bean paste
   (mien chiang) (opt.)
2 tbsp. sake or dry sherry
1 tbsp. sugar
salt to taste

1 small clove garlic,
   crushed
1 tsp. toasted sesame
   seed*
1 tsp. minced scallion
1 tbsp. oil
¼ tsp. cayenne pepper

Crush garlic with sugar and salt to a smooth paste. Combine with all other ingredients and dip broiled or fried beef slices in the sauce.

*See Glossary

New England Boiled Dinner

For Six

4 lbs. corned beef (brisket)
10 black peppercorns
1 firm white cabbage
   (medium size), cored
   and quartered

6 white turnips, peeled,
   quartered
6 small carrots, peeled
6 medium potatoes, peeled
6 small boiled beets

Wash the corned beef under running water, tie the piece to keep its shape. Put in a deep saucepan, cover with cold water and bring slowly to a boil. Boil for about 10 minutes. Remove scum from top, cover and cook gently for 3 hours. Add cabbage, turnips, carrots and potatoes, cook for another half hour until vegetables and meat are soft. Put meat in a serving dish, surround with vegetables and serve.

Chinese Steak

For Six

1 flank steak, 2 to 2½ lbs.
2 tbsp. oil
⅓ cup soy sauce
2 tbsp. honey
1 clove garlic, mashed

3 tbsp. sherry
½ tsp. powdered ginger
   root
1 tsp. hot mustard
pepper to taste

Trim the steak and score the surface in a diamond pattern. Blend all other ingredients. Put steak in a shallow pan, pour the soy sauce mixture over it, coat the steak on both sides with the mixture. Let stand for 4 to 6 hours, turning it once in a while.

Broil under a very hot broiler or over charcoal. Cut into very thin slices when serving.

Cabbage and Beef Hash

For Six

1 medium head
   white cabbage, cored
8 slices lean bacon
1½ lbs. potatoes,
   peeled, diced
½ cup fresh white
   breadcrumbs

1 lb. lean beef, chopped
1 tsp. paprika
¾ tsp. caraway seed
½ cup light cream
3 egg yolks
2 tbsp. flour
salt and pepper to taste

Cook cabbage in salted water for about 6 minutes until the outside leaves are soft. Drain cabbage, remove about 6 outside leaves and reserve. Shred the remaining cabbage. Line a casserole with bacon slices, cover with the whole cabbage leaves. Spread half of the diced potatoes on the leaves. Mix beef, breadcrumbs, paprika, caraway and season with salt and pepper. Place alternate layers of beef mixture and of shredded cabbage on top of the layer of potatoes. Cover with the remaining half of the potatoes. Blend all remaining ingredients, spread on top of casserole, cover and bake at 350° for about 1 hour until potatoes are done.

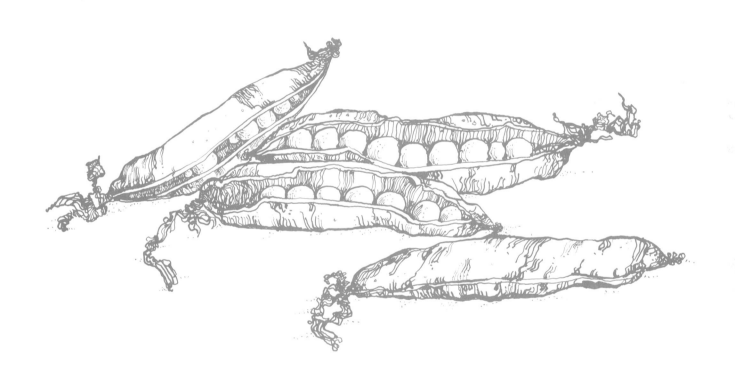

Salisbury Steak

For Four

2 lbs. ground lean beef,
   chuck or round
2 tbsp. minced onion
2 tbsp. minced parsley
1 tbsp. prepared mustard
¼ cup sherry wine

1 tbsp. paprika
salt and pepper to taste
2 tbsp. olive oil
½ lb. firm mushrooms,
   sliced
⅓ cup butter
salt and pepper to taste

Mix lightly all ingredients except mushrooms and butter. Shape into 4 patties. Brush patties with oil and broil to taste. Sauté sliced mushrooms in butter for 3 or 4 minutes, season them with salt and pepper and spoon over steaks when serving.

Chinese Green Pepper Steak and Rice

For Six

1½ lbs. sirloin steak, cut in strips ¼ inch thick
1 tbsp. paprika
2 cloves garlic, crushed
2 tbsp. butter
2 green peppers, cut in strips

1 cup sliced green onions
2 large fresh tomatoes, chopped
1 cup beef broth
¼ cup water
2 tbsp. cornstarch
2 tbsp. soy sauce
3 cups hot cooked rice

Sprinkle steak with paprika and allow to stand while preparing other ingredients. Cook steak and garlic in butter until meat is browned. Add onions, green peppers, tomatoes, and broth; cover and simmer about 15 minutes. Blend water with cornstarch and soy sauce. Stir into steak and cook until thickened. Serve over beds of fluffy rice.

Bucks County Beef Stew ▷

For Six

3 tbsp. oil
2 lbs. stewing beef, cut in 2-inch cubes
1 beef bouillon cube
2 tsp. salt
1 bay leaf
¼ tsp. crushed dried thyme leaves
4½ cups water
6 carrots
12 small white onions
¼ cup cornstarch

In skillet heat corn oil over medium heat. Add beef; brown on all sides. Add bouillon cubes, salt, bay leaf, thyme leaves and 4 cups of the water. Cover; bring to a boil. Reduce heat; simmer 1½ hours. Add carrots and onions. Simmer ½ hour or until tender. Mix cornstarch and remaining ½ cup water. Stir into beef mixture. Bring to a boil, stirring constantly; boil 1 minute.

Beef Stroganoff

For Four to Six
2 lbs. filet of beef,
   cut into thin strips
1 tbsp. minced onion
4 tbsp. butter
1 tbsp. flour

1½ cups beef broth
½ cup sour cream
2 tsp. tomato paste
½ cup sliced fresh
   mushrooms
salt and pepper to taste

Heat 2 tablespoons butter in a skillet, stir in flour and cook the roux over gentle heat while stirring, until the mixture bubbles. Gradually add beef broth, stir and simmer until the mixture is smooth and thickened. Remove from fire and rub through a fine sieve into a saucepan. Stir in tomato paste and mushrooms, simmer for a few minutes. Heat remaining butter in a large skillet, sauté meat and onion quickly — not more than 3 minutes or so — until nicely browned. Pour contents of the skillet into the simmering sauce, season with salt and pepper and blend well. Simmer for 15 minutes or cook in top of a double boiler over simmering water for 20 minutes. Blend in sour cream, heat through and serve.

Note: Other cuts of meat, such as lean sirloin can be used, but the filet, the tenderest of all beef cuts, is the classic one to use.

Greek Potato Casserole

For Six
8 medium potatoes
3 tbsp. butter
2 onions, sliced thin
¾ lb. ground beef

2 tomatoes, peeled, sliced
1 cup beef or chicken broth
pinch of thyme
pinch of oregano
salt and pepper to taste

Peel potatoes, cut into ½-inch thick slices. Heat 2 tablespoons butter in a skillet, sauté slices quickly on both sides and arrange them in a saucepan. Add the remaining butter to the skillet, add onions, sauté for 2 minutes, add meat and sauté while stirring for about 10 minutes until browned. Spread the meat and onions over the potatoes, top with tomato slices, sprinkle with thyme and oregano and season with salt and pepper. Add broth, cover tightly and cook gently for about 45 minutes until potatoes are done. Add more broth if needed.

Chopped Beef Casserole

For Four
6 medium-sized zucchini
   (about 1½ lbs.)
water
2 tbsp. olive oil
¾ lb. ground lean beef
1 large onion, grated
1 large green pepper,
   seeded and chopped

1 clove garlic, minced
2 medium tomatoes, peeled
   and sliced ½ inch thick
2 tbsp. fresh dill, chopped
1 tbsp. parsley, chopped
   (or 2 tsp. dried)
1 tsp. paprika
salt and pepper to taste
1 cup beef broth

Peel zucchini and cut into 2½ inch long pieces. Cook them in boiling water for 2 minutes. Drain and arrange the pieces in one layer in a saucepan. Heat oil in a skillet, add ground beef and onion, sauté quickly until light brown — 3 to 4 minutes. Stir while sautéing. Add garlic and green pepper, mix and sauté 3 minutes longer. Add tomato and cook another 2 minutes. Spread this mixture over zucchini, sprinkle with dill, parsley, mint and paprika, season with salt and pepper, add ½ cup broth, cover and cook gently for half an hour. Add more broth if needed.

Stir-fried Beef and Cabbage

For Four

1 lb. flank steak
2 cups Chinese cabbage, sliced
1 clove garlic, mashed
2 thin slices ginger root, minced
3 scallions

¼ cup beef broth
1 tbsp. soy sauce
1 tbsp. sherry
pepper to taste
2 tsp. cornstarch
3 tbsp. water
2 tbsp. oil

Cut cabbage at a slant into ¼ inch slices. Cut flank steak across the grain into ¼ inch thick slices, 2 inches long. Slice scallions lengthwise in half and then cut into 2 inch pieces. Heat one tablespoon oil in a wok, add ginger and garlic and stir-fry for a minute until starting to brown. Add cabbage and scallions, fry for another minute or two. Combine beef broth, soy sauce, sherry and pepper, add to wok, blend and cover. Cook for a minute. Remove vegetables and sauce from wok and reserve. Clean wok, heat 1 tablespoon oil and stir-fry beef over high flame for 1 minute. Add reserved vegetables and sauce and heat through. Dilute cornstarch in water, add to the pan and stir for a minute until thickened.

Ropa Vieja

For Four

1 flank steak (1½ to 2 lbs.)
1 carrot, peeled

For the sauce:

2 tbsp. lard or oil
1 medium onion, chopped
3 green peppers, seeded and chopped
2 cloves garlic, minced
1 tbsp. paprika

1 turnip, quartered
2 cloves

3 large tomatoes, peeled, seeded and chopped
¼ cup canned pimientos, chopped
1 small bay leaf
salt and pepper to taste

Put flank steak in a pan, cover with water, add carrot, turnip and cloves, cover and boil gently until meat is cooked and very soft (2 to 3 hours). Remove meat, drain and shred it with your fingers.

Heat lard in a heavy saucepan, sauté onion until it starts to color, add garlic and peppers, sauté for a couple of minutes. Then add meat and all other ingredients, bring to a boil and simmer for 15 minutes.

Savory Meat Balls

For Four

6 leeks (medium size)
1 lb. ground beef
1 cup soft white breadcrumbs
salt and pepper to taste
2 eggs, lightly beaten

1 tsp. paprika
2 tbsp. parsley, minced
1 tbsp. dill, chopped
3 tbsp. lemon juice
⅓ cup oil
1 tbsp. butter
¾ cup beef broth

Trim leeks, cut off and discard half of the green part, split them in half and wash well. Cook leeks in boiling water until soft. Drain well and mince very fine. Blend with meat, breadcrumbs, paprika, salt, pepper, eggs, parsley and dill. Knead until smooth. Shape into balls about 1 inch in diameter. Heat oil and fry meat balls while shaking the skillet until they are nicely browned.

Heat lemon juice, butter and ½ cup broth in a saucepan, add meatballs, cover and cook gently for about 25 to 30 minutes until meatballs are cooked. Shake pan occasionally and add more broth if needed. Spoon a little of the lemony sauce over the meatballs when serving.

Dill-Horseradish Pot Roast ◁

For Six
3 lbs. beef bottom round
¼ tsp. salt
few grains pepper
¼ cup dill pickle liquid
    drained from dill pickles
1 medium onion, peeled
1 cup sour cream
½ cup heavy cream, whipped
2 tbsp. prepared horseradish
½ cup sliced dill pickles, well drained

Trim excess fat from meat. In heavy pot, brown meat on all sides in its own fat. Sprinkle with salt and pepper; add pickle liquid and whole onion. Cover tightly and simmer about 2 hours or until tender. Pour off pan liquid; skim off fat. Measure ⅓ cup pan liquid; reserve. Pour remaining liquid back into pot to keep meat warm while preparing sauce.

To make sauce, gently fold together sour cream, whipped cream, reserved pan liquid and horseradish. Just before serving, mix in pickle slices. Serve with pot roast.

Spanish Beef Stew with Olives ▷

For Eight
2 tbsp. olive or salad oil
3½ lbs. beef stew meat,
    cubed
1 tsp. salt
⅛ tsp. pepper
2 medium onions, sliced
2 large cloves garlic,
    crushed
2 cups beef bouillon
2 cups dry red wine
    (or additional bouillon)
parsley
2 cups bouillon

4 tomatoes, peeled and
    quartered

*tie herbs in cheesecloth,
    as follows:*
    1 bay leaf
    4 parsley sprigs
    ½ tsp. thyme leaves

1½ cups Spanish stuffed
    green olives
2½ lbs. potatoes, peeled
    and halved
2 tbsp. flour

Heat oil in large kettle or Dutch oven. Add meat, a few pieces at a time, and brown well on all sides. Remove meat and season with salt and pepper. If drippings in kettle are too brown, drain off and add additional 2 tablespoons oil. Add onions and cook until tender and lightly brown. Add garlic, bouillon, wine, 1 of the tomatoes and the herbs. Add browned meat and bring to a boil. Cover and simmer or bake in 350⁰ oven 2 hours or until meat is tender. Add olives and potatoes and continue cooking 30 minutes. Remove meat and vegetables to serving dish; keep warm. Drain cooking liquid into saucepan and skim off fat; bring to a boil. Blend flour with 3 tablespoons water; stir into boiling liquid. Add remaining tomatoes and simmer 10 minutes. Pour liquid over meat and vegetables; top with tomatoes. Garnish with parsley.

Oxtail Ragout

For Four

1 large meaty oxtail,
   cut in pieces
salt and pepper to taste
¼ tsp. mace
pinch of allspice
2 tbsp. Applejack or brandy
2 tbsp. butter
2 carrots, peeled,
   coarsely chopped

1 large onion, minced
2 stalks celery
   (white part), chopped
1 bay leaf
pinch of thyme
½ tsp. rosemary, crushed
½ cup beef broth
½ cup dry red wine
2 tbsp. tomato paste

Put oxtail in a bowl, add salt, pepper, mace, allspice and Applejack; mix well and let stand for 30 minutes, drain.

Heat butter in a saucepan, sauté oxtail for about 7 minutes, until nicely browned on all sides. Remove from saucepan and keep warm. Add onion, carrots and celery to pan, sauté over gentle heat until vegetables are soft but not browned. Return meat to pan, add bay leaf, thyme, rosemary, broth, wine and tomato paste. Mix well. If needed to cover the meat, add a little more broth and wine. Cover and cook slowly for 4 to 5 hours or until meat is very soft.

It is best to cook this dish the day before you intend to serve it. When the meat is cooked, take off the fire, cool and refrigerate overnight. The next day remove the fat that has solidified on the top. Heat casserole until bubbling. Remove meat with a slotted spoon, reduce gravy by one third until nice and thick, return meat and heat through before serving.

Sweet and Sour Beef Balls

For Four

1 lb. lean beef
2 tbsp. onion, minced
1 tsp. fresh ginger root,
   minced
1 small clove garlic, minced
1 egg
1 tbsp. flour

salt to taste
1½ cups beef broth
2 tbsp. brown sugar
3 tbsp. soy sauce
4 tbsp. vinegar
pinch of cayenne pepper
2 tsp. cornstarch
1 tbsp. water

Grind beef very fine or mince with sharp knives. Blend with onion, ginger, garlic, the lightly beaten egg and flour. Do not handle too much. Shape into small balls. Bring broth to a boil in a deep, smallish saucepan. Drop beef balls, a few at a time into the broth and simmer, covered, until done. Remove them as they get done and keep hot. When all are cooked, add sugar, soy sauce, vinegar, salt and cayenne to the broth, stir well. Blend cornstarch and water, stir into broth to thicken and pour over beef balls.

Hamburger Hints

Ground round, ground chuck, or ground shoulder can be used for hamburgers.

Good round is lean, chuck has more fat and therefore often makes a juicier hamburger.

Broil thick large hamburgers, but better pan-broil thin patties.

For extra juicy hamburgers, add about 3 tablespoons ice water to each pound of meat and mix in lightly with a fork — or substitute tomato juice or dry red wine for water.

Add onions — finely minced or grated — and mix with the meat. Other good seasonings for blending into the meat include Worcestershire sauce, soy sauce, horseradish, a variety of mustards, spices and herbs, such as thyme, poultry seasoning, oregano, ginger, cumin and red pepper.

Another seasoning — blend ¼ cup soy sauce with 2 tablespoons brown sugar and a pinch of powdered ginger. Dip the unseasoned meat patties into the mixture just before broiling.

Place a slice of sharp cheese or a spoonful of well-seasoned various dressings between two thin hamburger patties, press edges together and broil.

Meat Balls and Mushrooms

For Four

2 lbs. lean chopped beef
1 cup dry unflavored
  breadcrumbs
2 eggs
1 medium onion, grated
1 large clove garlic,
  mashed
2 tbsp. parsley, minced
1 tsp. paprika

pinch of grated nutmeg
salt and pepper to taste
4 tbsp. fat
1 cup tomato sauce
½ cup beef broth
1 cup sliced mushrooms
1 tsp. paprika
1 tsp. sugar
salt to taste

Mix beef, breadcrumbs, eggs, onion, garlic, parsley, 1 teaspoon paprika, nutmeg, salt and pepper. Shape into 1½ inch balls. Heat fat in a heavy saucepan and brown meat balls on all sides. Pour fat off pan, add all other ingredients, cover and cook gently for 15 minutes.

Polish Beef and Vegetables

For Four

1½ lbs. brisket of beef,
  sliced
2 tbsp. flour
2 tbsp. butter or bacon
  drippings
¾ cup beef broth
salt and pepper to taste
2 medium onions, coarsely,
  chopped

3 carrots, peeled, sliced
1 parsnip, peeled, sliced
1 parsley root, peeled,
  diced (or ⅓ cup
  chopped parsley)
2 stalks celery, sliced
¾ cup sour cream
1 tbsp. chopped dill
  leaves

Heat butter or drippings in a saucepan. Sprinkle meat with flour and brown the slices on both sides. Add broth, cover and cook gently for one hour. Season with salt and pepper, add all vegetables, cover and cook for another 30 minutes. Correct seasoning, remove from fire, blend in sour cream and serve.

Fried Beef and Mushrooms

For Four

¾ lb. lean steak
1 clove garlic, crushed
½ tsp. grated fresh ginger
½ tsp. grated lemon peel
salt and black pepper to taste
1 tbsp. dark soy sauce

½ lb. fresh mushrooms,
  thickly sliced
3 tbsp. sesame oil
⅓ cup beef broth (or water)
2 tsp. cornstarch
1 tbsp. water

Slice beef paper thin across the grain or ask your butcher to do so on his meat slicer. Sprinkle with garlic, ginger, lemon peel, salt and pepper, and blend lightly. Heat oil in a wok, stir in beef and cook while stirring until beef browns lightly. Add mushrooms and soy sauce and stir fry 2 minutes longer. Add broth, reduce heat and cover. Cook gently for 2 minutes. Dissolve cornstarch in water, add to the wok, stir well, bring to a boil and simmer until thickened.

◊ Sukiyaki

For Six

2 lbs. lean sirloin or round steak
12 fresh mushrooms
2 whole canned bamboo shoots
8 scallions
1 medium onion, sliced thin
¼ lb. thin spaghetti, cooked
1 bunch watercress
1 square bean curd* (tofu)
½ cup mirin*
½ cup light soy sauce
¼ cup dashi*
2 tsp. sugar
1 piece of beef suet (about 1-inch
   cube)

Ask your butcher to slice the meat paper thin on his meat slicer. Cut mushrooms in thick slices, slice bamboo shoots about ⅛-inch thick, and cut watercress and scallions in 1½-inch pieces. Cut bean curd into 1-inch cubes. Rinse and drain cooked spaghetti. Arrange all these ingredients attractively on a large platter. Combine mirin, soy sauce, dashi and sugar.

Sukiyaki should be cooked at the table in a heavy iron skillet over a portable stove or in an electric skillet. Heat the skillet, rub with the piece of suet until well coated. Discard the suet. Add about ⅓ of the meat, stir and cook it for a minute. Add ¼ cup of the mirin sauce mixture, stir and add ⅓ of the mushrooms, bamboo shoots, bean curd and noodles in small heaps — do not mix these ingredients together. Cook for 3 minutes and add another ¼ cup sauce. Add scallions and watercress, cook for one more minute. Let each guest help himself from the skillet while you add more meat and vegetables as the skillet is being emptied.

*See Glossary

Stir-fried Shredded Beef

For Three
¾ lb. flank steak, shredded
2 tbsp. soy sauce
1 tsp. sherry
1 small clove garlic, minced
1 slice fresh ginger, shredded
1 tsp. hoisin sauce
2 scallions, chopped
1 cup shredded celery
¼ cup shredded bamboo shoots
½ cup shredded carrot
3 tbsp. oil
½ tsp. dried red (hot) pepper

Add soy sauce, sherry, hoisin sauce and garlic to beef; mix well. Heat 1½ tablespoons oil in a wok, add beef and stir-fry about 2 minutes until it starts to turn brown. Remove beef from wok and keep warm. Add remaining oil to wok and heat. Add ginger root, stir for a few seconds; add scallions and carrots; stir-fry for 1 minute. Add bamboo shoots, celery and red pepper; fry 1 minute more. Return beef, stir to heat through.

◊ Beef Borscht

For Eight
2 lbs. beef for stew
4 cups water
2½ tsp. salt
¼ tsp. pepper
1 bay leaf
2 cups thinly sliced celery
1 medium onion, chopped
1 clove garlic, chopped
1 tbsp. vinegar
2 tsp. sugar
¼ tsp. thyme
½ medium cabbage, thinly sliced
1 jar (16 oz.) sliced beets
2 tbsp. flour
sour cream

Cut beef for stew into 1-inch pieces and place in Dutch oven or large pot. Add water, salt, pepper, and bay leaf; cover tightly and simmer 1½ hours. Remove bay leaf. Add celery, onion, garlic, vinegar, sugar and thyme and simmer, covered, 15 minutes. Add cabbage and continue to cook, covered, 15 minutes or until meat and cabbage are tender. Drain beets; re-serve liquid, combine with flour to blend, stir into soup and cook, stirring constantly to thicken slightly. Add beets and simmer 3 to 5 minutes. Serve sour cream to top individual servings of soup.

Veal Piccata

For Four
1½ lbs. veal scaloppine,
    pounded thin (about
    12 pieces)
5 tbsp. butter
2 tbsp. oil

flour
salt and pepper to taste
3 tbsp. lemon juice
2 tbsp. parsley, minced
2 tbsp. dry white wine
very thin lemon slices

Dredge scaloppine very lightly in flour and shake off the excess. Heat 3 tablespoons butter and the oil in a skillet. When the fats start foaming, add the meat, not too many pieces at a time, brown them quickly on one side, turn and brown the other side. This should take not more than a minute or two.

As they are done, remove them to a warm platter and season with salt and pepper. Take skillet off the flame, add lemon juice and wine, scrape the pan to deglaze. Swirl in the remaining butter, then add parsley, blend and return scaloppine to the sauce. Return skillet to stove, heat through very briefly. Put meat on a hot serving platter, sauce over it and garnish with lemon slices and a little chopped parsley.

Roast Veal Shank

For Four
2 veal shanks,
    about 2½ lbs. each
salt and pepper to taste

2 tbsp. flour
4 tbsp. butter
1 cup chicken broth
1 tbsp. flour

Wipe shanks with a damp cloth. Season with salt and pepper, sprinkle with flour. Heat butter in a roasting pan and brown shanks on all sides. Add ½ cup chicken broth, roast in 375⁰ for about 1½ hours or until meat is tender. Baste quite often adding more broth as needed. When done, remove shanks to serving platter, stir flour into roasting pan, add more liquid if needed, and make a pan gravy to be served with the meat.

Note: Cold roasted veal shanks are the juiciest of all cooked veal cuts and are excellent to serve for lunch or at picnics.

Spaghetti with Veal and Peppers   ⇨

For Eight

2 lbs. boneless veal
   shoulder, cut in strips
flour
¼ cup butter
⅓ cup olive oil
4 medium green peppers,
   cut in strips
2 small onions, sliced

4 cloves garlic, minced
2 cans (19 oz. each)
   tomatoes
2 cans (8 oz. each)
   tomato sauce
salt and pepper to taste
1½ tsp. basil
¼ to ½ tsp. oregano
1 lb. spaghetti

Coat veal with flour; brown in butter and oil in large skillet. Remove meat; sauté green peppers and onion about 5 minutes. Return meat; add garlic, tomatoes, sauce, salt, herbs and pepper. Simmer covered 1 hour, stirring occasionally, until meat is tender.

Cook spaghetti until tender. Drain in colander. Serve with veal and pepper sauce.

Veal Cutlets Milanese

For Four

1½ lbs. veal scalloppine
2 eggs, lightly beaten
   with 1 tbsp. milk
6 tbsp. butter
2 tbsp. olive oil

1½ cups (approx. fine
   white dry breadcrumbs,
   unflavored
salt
lemon wedges

Have veal cut about ¼ inch thick and then well flattened. Dip each cutlet in beaten eggs, then in breadcrumbs. Press crumbs gently with your hands into the meat, then shake off excess crumbs. Letting the cutlets rest after breading will make the breading adhere better.

Heat butter and oil in a skillet. The fats should be about ¼ inch deep. Cook the cutlets over medium heat until golden brown, turn when one side is done. Drain on paper towel, sprinkle with salt and serve garnished with lemon wedges.

Veal Cutlets with Parmesan

Proceed as for veal cutlets Milanese, but mix ¼ cup Parmesan cheese with the breadcrumbs before breading the meat.

Wiener Schnitzel (Vienna Veal Cutlet)

For Four

4 veal cutlets, cut from the
   leg, about ¼ inch thick
salt to taste
¾ cup flour
2 eggs beaten with
   2 tbsp. water

1 cup fine white
   breadcrumbs
¾ cup lard (or ½ cup
   butter and ¼ cup oil)
lemon wedges
parsley

Veal cutlets are very popular in Viennese cooking and are prepared in many different ways. The best known is the breaded veal cutlet — Wiener Schnitzel. It is a shallow fried cutlet, *never* served with any sauce or melted butter or garnishes other than a lemon wedge.

Pound and flatten the cutlets to about half their thickness. Season with salt, dredge in flour, dip in beaten eggs and then roll in breadcrumbs. Shake off excess crumbs and let cutlets stand for half an hour. Heat fat in a skillet — the fat should be about ½ inch deep — and sauté cutlets until golden brown on one side, turn and cook the other side. Drain on paper towel. Garnish with lemon wedges and parsley.

Schnitzel Holstein

Prepare Wiener Schnitzel as above and top each with one fried egg and a strip of anchovy filet before serving.

Italian Stuffed
◁Breast of Veal

For Six
1 breast of veal
6 tbsp. olive oil
½ cup uncooked rice
2 cups fresh breadcrumbs
lukewarm milk
¼ cup salt pork, finely
    diced and blanched
½ cup chicken livers
½ cup grated Provolone cheese
½ lb. spinach, blanched and
    finely chopped
2 egg yolks
½ tsp. dried basil
pinch of grated nutmeg
1 large onion, chopped
2 carrots, peeled and chopped
1 leek, white and green part,
    washed and chopped

Have butcher bone veal for stuffing.

Heat 1 tablespoon oil in a casserole, add the rice and stir until the rice becomes translucent. Add ¾ cup of water and a little salt. Cover tightly and cook for about 17 minutes or until rice is tender.

Soak the breadcrumbs in lukewarm milk. Squeeze them dry. Mince together the salt pork and the chicken livers. Mix them with the cooked rice, the breadcrumbs, spinach, grated cheese, egg yolks and basil. Season with salt, pepper and nutmeg. Stuff the breast of veal with this mixture and sew the opening closed.

Put the chopped vegetables in a casserole with the remaining oil and veal bones. Place the stuffed breast of veal on top and cook over high heat for 7 or 8 minutes. Cover the casserole and transfer it to a preheated 350⁰ oven. Bake for about 2½ hours. After 1 hour cooking time, pierce the meat in three places with a needle. Baste occasionally.

Drain the cooked meat, place it on a large serving dish. Skim the fat off the pan juices and strain the juices over the meat. Chill until serving time. Serve cold, garnished with tomato slices and black olives.

Veal and Mushrooms

For Four

2 lbs. veal (shoulder or boneless shank) cubed	½ cup chicken broth
1 lb. firm small mushrooms	¼ cup sour cream
2 tbsp. butter	¼ cup tomato purée
1 medium onion, chopped	salt and pepper to taste
	1 tbsp. flour

Heat butter in a saucepan, sauté veal cubes for 2 minutes while stirring, add mushrooms and sauté while stirring until lightly browned. Add onion, cook 5 minutes longer. Sprinkle with flour, stir, add chicken broth, cover and cook gently for 45 minutes until meat is tender. Blend in sour cream, tomato purée, season with salt and pepper, let come to a simmer and serve.

Ossobuco

For Four

4 meaty pieces of shin of
  veal, with bone, each
  about 4 inches long
flour
salt and pepper to taste
3 tbsp. butter
3 tbsp. olive oil
½ cup carrots, minced
½ cup onion, minced

1 large clove garlic, minced
1 tbsp. parsley, chopped
¾ cup dry white wine
¾ cup chicken broth
¼ tsp. thyme
2 strips lemon peel
¼ tsp. rosemary
2 tbsp. tomato paste
½ cup celery, minced

Dredge meat in flour, shake off excess, season with salt and pepper. Heat half the butter and oil in a heavy skillet or dutch oven. Brown the meat on all sides. Remove from pan, which ideally should just be big enough to contain the shank pieces standing upright. Pour off the fat and add the remaining oil and butter. Add all the vegetables, sauté while stirring until they are lightly browned. Add wine and chicken broth, place meat on top of vegetables, add all other ingredients, cover tightly and simmer for about 1½ hours or until meat is done. Baste every 15 minutes. When meat is done remove to hot serving platter, strain the sauce and reduce quickly if too thin.

Veal Birds ⇨

For Four

8 slices of veal cutlets, ¼ inch thick
salt and pepper to taste
flour
3 tbsp. oil
1 tbsp. butter
1 tbsp. lemon juice
1 cup Madeira wine
1 tbsp. cornstarch blended
  with 2 tbsp. water

For the stuffing:

⅓ lb. ground veal
⅓ lb. lean pork, ground
⅓ smoked ham, ground

Combine the stuffing ingredients. Flatten the veal cutlets (or ask your butcher to do it). Season them with salt and pepper, put a little of the stuffing on each. Roll them up and tie them securely with kitchen string. Dust with flour, and sauté them in the combined oil and butter over high heat until golden on all sides. Reduce the heat, cover and simmer for 15 minutes.

Transfer veal serving dish and keep hot. Stir the Madeira and the lemon juice into the pan juices, boil for a few minutes, stir to deglaze, then add the cornstarch mixture. Cook stirring until thickened. Coat the veal birds with the sauce and serve.

Veal Cutlets à la Russe

For Four
4 loin veal chops, cut ¼
    inch thick
softened butter, the weight
    of the boned chops
salt and pepper to taste
pinch of grated nutmeg

fresh white breadcrumbs
    soaked in milk, squeezed
    dry, also the weight of
    the boned chops
flour
6 tbsp. butter
1 lemon, sliced

Bone and trim the chops, reserve the bones. Grind the meat (or have your butcher do it), using the finest blade of the grinder. Weigh the meat and then beat into the ground meat the same weight of softened butter and of fresh white breadcrumbs soaked in milk and squeezed dry. Season with salt, pepper and nutmeg.

Divide the mixture into four pieces and form them in the shape of the original chops around the bones. Dust lightly with flour and sauté in hot butter in a skillet until golden brown on both sides.

Place on a serving dish and garnish with lemon slices.

Saltimbocca Romana

For Four
1½ lbs. scallopine (veal
    cutlets, cut very thin)
¼ lb. prosciutto
    (or lean bacon)
2 tbsp. butter

fresh sage leaves (or 1
    tsp. dried sage)
2 tbsp. olive oil
salt and pepper to taste
½ cup chicken broth

Cut the veal cutlets in 4-inch squares. Sprinkle a little sage on each square, put a slice of prosciutto or bacon on top and fasten to veal with a toothpick. Season with salt and pepper. Heat butter and oil in a skillet and brown the meat quickly on both sides. This should not take longer than 2 or 3 minutes. Remove the saltimbocca as they get done to a hot serving platter, then add broth to the skillet, scrape and deglaze the skillet, reduce the gravy if too thin, and pour over meat.

Blanquette of Veal

For Four
2 lbs. veal from shoulder
    or breast, cut into 1½
    inch pieces
3 medium carrots, sliced
12 small white onions,
    peeled
1 clove garlic, chopped
1 stalk celery
3 sprigs parsley
1 bay leaf

salt and pepper to taste
2 cups chicken broth
    (or water)
2 tbsp. shallots, minced
3 tbsp. butter
12 small firm mushrooms
3 tbsp. flour
2 egg yolks
⅓ cup heavy cream
1 tsp. lemon juice
minced parsley

Put meat, carrots, onions and garlic in a casserole. Tie celery, parsley and bay leaf together and add to the meat, season with salt and pepper and add chicken broth. Let it come to a boil, turn heat low and simmer for a few minutes. Take scum off the surface, cover the casserole and simmer for an hour or more, until meat is done. Sauté shallots in a skillet in 2 tablespoons butter until soft but do not let brown. Add mushrooms and sauté until they take on color. Remove mushrooms and add them to the casserole. Add remaining butter to the skillet, stir in the flour and cook the roux, stirring for a couple of minutes. Then add gradually ¾ cup sauce from the casserole to the roux, stir constantly until smooth. Blend egg yolks and crème fraîche and add, while whisking, to the skillet. Heat through but do not let boil. Stir this sauce into the casserole, let it thicken for a few minutes. Stir in lemon juice, correct seasoning. Remove the tied celery and parsley, sprinkle blanquette with parsley before serving.

Paprika Schnitzel

For Four
2 lbs. veal cutlets,
    pounded thin
salt and pepper to taste
2 tbsp. flour
5 tbsp. butter
1 small onion, minced

2 tsp. paprika
2 tsp. flour
¾ cup chicken broth
    (approx.)
salt
½ tsp. caraway seed
¾ cup sour cream

Score the edges of the cutlets, season with salt and pepper, sprinkle with flour. Heat butter in a saucepan, brown cutlets quickly on both sides, remove from pan and keep warm. Add onion to pan, sauté until very soft, stir in paprika and flour and add gradually enough chicken broth to make a sauce. Season with salt, add caraway and return meat to pan. Cover and simmer until meat is done — about ½ hour. A few minutes before serving, blend in sour cream and heat through.

Veal Cutlets à la Crème

For Four
4 veal cutlets pounded
    thin (about ¼ lb. each)
2 tbsp. lemon juice
salt and pepper to taste
2 tbsp. butter

4 tbsp. dry vermouth
½ cup crème fraîche*
    or heavy cream
½ tsp. tarragon
finely minced parsley

Sprinkle the cutlets with lemon juice, season with salt and pepper and sauté them in butter for 3 minutes on each side. Then add the vermouth, cook for another minute. Reduce the heat and stir in the crème fraîche, parsley and the tarragon. Simmer for 5 minutes, stirring once in a while. Correct seasoning and serve.

*See Glossary

Roast Loin of Veal (Nierenbraten)

For Six
4 lbs. veal loin with
    kidneys
salt

4 tbsp. butter
1 cup chicken broth
1 tbsp. flour
1 tbsp. parsley, minced

Have butcher trim and bone loin, cut kidneys lengthwise in half and place them in the boned roast. Roll roast and tie securely. Season meat with salt. Heat butter in a roasting pan and brown the meat on all sides. Add ½ cup chicken broth and roast at 375⁰ for about 1¾ to 2 hours or until meat is tender. Baste frequently and add more broth if necessary. When done, remove meat to hot serving platter, removing strings. Stir flour into roasting pan, add more broth if needed, and cook quickly on top of the stove to make a pan gravy. Sprinkle meat with parsley, serve gravy separately.

Veal and Okra Stew

For Four
1 large onion, minced
1 medium onion,
    sliced thin
2 cloves garlic, minced
3 tbsp. butter
2 lbs. veal shoulder, cubed
1½ cups chicken broth
    (or water)

1 tbsp. tomato paste
1½ lbs. fresh okra (or
    2 packages frozen)
    trimmed
2 tomatoes, peeled,
    seeded and chopped
salt and pepper to taste
1 tbsp. lemon juice

Heat butter in a saucepan, add minced onion and sauté until light golden, add sliced onion, garlic and meat, sauté until lightly browned. Add okra (if frozen okra is used drain well before adding), sauté 3 minutes longer. Add all other ingredients, mix well, cover and cook gently for 1½ hours or until meat is tender. Add a little more liquid if needed.

Veal and Peppers

For Four
2 tbsp. butter
1 tbsp. oil
1½ lbs. boneless veal
(shoulder or rump) cubed
salt and pepper to taste
1 medium onion,
sliced thin

4 firm ripe tomatoes,
peeled, seeded, chopped
1 tsp. dried basil, crumbled
½ tsp. marjoram
4 large sweet peppers
(green or red or mixed)
3 tbsp. olive oil

Heat butter and oil in a saucepan, add veal cubes and brown. Season with salt and pepper, add onion, stir well and cook over medium heat for 5 minutes. Add tomatoes, basil and marjoram, mix well, cover and simmer for 20 minutes. Cut caps off peppers and discard. Remove seeds and membranes; quarter peppers lengthwise. Heat olive oil in a skillet and fry peppers for 5 minutes or more until soft. Then add to the veal, cover again and simmer another half hour or until meat is cooked. Correct seasoning before serving.

Veal Marengo

For Four
2 lbs. shoulder of veal or
boneless veal shank
1½ tbsp. olive oil
1½ tbsp. butter
1 medium onion, chopped
3 tomatoes, peeled,
seeded and chopped

12 small firm mushrooms
2 tbsp. flour
½ cup dry white wine
1 cup chicken stock
1 clove garlic, minced
salt and pepper to taste
3 tbsp. Cognac
minced parsley

Cut the veal in fairly large cubes, heat oil and butter, add veal, onion and tomato. Sauté over medium heat for 15 minutes, stirring occasionally. Then add mushrooms. Continue cooking until most of the liquid has evaporated. Stir in flour, add wine, chicken stock and garlic, season with salt and pepper, stir well. Cover and simmer for about one hour or until meat is tender. Uncover, reduce sauce if too thin, add Cognac and flame. Sprinkle with parsley before serving.

Carbonnade of Veal

For Six
4 lbs. rump of veal
1 cup olive oil
1 tbsp. dried thyme
6 tbsp. butter

salt and pepper to taste
4 shallots, minced
½ lb. smoked ham or
prosciutto ham, diced
2 lbs. fresh spinach

Marinate veal in oil and thyme for 12 hours. Drain.

Heat half the butter and 2 tablespoons of the oil marinade in a saucepan. Brown veal over high heat on all sides. Season with salt and pepper, cover pan and simmer over low heat for 1½ hours or until meat is tender. Put meat on a serving dish and keep hot.

Add shallots and ham to saucepan, cook them for 5 minutes, remove with a slotted spoon and put on top of veal. Add remaining butter and spinach to the saucepan, stir well and cook for 6 to 8 minutes until spinach is tender. Correct seasoning and garnish the veal with spinach.

Veal Paprika

For Four
2 lbs. boneless veal,
breast or shoulder,
cubed
1½ tbsp. butter
1 large onion, minced
½ tbsp. paprika
1 clove garlic, crushed

1 tbsp. flour
salt and pepper to taste
½ cup broth or water
1 ripe tomato, peeled,
seeded and chopped
1 green pepper, seeded
and diced
1 cup sour cream

Heat butter in a heavy saucepan, add onion and sauté until light golden. Blend in paprika, garlic, salt, pepper, cubed veal and ¼ cup broth. Cover and cook gently for half an hour. Check from time to time and add a few tablespoons of liquid if needed. Add tomato, green pepper, cover and cook about 20 minutes longer or until meat is cooked. Stir flour into sour cream, add to the stew, mix well and barely simmer for 10 more minutes. Do not let boil.

Lamb

◊ Shish Kebab

For Six
2 lbs. boned leg of lamb,
   cut into 1½ inch cubes
2 tbsp. lemon juice
1 tbsp. vinegar
4 tbsp. olive oil
1 medium onion, grated
salt and pepper to taste
1 bay leaf
2 or 3 green peppers, seeded
   and cut into 1½ inch squares

Blend all ingredients except green peppers, mix well with meat and let stand for 3 to 4 hours. Thread on skewers, alternating a meat cube and a piece of pepper. Broil over hot charcoal, about 3 inches from the fire about 3 to 4 minutes on each side, turning the skewers to brown meat evenly.

Lamb Chops Champvallon

For Two

4 tbsp. cooking oil
4 tbsp. butter
3 tomatoes, peeled,
   seeded and chopped
3 potatoes, peeled and
   thinly sliced

½ tsp. dried thyme
1 bay leaf
salt and pepper to taste
2 large lamb chops,
   trimmed
2 onions, minced
1 clove garlic, minced

Heat half the oil and half the butter in a casserole, add the tomatoes and cook until they are soft. Then add the potatoes, thyme, bay leaf and garlic. Add salt and pepper to taste and just enough hot water to cover the potatoes. Cover and simmer over low heat for about 20 minutes. When the potatoes are done they should have absorbed all the water. If not, uncover and boil the water away.

Put remaining oil and butter in a skillet, season chops and brown them quickly on both sides. Add onions and continue cooking until onions are golden brown and the chops are done to your taste. Then place chops on top of the potatoes, spread onions on top and pour pan juices from skillet over the chops. Cover the casserole and simmer for another 2 minutes.

Italian Spring Lamb ▷

For Six

1 leg of lamb, about 6 lbs.
salt and pepper
2 cloves garlic, mashed
⅓ cup dry red wine
2 tbsp. chopped fresh basil or 2 tsp.
   dried basil
2 tbsp. grated Parmesan cheese
⅓ cup olive oil

Sprinkle lamb on all sides with salt and pepper. Place lamb in a shallow roasting pan. Beat remaining ingredients in a bowl until thick and well blended. Brush some of the wine mixture over lamb. Roast in a preheated oven at 350⁰ for about 1¾ hours for pink lamb and 2½ hours for well-done lamb. Brush lamb with wine mixture every 30 minutes during cooking. Garnish with additional sprigs of fresh basil if desired. Allow cooked lamb to stand 10 minutes before carving.

Serve garnished with a vegetable medley of cooked zucchini slices and onions, artichoke hearts and roasted red pepper pieces if desired.

New England Lamb Stew

For Two
1 lb. boneless lamb shoulder
  or leg, cut in 1″ cubes
butter or cooking oil
¼ onion, thinly sliced
¼ green pepper, chopped
1 stalk celery, sliced
1 small clove garlic,
  crushed
1 cup bouillon
1 large potato, quartered
1 large carrot, peeled
  and sliced
1 small turnip, peeled,
  diced

1 cup whole tomatoes
⅛ tsp. sage
⅛ tsp. marjoram
⅛ tsp. thyme
¼ bay leaf, crushed
½ tsp. Worcestershire sauce
½ tsp. prepared horseradish
1 tbsp. molasses or brown
  sugar
salt and pepper to taste
½ cup whole kernel corn
½ cup frozen green beans,
  thawed
2 tbsp. flour
¼ cup water

In large dutch oven or heavy pot, cook lamb in 1 tablespoon butter over medium heat, until browned, stirring frequently; remove lamb. Add onion, green pepper, celery and garlic, adding more butter if necessary. Continue cooking and stirring until onion is lightly browned. Add bouillon, lamb cubes, potato, carrot, turnip, tomatoes, seasonings, molasses, and salt and pepper to taste. Heat to boiling; simmer, covered, for 20 to 30 minutes, or until meat and vegetables are tender. Add corn and beans. Cook 5 minutes, or until beans are tender. Blend flour with water; gradually stir into lamb mixture — stir — simmer 5 minutes.

Stuffed Leg of Lamb

For Six
1 leg of lamb (about 5 lbs.)
¼ lb. ground veal
¼ lb. ground lean pork
6 chicken livers, chopped
1 cup fresh white
  breadcrumbs
salt and pepper to taste

pinch of cayenne pepper
pinch of dried thyme
1 tsp. crushed dried
  rosemary leaves
2 tbsp. parsley, minced
1 clove garlic, minced
3 carrots, peeled, chopped
1 medium onion, chopped

Bone and butterfly the leg of lamb or have your butcher do it. Trim off most of the fat. Make the stuffing: mix veal, pork, chicken livers, breadcrumbs, parsley, cayenne, salt and pepper. Lay the boned leg of lamb flat. Sprinkle the surface with thyme and rosemary, spread the filling over the meat, roll it up and tie it in a neat roll or fasten it securely with skewers. Spread carrots, onion and garlic in the bottom of a baking dish or small roasting pan, add a little water and cook in a preheated 375° oven for about one hour or according to taste.

Roast of Mock Venison

For Eight
1 heavy leg of lamb
1 bottle Burgundy-type
  dry red wine
juice of 2 oranges
1 medium onion,
  thinly sliced
1 bay leaf
1 tsp. celery seed

1 carrot, sliced
3 cloves garlic, crushed
1 tsp. whole peppercorns
¼ cup juniper berries,
  crushed
¼ cup olive oil
1 tbsp. salt
¼ cup brandy

Trim all fat off the lamb. The surface must be all red meat, no fat or skin remaining. Put half the wine and all other ingredients except brandy in a saucepan, bring to a boil and simmer for 2 or 3 minutes. Place meat in a dish not much larger than the leg of lamb, pour the hot marinade over it, add the remainder of the wine and the brandy. Cover tightly and refrigerate for 3 to 4 days, turning the meat 2 or 3 times daily. Remove a few hours before cooking to bring to room temperature. Pat meat dry, rub surface with oil and roast at 350° for 17 to 19 minutes per pound, depending on the doneness desired. Baste occasionally with the marinade. Serve with roasted potatoes.

Irish Stew

For Six

3 lbs. breast of lamb, cut into 2-inch pieces
flour
3 tbsp. butter
1 medium onion, chopped
2 stalks celery, cut crosswise into 1-inch pieces
2 carrots, peeled, cut into ½-inch thick rounds

1 cup peeled, diced turnips
6 medium potatoes, peeled, quartered
1½ cups coarsely shredded cabbage
1 tomato, peeled, seeded, chopped
5 cups water or chicken broth
½ tsp. whole peppercorns
salt to taste

Dredge lamb pieces with flour. Heat butter in a heavy saucepan or dutch oven, add lamb and sear for a few minutes, but do not let brown. Add onion and sauté gently for a few minutes, stirring occasionally. Add all other ingredients, cover tightly and simmer for about 1½ hours or until meat is tender. Serve in soup plates.

Lamb and Leek Casserole ▷

For Four

2 lbs. lamb (leg or shoulder), cut in 1½ inch cubes
4 tbsp. butter
8 leeks, washed, white part only
8 scallions, white part only
1 large tomato, peeled, seeded and chopped
1 small clove garlic, minced
1 tbsp. fresh dill, chopped
4 potatoes, peeled and sliced ¼ inch thick
1 tsp. paprika
salt and pepper to taste
1½ cups chicken broth (or water)

Heat butter in a heavy casserole, sauté lamb cubes to brown on all sides. Cut white part of leeks crosswise in half, place on top of lamb, also scallions. Spread chopped tomato on top, sprinkle with garlic and dill, cover with sliced potatoes. Season with salt and pepper, sprinkle with paprika, add chicken broth. Bring to a boil, cover and cook over low heat for 1½ hours until meat is done and most of the liquid absorbed.

Mexican Roast Leg of Lamb

For Six to Eight

1 leg of lamb, 5 to 6 lbs.
  well trimmed
2 tbsp. olive oil
1½ tsp. chili powder
1½ tsp. oregano
1 tsp. rosemary, crushed
1 tsp. caraway seed, crushed

2 tsp. paprika
2 tsp. Dijon mustard
1 tsp. brown sugar
salt and pepper to taste
2 tbsp. dry sherry wine
¼ cup lemon juice
¼ cup olive oil

Combine all ingredients except meat, lemon juice and ¼ cup olive oil to make a smooth paste. With a sharp knife make small incisions all over the lamb and rub the paste in the incisions. Blend lemon juice and olive oil, coat the lamb with the mixture and refrigerate for 24 hours. Turn two or three times while the lamb is marinating. Remove lamb from refrigerator 3 hours before cooking. Wipe off excess marinade, roast at 350⁰ for 17 minutes per pound for pink meat and about 20 minutes per pound for well done.

Lamb Chops in Tomato Sauce

For Four

8 lamb chops, well trimmed
2 tbsp. butter
1 large onion, sliced thin
1 large clove garlic, minced
salt and pepper to taste

3 large ripe tomatoes,
  skinned, seeded, chopped
pinch of ground cardamom
½ tsp. rosemary, crumbled
1 cup chicken broth
  (or water)

Heat butter in a skillet, sauté chops quickly until lightly browned on both sides. Remove from skillet. Sauté onion in the skillet until golden, add tomatoes, garlic, cardamom, rosemary, salt, pepper and ½ cup of broth. Mix well, simmer 5 minutes. Arrange chops in one layer in a large saucepan or deep skillet, pour sauce over chops, cover and cook gently for about 45 minutes to 1 hour until chops are tender. Turn chops once in a while and add more·broth as needed.

Leg of Lamb Hunter's Style

For Four

½ leg of lamb
   (about 3 lbs.)
1 tbsp. vinegar
2 carrots, sliced
1 parsnip, sliced
3 stalks celery, sliced
1 medium onion, chopped
4 tbsp. butter

2½ cups water
6 peppercorns
1 small bay leaf
small pinch allspice
small pinch thyme
salt to taste
1½ tbsp. flour
1 cup sour cream

Trim fat off the meat. Heat butter in a heavy saucepan or casserole, add vegetables and sauté for 2 or 3 minutes, add meat and brown on all sides. Add 1½ cups water and all other ingredients except flour and sour cream. Cover and simmer for 1 hour. Skim off fat, add remaining water and cook uncovered in a 350° oven for 45 minutes. Remove meat and keep hot. Strain gravy and rub vegetables through the strainer. Return to pan, stir in flour, blend in sour cream, heat through but do not let boil. Pour over meat and serve.

Lamb and Pea Casserole

For Four

2 lbs. lean lamb
   (shoulder or leg)
2 tbsp. butter
2 medium onions, chopped
½ cup tomato puree
½ cup chicken broth

1 tbsp. fresh mint, chopped
   (or ¾ tsp. dried mint)
½ tsp. lemon juice
½ tsp. sugar
2 cups green peas
salt and pepper to taste

Cut lamb into 2 inch cubes. Heat butter in a saucepan, add lamb and onions and sauté until meat and onions are lightly browned. Add all other ingredients except peas, mix, bring to a boil, cover and cook gently for one hour until meat is nearly cooked. Add peas, cover and cook another 30 minutes.

Lamb Pilaf

For Four

1½ lbs. shoulder or leg
   of lamb, cubed
1 medium onion, chopped
1 clove garlic, minced
4 tbsp. butter
1½ tsp. paprika

3 cups beef broth or
   water
salt and pepper to taste
¼ tsp. caraway seed
1 cup long grain rice
½ cup grated Parmesan
   cheese

Heat butter in a saucepan, sauté onion until light golden, add meat and brown lightly. Add garlic, paprika, 1 cup broth, salt, pepper and caraway; mix, cover and cook gently for 1 hour or until meat starts to get tender. Add rice, mix well and add enough liquid to stand 1 inch over the food. Cover and simmer 20 to 25 minutes longer until rice is cooked. Sprinkle with grated cheese when serving.

Garden Kebab

For Four to Five

2 lbs. lean boneless lamb,
   cut in 1½ inch cubes
5 tbsp. butter
2 large carrots, peeled
   and sliced
4 firm tomatoes,
   peeled and diced

1 cup fresh green peas
8 small white onions, peeled
salt and pepper to taste
1 tsp. vinegar
1 tbsp. parsley, chopped
1 tbsp. fresh dill, chopped
½ cup chicken broth
   (or water)

Heat butter in a saucepan, add meat and sauté while stirring until meat is browned. Add carrots, mix, cover tightly. Reduce heat and simmer for about 45 minutes. Stir or shake pan once in a while to prevent scorching. Add tomatoes, peas, onions, salt, pepper, vinegar and ¼ cup broth. Cover and cook over gentle heat for 30 minutes or until meat is tender. Add more broth if needed. When meat is cooked, add parsley and dill, cook for another minute and serve.

Lamb and Vegetable Stew

For Six

1½ lbs. lamb shoulder
  cut into 1½ inch cubes
2 tomatoes, peeled, seeded
  and chopped
1 large clove garlic,
  chopped
1 yellow summer squash,
  sliced
1 zucchini squash, sliced
1 turnip, diced

1 cup sliced mushrooms
1 large carrot, sliced
2 cups water or bouillon
½ cup diced green pepper
½ cup chopped onion
½ cup canned or frozen corn
2 tsp. salt
½ tsp. dried thyme
½ bay leaf, crushed
¼ cup flour
2 tbsp. butter or margarine

Place lamb, tomatoes, garlic, summer squash, zucchini, turnip, mushrooms, carrots, green pepper, onion, salt, thyme, bay leaf, and water or bouillon in electric slow cooker. Cover; then cook at low for about 8 hours or until lamb and vegetables are very tender. Turn cooker to high. Blend flour and butter together and shape into 1-inch balls. Drop flour butter balls into stew. Cook, stirring several times, until thickened.

Broiled Lamb Chops

For Four

8 well-trimmed lamb chops
  about 1 to 1½″ thick
1 medium onion,
  finely grated
1 small clove garlic, crushed

3 tbsp. olive oil
½ tsp. thyme
½ tsp. rosemary, crumbled
salt and pepper to taste
½ tsp. lemon juice

Combine all ingredients except chops and blend well. Rub the mixture into the chops, let them stand for 2 hours. Broil over hot charcoal, about 3 inches from the fire for 5 minutes on each side. Garnish with parsley and serve.

Braised Leg of Lamb

For Four

½ leg of lamb
  (about 3 lbs.)
1 cup dry white wine
¼ cup onion, chopped
¼ cup carrot, chopped
¼ cup celery, chopped

2 cloves garlic, crushed
½ tsp. rosemary, crushed
1 tbsp. juniper berries
1 anchovy filet, mashed
salt and pepper to taste
2 tbsp. brandy

Trim most of the fat off the lamb. Place lamb in a heavy casserole or dutch oven, add all ingredients except brandy, cover tightly and cook gently for about 1½ hours. Turn several times while cooking. Then remove lid to allow some steam to escape and cook another 1½ hours. The meat should be quite tender. Remove meat from pot, skim off fat and reduce sauce quickly. The sauce should be rich and creamy. Return meat to sauce, heat through, pour brandy over it, flame and serve.

Souvlaki (Greek Kebabs)

For Four to Five

2 lbs. boneless leg of lamb,
  cut in 1½ inch cubes
½ cup olive oil
4 tbsp. lemon juice
¼ cup white wine
salt and pepper to taste
½ tsp. oregano

2 cloves garlic, minced
1 bay leaf
6 small onions, peeled
  and cut in half
3 firm tomatoes, quartered
2 green peppers, cut
  in 1½ inch squares

Put lamb cubes in a bowl. Combine oil, lemon juice and wine, pour over meat. Sprinkle with salt, pepper, oregano, garlic; add bay leaf. Put onions and tomatoes on top of meat, cover with a plate and weigh down. Place in refrigerator and marinate overnight. Let meat come to room temperature. Thread meat on oiled skewers, alternating with pieces of pepper, tomato and onion. Broil over hot charcoal for about 10 to 12 minutes or to taste, turn to brown on all sides and baste occasionally.

Shoulder of Lamb Landaise

For Four
1 shoulder of lamb, boned
  (about 3 lbs.)
¼ lb. veal, ground
¼ lb. lean pork, ground
¼ lb. chicken livers, minced
1 cup fresh white
  breadcrumbs

2 tbsp. parsley, minced
1 tbsp. brandy (opt.)
salt and pepper to taste
3 tbsp. oil
3 tbsp. butter
4 firm tomatoes, cored
3 cups cooked, buttered
  leaf spinach

Have butcher bone the shoulder, and trim off any fat. Blend the veal, pork and livers (or ask your butcher to grind them together), add breadcrumbs, parsley and brandy, salt and pepper and mix well. Spread the shoulder of lamb flat, place filling in the center and roll up. Tie securely with kitchen string. Heat oil and butter on top of the stove and brown the rolled lamb on all sides. Roast in a 400° oven for about 1 hour. Baste frequently and turn several times to cook evenly on all sides. When meat is three-quarters done, place tomatoes in the pan, baste them and finish cooking.

Before serving, remove string, put the meat on a hot serving platter and spoon the pan juices over the meat. Surround the meat with mounds of hot buttered spinach and top each mound with a tomato.

Navarin of Lamb

For Four to Six
2½ lbs. lean lamb, cubed
2 tbsp. flour
1 tbsp. cooking oil
1 tbsp. butter
1 small bay leaf
pinch of thyme
1 cup chicken broth
1 tomato, peeled, seeded,
  chopped
2 cloves garlic, minced

2 tbsp. butter
8 small white onions, peeled
2 white turnips, peeled,
  quartered
3 small carrots, peeled,
  cut lengthwise in half
½ cup Frenched string beans
½ cup green peas
8 small new potatoes, peeled
salt and pepper to taste

Heat oil and 1 tablespoon butter in a saucepan, sprinkle meat with flour and sauté until lightly browned. Pour off fat, add chicken broth, bring to a boil and stir to deglaze the pan. Do not let scorch. Add bay leaf, thyme, tomato and garlic, cover and simmer gently.

In another pan sauté onions and turnips in 2 tablespoons butter until golden brown, add to the simmering stew together with the carrots, beans and potatoes, salt and pepper. Cover and simmer for 30 minutes, then add peas and continue cooking for 15 minutes or more until meat is done.

Lamb and Broccoli with Lemon Sauce

For Four
2 lbs. lean boneless
  shoulder of lamb,
  cubed
2 tbsp. butter
1½ cups chicken broth
  (or water)

1 large onion, chopped
salt and pepper to taste
2 bunches broccoli
2 large eggs
1½ tbsp. flour
2 tbsp. lemon juice

Heat butter in a saucepan, add meat and onions and brown nicely. Add broth, season with salt and pepper, cover and cook gently for 45 minutes.

Wash broccoli, cut off florets and discard tough stems. Add broccoli to meat, cover again and cook for another half an hour to 45 minutes until meat and vegetables are cooked. Remove pan from heat and let cool slightly. Beat eggs well, blend in flour and lemon juice while beating. Continue beating and add gradually one cup of the broth from the stew. When smooth, return mixture to the saucepan, blend gently into the rest of the sauce, simmer 2 minutes and serve.

Lamb Pörkölt

For Six
1 large onion, minced
¼ cup smoked bacon, diced
1 tbsp. paprika
½ cup broth or water
3 lbs. boneless lamb shoulder or boned shanks, well trimmed and cubed
½ tsp. caraway seeds, crushed

salt and pepper to taste
½ tsp. marjoram
1 tbsp. vinegar
2 large cloves garlic, crushed
2 ripe tomatoes, peeled, seeded and diced
1 large green pepper, seeded and diced
6 potatoes, peeled and diced
pinch of cayenne pepper

Fry bacon in a heavy kettle until browned. Add onion and sauté until golden brown. Stir in paprika, add broth and blend. Add meat, salt, pepper, caraway, marjoram, vinegar and garlic. Cover, cook gently for about 1 hour until meat is nearly cooked. Add all other ingredients, some more broth if needed, cover and cook until meat and potatoes are done.

Ground Lamb Greek Style

For Six
1½ lbs. ground lean lamb
1 clove garlic, mashed
1 tbsp. fresh mint leaves, minced

2 tbsp. lemon juice
1 egg, lightly beaten
salt and pepper to taste
small egg tomatoes
¼ cup oil

Blend all ingredients except tomatoes and oil. Oil skewers and press meat around skewers in sausage shape, each about 1½ inches in diameter and 3 inches long. Alternate meat with egg tomatoes and finish each skewer with a tomato. Broil over hot coals for 5 to 7 minutes, turning and brushing with oil frequently.

Lamb Shank Casserole

For Four
4 lamb shanks, all fat trimmed off and each cut in two
flour
2 carrots, peeled, sliced ¼-inch thick
1 cup tomatoes, fresh or canned, peeled, seeded and chopped

2 large onions, sliced thin
2 tbsp. oil
1 large clove garlic, chopped
1 lb. small potatoes, peeled
1 tbsp. parsley, chopped
½ tsp. rosemary, crushed
1 tsp. sugar
⅔ cup beef broth
¼ cup dry white wine
salt and pepper to taste

Dredge meat in flour, brown quickly on all sides in hot oil. Remove meat and place in a heavy casserole or dutch oven. Sauté onion rings in the skillet meat was browned in until they are limp. Add carrots and garlic and sauté 2 or 3 minutes longer. Add vegetables to meat, pour fat off skillet and deglaze the skillet with beef broth. Add broth and all other ingredients to meat, simmer over very low heat for 3 to 4 hours.

Stuffed Lamb Roll

For Four
1½ lbs. lean ground lamb
¾ cup mushrooms, chopped
¼ cup butter
1 tbsp. chives, chopped
1 tbsp. mint leaves, chopped

1 clove garlic, crushed
1 tsp. lemon juice
salt and pepper to taste
1 cup soft white breadcrumbs (approx.)

Sauté mushrooms in butter over low heat for about 3 minutes until soft. Add herbs, garlic, lemon juice, salt and pepper, sauté another minute and remove from fire. Blend with enough breadcrumbs to form a stiff paste. Roll out ground meat on wax paper to a rectangular sheet not more than ¼ inch thick. Spread mushroom paste evenly on meat. Roll up meat by lifting one side of the wax paper. Cut the roll in 2-inch slices, press ends of the slices to seal and broil until meat is nicely browned.

Other Meat Dishes

Broiled Pork Filets Sweet and Sour

For Four
1½ lbs. pork tenderloin
1 tbsp. prepared hot
   mustard
3 tbsp. sherry wine

1 tsp. sugar
2 tbsp. soy sauce
1 clove garlic, crushed
1 tbsp. oil
salt and pepper to taste

Cut filets lengthwise in half and trim off all fat. Blend remaining ingredients and rub into the meat. Let stand for 2 hours. Broil meat slowly for 25 to 30 minutes over charcoal or under a broiler, turn it frequently and brush a few times with oil. Slice thin when serving.

Philippine Roast Pork

For Six to Eight
4 lbs. lean pork loin
   (or shoulder)
2 tbsp. flour
1 clove garlic, crushed
1 tsp. salt
pepper to taste
2 tbsp. light soy sauce

½ tsp. powdered ginger
1 tbsp. lime juice
3 pineapple rings, cut
   in half
⅓ cup sugar
½ cup pineapple juice
3 tbsp. vinegar

Sprinkle pork with flour, brown quickly on all sides in a skillet. Combine and blend garlic, salt, pepper, soy sauce, ginger and lime juice and rub well into the roast. Place in roasting pan and cook in preheated 350° oven, 30 minutes per pound. About 45 minutes before the roast is done, place pineapple rings on top of meat, sprinkle with sugar and finish roasting. During cooking baste once in a while with a mixture of pineapple juice and vinegar.

Serve garnished with pineapple rings and pan gravy.

Aromatic Pork Chops

For Four
4 loin pork chops
   (about 1¼ inches thick)
2 tbsp. butter
salt and pepper to taste
1 tbsp. grated onion
1 tbsp. tomato paste

½ cup dry white wine
¼ cup sherry
1 small clove garlic, crushed
½ tsp. marjoram
1 tbsp. lemon juice
1½ tbsp. anisette or other
   anise flavored cordial

Trim most of the fat off the chops. Heat butter in a skillet and sauté chops for about 15 minutes on each side over gentle heat, until well cooked. Remove to hot serving platter. Add all other ingredients except anisette to skillet, scrape and deglaze the pan, let come to a boil and cook over moderate heat for 5 minutes until well blended and slightly thickened. Correct seasoning. Add anisette, blend, simmer for 1 minute, then pour sauce over chops and serve.

Ham Steak with ◁ Wine Sauce

For Six to Eight
1 tbsp. cornstarch
¼ cup currant jelly
¾ cup dry red wine
2 tsp. orange juice
1 boneless fully-cooked ham
    steak, about 1¾ lbs.

Blend cornstarch, jelly, wine and orange juice in small saucepan. Cook and stir over medium heat until sauce is thickened and clear. Place ham slice on grill or broiler rack. Brush ham with some sauce. Cook, 4 inches from heat source, 10 minutes on each side brushing 2 or 3 times with sauce. Or, place ham on rack in shallow roasting pan. Bake in 325⁰ oven 30 minutes, brushing 2 or 3 times with wine sauce.

Serve ham steak with remaining wine sauce, surround with scrambled eggs.

Pork Chops Charcutiere

For Two
4 lean pork chops,
    center cut, ½ inch thick
1 tbsp. fat or oil
1½ tbsp. butter
¼ cup chopped onion
1 tbsp. flour
¾ cup beef broth

½ cup dry white wine
1 tbsp. tomato paste
1 clove garlic, minced
1 tbsp. prepared mustard
1 tbsp. Worcestershire sauce
2 tbsp. sour gherkins,
    thinly sliced
salt and pepper to taste

Trim chops, season with salt and pepper. Heat fat in skillet, brown chops quickly on both sides. Cover, reduce heat and cook until meat is tender, about 30 minutes. In the meantime, prepare the following sauce: Heat butter, add onion and sauté until limp. Stir in flour and cook while stirring until the mixture is light brown. Still stirring, add broth and wine gradually and cook until mixture is smooth. Add tomato paste, garlic, mustard and Worcestershire sauce, blend and simmer for 15 minutes. Remove chops from skillet, pour off all fat, add the sauce to the skillet, stir and simmer gently until all browned particles in the skillet have dissolved. Return chops to skillet, heat through, add gherkins and serve with plain boiled potatoes. Sprinkle a pinch of caraway seeds over potatoes when serving.

Broiled Pork (Sate Babi)

For Four
1½ lbs. boneless lean pork (loin or tenderloin)
1 medium onion, chopped
1 large clove garlic
2 tbsp. lemon juice
1 tsp. chopped fresh ginger
½ tsp. ground coriander
2 tbsp. dark soy sauce
2 tbsp. sherry wine
salt and pepper to taste
pinch of cayenne pepper (opt.)
2 tbsp. honey (or light brown sugar)
3 tbsp. oil

Cut pork into 1-inch cubes. Put all other ingredients except oil in a food processor or blender and process until smooth. Pour the mixture over the pork cubes, mix in 2 tablespoons oil and marinate for 2 hours. Thread pork on small skewers, (or bamboo skewers previously soaked in water). Leave space between the meat cubes. Broil over medium charcoal fire or under a pre-heated broiler, not too close to the fire, for about 5 to 6 minutes on each side, turning a few times, until the meat is well done and evenly browned. Brush with more oil when broiling.

Serve with **Sate Sauce.**

About One Cup Sate Sauce
2 tbsp. oil
1 medium onion, minced
2 cloves garlic, crushed
1 tsp. grated lemon peel
⅓ cup peanut butter
⅛ tsp. cayenne pepper (or to taste)
2 tbsp. sugar
¾ cup chicken broth
salt to taste

Heat oil in a saucepan, sauté onion until golden brown, add garlic and sauté 2 minutes longer. Stir in all other ingredients, blend well and simmer until the sauce is thick and smooth. Serve as a dip with sates.

Chinese Roast Pork

For Four
2 lbs. pork tenderloin or boned loin
1 large clove garlic, crushed
1 tbsp. grated onion
1 very thin slice ginger root, minced
3 tbsp. soy sauce
1½ tbsp. sherry
1 tbsp. hoisin sauce
freshly ground pepper to taste
2 tsp. sugar
¼ tsp. ground anise
½ tsp. (scant) cinnamon
pinch of allspice
2 tbsp. oil
2 tbsp. honey

Put pork in a pan. Blend all ingredients except honey and oil, add to the pork, coat the meat with it and let marinate for at least 3 hours. Drain and reserve the marinade. Place a shallow pan with water in bottom of the oven. Preheat oven to 425°. Put meat on a rack in a shallow roasting pan. Cook at 425° for 15 minutes. Blend 2 tablespoons of the marinade with the oil and brush the meat on both sides with it. Reduce heat to 350° and continue roasting for 20 minutes. Then brush both sides of meat with honey and roast 20 minutes longer.

To serve, cut into ¼ inch thick slices.

Pork Chops in Dill Sauce

For Four
8 pork chops, about ¾ inch thick
salt and pepper to taste
½ cup flour
2 tbsp. lard
1 medium onion, chopped
1 clove garlic, minced
½ tbsp. paprika
1 cup sour cream
1 tbsp. flour
3 tbsp. fresh dill, chopped

Season chops with salt and pepper, dredge lightly in flour. Heat lard in a heavy pan and brown chops lightly on both sides. Remove and reserve. Add onion to pan, sauté until light golden, add garlic, stir in paprika and about ½ cup water. Mix well and let simmer for a couple of minutes. Return chops to pan, cover and cook gently for about 45 minutes until chops are almost cooked. Turn a few times during cooking and add more water if too dry. Blend flour into sour cream, stir in chopped dill, add to mixture in pan and blend with pan juices. Simmer very gently until meat is done.

Lion's Head

For Four
1½ lbs. pork (ham or
  shoulder)
5 dried Chinese
  mushrooms
⅓ cup bamboo shoots,
  chopped
1 large clove garlic, mashed
2 thin slices fresh ginger,
  minced
4 scallions, chopped
salt and pepper to taste

1 tsp. sugar
2 tbsp. sherry
1 tsp. cornstarch
1 egg, beaten
oil for deep frying
1 cup chicken broth
4 tbsp. soy sauce
1 small Chinese cabbage
  (about ¾ lb.)
1 tbsp. oil
2 tsp. cornstarch
1 tbsp. water

Chop the pork quite fine. Soak mushrooms in warm water
for half an hour, remove and discard stems, squeeze dry
and mince caps. Put chopped meat in a bowl. Add mushrooms, bamboo shoots, garlic, ginger root and scallions. Also, salt, pepper, sugar, sherry, 1 teaspoon cornstarch and egg. Stir to blend mixture. Do not stir too much or the mixture will become too heavy. Shape into four balls. Heat oil in a deep pan and fry the pork balls for about 4 minutes or until lightly browned. Drain on paper towel and put them in a saucepan. Add broth and soy sauce, bring to a boil, reduce heat, cover and simmer for 25 minutes. Trim cabbage, cut into broad slices. Heat 1 tablespoon oil in a wok and stir-fry cabbage for a few minutes until soft. Then place cabbage on top of simmering pork balls, cover and simmer for 10 more minutes. Dilute cornstarch with water, add to sauce, stir until thickened. Put cabbage on serving dish, the pork balls on top, and cover with the sauce.

Savory Pork Stew

For Six
2 tbsp. oil
2½ lbs. lean pork (loin or
  tenderloin) cut in strips
  about 2 inches long
1 medium onion, sliced
  thin
1 cup sliced fresh
  mushrooms

1 clove garlic, minced
½ tsp. grated lemon peel
2 cups chicken broth
1 tsp. curry powder
pinch of cayenne pepper
2 tsp. lemon juice
2 tsp. cornstarch
salt to taste
½ cup heavy cream

Heat oil in a heavy saucepan, sauté pork strips over medium heat until nicely browned on all sides — about 5 minutes. Remove pork and reserve. Add onion to casserole, sauté until soft but not browned; add mushrooms and lemon peel, mix well; add chicken broth, curry, cayenne, salt and lemon juice, blend. Return meat to pan, cover and simmer gently for about 45 minutes until meat is tender. Dissolve cornstarch in 2 tablespoons water, add to the stew, stir and cook over very low heat until slightly thickened. Add cream, blend, heat through and serve.

Pork Adobo

For Six
2 lbs. lean pork loin,
  boned, cut in 2-inch
  cubes
8 cloves garlic

⅔ cup rice (or white)
  vinegar
1 cup chicken broth
salt and pepper to taste
oil for frying

Blend all ingredients except oil and let stand for 1 to 2 hours. Place all these ingredients in a heavy saucepan, bring to a boil, then cook gently for about 45 minutes to one hour or until pork is cooked. Remove pork with a slotted spoon and reserve. Reduce liquid in pan until well thickened. Strain into a bowl and keep hot.

Heat oil in a skillet, fry the pork cubes quickly until nicely browned and crisp on all sides. Put on a hot serving plate, spoon the reserved sauce over it and serve.

Mexican Pork Roast

For Six to Eight

center cut loin of pork
  (4 lbs.)
½ tsp. thyme
1 tsp. rosemary, crushed
1 tsp. dried marjoram
1 tbsp. paprika
1 large clove garlic, mashed

1 tsp. chili powder
1 tsp. meat extract
  (Bovril or other)
salt and pepper to taste
1 cup dry white wine
⅓ cup sherry wine
½ cup guava jelly
1½ tbsp. oil

Have butcher bone the loin, remove all fat down to the bare meat. Tie the roast in a roll. Mash garlic with a little salt or through a garlic press, add all herbs, crush and blend them into the garlic paste. Add paprika, oil, chili powder, meat extract, salt and pepper; blend well and rub this mixture into the roast.

Place pork in a roasting pan — do not use a rack — add ½ cup white wine to the pan and put in a preheated 400° oven. After 15 minutes reduce the temperature to 350°. Continue roasting for 25 minutes per pound (weighed after boning and trimming). Baste frequently and add more wine if more basting liquid is needed.

Melt guava jelly over a low flame, combine with sherry wine. 15 minutes before roast is done spread the guava mixture on top of the roast and increase oven temperature to 400°. When done remove roast to hot serving platter and remove strings. Add a little more wine or water to the roasting pan to make a pan gravy.

Serve with plain saffron rice surrounding the roast.

Stir-fried Curried Pork ▷

For Four

¾ lb. lean pork
1 medium onion, sliced thin
1 green pepper, sliced
1 clove garlic, mashed
½ tsp. ginger root, minced
2 tbsp. oil
½ tsp. salt
1½ tsp. curry powder
1 tbsp. sherry
1 tsp. lemon juice
⅓ cup chicken broth
2 tsp. cornstarch
1½ tbsp. water

Cut pork across grain in thin strips. Heat oil in a wok, add salt, stir-fry pork for 2 to 3 minutes until all traces of pink have disappeared. Add pepper, onion, garlic and ginger, stir-fry about 2 minutes or until vegetables have softened. Add curry powder and stir-fry 2 minutes over low heat. Add broth, sherry and lemon juice, mix well and fry 5 minutes over medium heat. Add cornstarch, diluted with water, and stir until thickened.

Braised Pork Loin

For Six

3 lbs. loin of pork, boned
2 cloves garlic, crushed
2 medium onions, sliced
1 small bay leaf

1 pinch dried rosemary
salt and pepper to taste
¾ cup dry red wine
¼ cup orange juice

Trim pork, remove as much excess fat as possible, tie it to keep its shape. Put onion and garlic in a heavy casserole, place meat on top and add bay leaf and rosemary, sprinkle with salt and pepper and ¼ cup wine. Roast in 350⁰ oven for 30 minutes. Then add remaining wine and orange juice, cover and cook for 1½ hours. Turn meat once or twice while cooking.

Barbecued Ribs

For Six

3 lbs. meaty spare ribs
½ cup ketchup
½ cup chili sauce
1 tbsp. dry mustard

1 tbsp. A-1 sauce
1 tbsp. oil
2 dashes Tabasco sauce
salt and pepper to taste

Precook ribs in a 350⁰ oven for 45 minutes. Drain off all fat. Blend all other ingredients. Brush the ribs on both sides with the mixture and let stand for 45 minutes to an hour. Broil over or under low heat for about 45 minutes until meat is tender and nicely browned. Turn the ribs once in a while and brush with remaining barbecue sauce.

Pork Balls

For Four

1 slice ginger root, minced
1 tbsp. scallion, white
    part only, minced
6 water chestnuts, minced
1 clove garlic, minced
1½ tbsp. cornstarch

1 tsp. sugar
¼ tsp. pepper
1 dash Tabasco sauce
1 tbsp. soy sauce
2 tbsp. ketchup
1 lb. lean ground pork
oil for frying

Mix all ingredients, except oil, without handling too much. Shape into balls the size of a golf ball. Fry, a few at a time, in hot, deep oil until they are golden brown. Serve with a variety of sauces and dips.

Pork Chops in Paprika Sauce

For Four

8 lean pork chops,
    ¾ inch thick
2 tbsp. flour
1½ tbsp. lard
1 medium onion,
    sliced thin
2 tsp. paprika
salt and pepper to taste
1 tbsp. tomato paste

½ tsp. caraway seed,
    crushed
2 cloves garlic, crushed
¼ cup water
1 green pepper, seeded,
    diced
1 ripe tomato, peeled,
    seeded, diced
8 potatoes, peeled, sliced

Flatten pork chops slightly, score edges, dust with flour. Heat lard in a saucepan, sauté the chops quickly, brown on both sides. Remove chops and reserve. Add onion to pan, sauté until light golden, stir in paprika, salt and pepper, tomato paste, caraway, garlic and water. Mix and simmer for a couple of minutes. Return chops to pan, cover and cook gently for 30 minutes. Add green pepper, tomato and potatoes, also more water if needed. Cover and cook 30 minutes longer or until meat is soft and cooked.

Pork Pörkölt

For Six
2 tbsp. lard
2 large onions, chopped
2½ lbs. lean pork shoulder, cubed
½ cup chicken broth or water

½ tbsp. paprika
1 tbsp. tomato paste
2 green peppers, seeded and cut into thin strips
3 large tomatoes, peeled, seeded and diced
salt and pepper to taste

Heat lard in a heavy saucepan, sauté onions until golden brown, stir in paprika and cubed pork. Sauté for a few minutes until meat is seared. Add broth and tomato paste, stir well, bring to a boil. Cover and cook gently for 1 hour. Stir occasionally and add more liquid if needed. Add peppers and tomatoes, season with salt and pepper and cook 20 minutes longer.

Braised Pork Chops

For Four
2 tbsp. oil
4 thick pork chops
1 small onion, thinly sliced
1 clove garlic, minced
⅓ cup soy sauce

2 tbsp. sherry
1½ cup chicken broth
½ tsp. sugar
1 lb. spinach, washed and trimmed
2 tbsp. oil

Heat oil in a heavy casserole, brown pork chops quickly on both sides. Remove from pan and keep warm. Pour off most of the fat, stir-fry onions and garlic for 1 minute. Return pork chops, add soy sauce, sherry, broth and sugar. Bring to a boil, cover and simmer for half an hour. Turn chops over and simmer covered for another half hour. Heat 2 tablespoons oil in a wok, stir-fry spinach for a minute or two, just before pork is cooked. Put pork on a serving platter, surround with spinach and pour sauce over the meat.

Szekely Pork Goulash

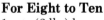

For Six
4 tbsp. lard or butter
1 large onion, chopped
2 lbs. pork shoulder, cut
    in large cubes
1 tbsp. paprika
1 clove garlic, crushed
1 tbsp. tomato paste
1 tsp. caraway seed
salt and pepper to taste
¾ cup water
2 lbs. sauerkraut, drained
½ cup sour cream

Heat lard in a heavy kettle or saucepan, add onion and sauté until light golden. Add pork, stir and cover. Cook for about 5 minutes. Stir in paprika, garlic, caraway, tomato paste, salt, pepper and water. Cover and cook gently for half an hour. Stir occasionally and add more water if needed. Squeeze sauerkraut as dry as possible, add to meat, mix well, cover. Cook for about 45 minutes until meat and sauerkraut are cooked. Just before serving, stir in sour cream.

Sweet Ham Steak

For Eight to Ten
1 can (3 lb.) ham
2 medium oranges
¾ cup sweet pickle liquid
    (drained from sweet
    mixed pickles)

½ cup apple jelly
1 tbsp. instant minced onion
1 tsp. grated orange peel
½ tsp. ginger
¼ tsp. garlic powder
2 cups sweet mixed pickles

Remove any gelatin from ham; discard. Place ham on its side and cut in half lengthwise; set aside while preparing sauce.

Grate enough peel from 1 orange, to equal 1 teaspoon; reserve. Peel and section both oranges. In small saucepan, combine pickle liquid, apple jelly, minced onion, orange peel, ginger and garlic powder. Cook over low heat, stirring constantly until jelly melts. Add pickles and orange sections; keep warm.

Place ham halves on grill or broiler pan. Brush with some sauce. Cook, 4 inches from heat source, 10 minutes on each side, brushing 2 or 3 times with sauce. Garnish ham with some pickles and orange sections. Serve with remaining sauce.

Gipsy Goulash

For Six
½ cup lean bacon, diced
1 lb. onions, chopped
1 clove garlic, minced
1½ lbs. beef shin, cubed
1 lb. lean pork, cubed
1 lb. lamb shoulder, cubed

1 tbsp. paprika
½ tsp. caraway seed
½ tsp. marjoram
salt and pepper to taste
1½ tbsp. vinegar
1 tbsp. tomato paste
1 cup beef broth

Sauté bacon in heavy saucepan or kettle until golden, add onion and garlic and cook until onions are soft. Add beef, sauté a few minutes, add paprika, caraway, marjoram, salt, pepper, vinegar, tomato paste and ½ cup broth. Cover and cook gently for 30 minutes. Add other meats, mix well, add remaining broth if more liquid is necessary, cover again and cook for one hour longer or until meats are soft.

Pork Chops Gitane

For Four
8 pork chops, about
    ½ inch thick
1 tbsp. butter
1 cup firm mushrooms,
    sliced
⅔ cup tomato sauce
    (canned can be used)
⅓ cup cooked ham,
    julienne cut (in strips)

2 tbsp. white onion,
    chopped
⅓ cup cooked smoked
    tongue, julienne cut
1 tbsp. parsley, minced
1 small clove garlic,
    crushed
4 tbsp. dry sherry
salt and pepper to taste

Trim most fat off the chops. Melt butter in a casserole and brown chops on both sides, cover and cook over medium heat until almost done — about 15 minutes. Then add mushrooms, tomato sauce, onion and garlic, cover again and cook for 10 minutes, until meat is soft. Add all other ingredients, simmer for 5 more minutes.

Basque Pork Casserole

For Six
3 lbs. pork tenderloin,
    sliced ¾ inch thick
flour
salt and pepper to taste
¼ cup oil
2 large cloves garlic,
    minced

2 medium onions, sliced
4 large tomatoes, peeled,
    seeded, chopped
1 cup chicken broth
½ cup dry white wine
¼ tsp. Spanish saffron
1 tsp. tarragon
2 tbsp. minced parsley

Dredge meat with flour, season with salt and pepper. Heat oil in a skillet, brown the pork on all sides. Remove pork and reserve. Add onion to the pan, sauté for about 5 minutes, then add garlic and sauté until onions are golden brown. Add tomatoes, broth and wine and cook another 5 minutes. Place browned pork in a saucepan, pour sauce over it, add saffron and tarragon. Mix well, cover and simmer for one hour or more until meat is tender. Sprinkle with parsley before serving.

Indonesian Broiled Spareribs

For Four
2½ lbs. lean spareribs
½ cup light soy sauce
1 tbsp. grated fresh ginger
2 cloves garlic, crushed

½ cup pineapple juice
¼ cup sherry
salt and pepper to taste
pinch of cayenne pepper
pinch of ground nutmeg

Separate ribs. Blend all other ingredients, rub the mixture into the ribs and marinate for 3 to 4 hours. Place under a broiler and broil at a fairly low heat for about 15 to 20 minutes on each side. Baste frequently with the marinade.

Korean Pork and Spinach

For Four

1 lb. fresh spinach
½ lb. lean pork
  diced small
1 large clove garlic, minced
2 tbsp. oil
2 tbsp. light soy sauce

salt and pepper to taste
½ tsp. grated fresh ginger
4 scallions, chopped
1 egg, lightly beaten
1½ tbsp. toasted sesame
  seed*

Wash spinach, discard tough stems and wilted leaves, drain well. Heat oil in a wok, add pork and garlic and stir fry until pork is seared. Add spinach, soy sauce, salt, pepper and ginger; stir fry for a minute, cover and simmer for a few minutes until spinach is just tender. Add, while stirring, scallions and egg; blend well and stir fry for 2 minutes longer. Sprinkle with sesame seeds when serving.

Ham Casserole

For Four

butter
3 large potatoes, peeled,
  sliced thin
4 slices cooked ham
  (sliced fairly thick)
salt and pepper to taste
½ tsp. basil
¼ tsp. thyme
¼ tsp. mace

3 hard-boiled eggs, sliced
1 medium onion, very
  thinly sliced
½ cup firm mushrooms,
  sliced
½ cup sour cream
½ cup soft white
  breadcrumbs
½ cup grated Swiss cheese

Cover the bottom of a well-buttered casserole with the sliced potatoes. Then add a layer of ham, sprinkle with salt, pepper and the mixed herbs, cover with a layer of sliced eggs, a layer of mushrooms and a layer of sliced onions. Spoon the sour cream over it, cover and bake at 375⁰ for about ½ hour. Remove from oven, mix breadcrumbs with grated cheese, spread mixture on top of casserole and return to oven. Bake uncovered until top is well browned.

Pungent Spareribs

For Four

2 lbs. meaty, lean
  spareribs
1 tsp. grated fresh ginger
2 cloves garlic
1 tsp. salt
½ tsp. ground coriander
2 tbsp. oil

½ cup beef broth
  (or water)
3 tbsp. dark soy sauce
3 tbsp. medium dry
  sherry wine
2 tsp. lemon juice
cayenne pepper to taste
1 tbsp. light brown sugar

Have ribs separated lengthwise and then cut into 2-inch long pieces. Crush garlic with salt to a paste, blend with ginger and coriander, rub into the meat and let stand for an hour. Heat oil in a wok, stir fry ribs for 6 to 8 minutes until nicely browned. Mix all other ingredients, pour over the meat, stir and bring to a boil. Cover the wok and cook gently until meat is soft, about 45 minutes more. Uncover, reduce liquid in wok and serve.

Braised Sweet Sour Pork

For Six

2 lbs. lean pork, cubed
1 large clove garlic,
  minced
1 cup chicken broth
2 tbsp. light soy sauce

2½ tbsp. light brown sugar
½ tsp. grated fresh ginger
salt and pepper to taste
⅓ cup mild vinegar
  (rice or malt vinegar)
1 small bay leaf

Put all ingredients in a saucepan, bring to a boil, cover and simmer gently for about 1 hour until pork is cooked.

Stir-fried Pork and Vegetables   ▽

For Four

4 dried Chinese mushrooms	½ cup bean sprouts,
⅔ lb. lean pork	washed and dried
½ cup bamboo shoots	1½ tbsp. sherry
5 water chestnuts	salt and pepper to taste
3 scallions, trimmed	½ cup chicken broth
1 clove garlic, mashed	1 tbsp. soy sauce
4 firm fresh mushroom caps	1 tbsp. cornstarch
4 tbsp. oil	3 tbsp. water

Soak mushrooms in hot water for ½ hour. Remove and discard stems and slice caps in strips. Slice pork across grain into ⅛ inch thick slices. Slice bamboo shoots and water chestnuts ¼ inch thick. Cut scallions diagonally into 1 inch pieces. Slice fresh mushrooms ¼ inch thick.

Put 2 tablespoons oil and salt in a wok and heat. Add garlic stir-fry 30 seconds, then remove and discard garlic. Add Chinese mushrooms, bamboo shoots, water chestnuts, and fresh mushrooms and stir-fry for one minute. Add bean sprouts and fry one minute longer. Remove vegetables from wok and reserve. Add remaining oil, heat, add scallions and stir-fry for half a minute, then add pork and fry 3 minutes. Stir in sherry and pepper. Return the vegetables, add chicken broth, soy sauce, bring to a boil and cook covered for 2 minutes. Then add the cornstarch dissolved in water and stir until the mixture thickens and serve.

◁ Roast Loin of Pork

For Six

4 lbs. center cut pork loin
salt and pepper
½ tsp. caraway seeds, crushed
2 tbsp. lard or butter
½ lemon, cut in very thin slices
1 cup beef broth (or water)
1 tbsp. flour
1 clove garlic

Trim roast, season with salt and pepper, rub with garlic and sprinkle with caraway seeds. Melt lard in saucepan, put meat in pan and put lemon slices on top of roast. Roast in 375° oven for about 2 hours until meat is cooked. Baste frequently with a little beef broth and pan juices. Remove cooked roast to serving platter, skim fat off pan juices, stir in flour and more broth, make a pan gravy.

Roast Fresh Ham with Herbs

For Ten to Twelve

1 fresh whole ham, bone-in,
    about 10 to 12 lbs.
salt and pepper
2 cloves garlic, cut
    into slivers

1 small onion, grated
1 tsp. crumbled thyme
1 tsp. crumbled marjoram
1 cup dry white wine
sautéed cherry tomatoes
    and fresh mint for garnish

Sprinkle ham on all sides with salt and pepper. Cut small slits about ½ inch deep all over ham and stuff each slit with garlic. Combine onion, thyme and marjoram. Rub ham with onion mixture. Place ham in a shallow roasting pan. Pour wine over ham. Roast in a preheated 325° oven for 25 minutes to the pound or until internal temperature on a meat thermometer registers 170°. Spoon pan juices over ham every 30 minutes during cooking time.

Crown Roast of Pork

For Four

center cut loin of pork,
    8 ribs, tied into a crown
2 tbsp. oil
1 clove garlic, crushed

½ tsp. salt
pepper to taste
1 tsp. paprika
1 tsp. lemon juice
1 cup dry white wine

Ask your butcher to trim most of the fat off the roast before preparing the crown. Combine all ingredients except wine, blend into a paste and rub the outside of the roast with the mixture. Let stand for one hour. In the meantime prepare the

Stuffing

3 sweet Italian sausages
2 tbsp. minced onion
⅓ cup celery, white
    part only, minced
1 small clove garlic, minced
1 tsp. paprika
pinch of dried thyme

½ tsp. dried rosemary,
    crushed
½ tsp. marjoram
salt and pepper to taste
2 cups white breadcrumbs
½ cup apples, chopped
½ cup dry white wine

Strip sausage meat out of casing. Sauté in a skillet for 3 minutes until lightly browned, break up lumps with a fork. Drain off all fat. Add onion and celery, stir and sauté 2 minutes longer. Add herbs and spices, blend well, remove from fire, mix with breadcrumbs, apples and wine.

Place the unstuffed crown roast in a roasting pan, the frenched rib bones pointing up. Wrap the end of each bone in aluminum foil to prevent charring. Preheat oven to 450°, put roast in oven, reduce heat immediately to 350°. Allow 30 minutes per pound cooking time. Add ½ cup wine, baste occasionally and add more wine if needed.

One and a quarter hours before roast is done, remove from oven and stuff the cavity. Return to oven and continue roasting and basting. When done, remove roast to a serving platter, remove foil from bones. Skim fat off pan, add more liquid to make a pan gravy. Serve with roasted or baked potatoes.

Braised Spareribs and Pineapple

For Four

2 lbs. spareribs
1 clove garlic, minced
1 tsp. fresh ginger, minced
¼ cup soy sauce
¼ cup pineapple juice
3 tbsp. honey
¼ cup vinegar
½ cup chicken broth

2 tbsp. oil
1 tbsp. flour
1 cup canned pineapple
    chunks, drained
pinch of cayenne pepper
1 tbsp. cornstarch
1 tbsp. sherry
2 tbsp. water

Cut ribs apart and chop into 2½ inch pieces. Put in a bowl, add garlic, ginger and soy sauce, mix well and let stand for an hour. Blend pineapple juice, honey, vinegar, cayenne and chicken broth. Heat oil in a heavy saucepan. Drain ribs and stir-fry until well browned. Stir in flour and the pineapple juice mixture, bring to a simmer, cover and cook gently for 45 minutes. Blend cornstarch, sherry and water. Add pineapple chunks to meat, stir gently until heated through, stir in cornstarch mixture to thicken.

Glazed Loin of Pork

For Five to Six

3 to 4 lbs. center cut loin
    of pork
½ tsp. dried thyme,
    crushed
1 tsp. dried rosemary,
    crushed
1 tsp. dried marjoram,
    crushed

1 tsp. paprika
1 large clove garlic, mashed
1½ tbsp. cooking oil
1 tbsp. soy sauce
salt and pepper to taste
1 cup dry white wine
¼ cup medium dry sherry
    or port wine
½ cup mango chutney

Have butcher bone the loin, remove all the fat down to the bare meat and tie the roast into a roll. Mash garlic with a little salt to make a paste, add the crushed herbs and blend them with the garlic paste. Add pepper, paprika, soy sauce and oil, blend well and spread the mixture over the roast. Place meat in a roasting pan, add ½ cup white wine and put in a pre-heated 400⁰ oven. Roast for 15 minutes, then reduce heat to 350⁰. Continue roasting for 25 minutes per pound of meat (weighed after boning and trimming). Baste frequently and add more wine if more basting liquid is needed.

Combine chutney with sherry or port, cut up larger pieces of chutney. Fifteen minutes before roast is done, spread chutney mixture on top, increase oven heat to 400⁰ and finish cooking.

Small peeled potatoes put into the roasting pan when you start the meat will be done to perfection by serving time. Turn them once or twice during cooking.

Belgian Fricadelles

For Six

2 lbs. pork, ground
2 tbsp. white onions,
    minced
1 tbsp. butter
6 slices white bread,
    crust trimmed off
½ cup milk
1 tsp. salt
¼ tsp. pepper
pinch of grated nutmeg
½ cup good ale
3 egg yolks

3 egg whites, beaten stiff
flour
2 tbsp. butter
12 small white onions,
    peeled
12 small new potatoes,
    peeled
1 small bay leaf
1 clove garlic, minced
pinch of thyme
ale
beef broth
salt and pepper to taste

Sauté minced onion for 2 or 3 minutes in 1 tablespoon butter. Do not brown. Soak bread slices in milk, squeeze dry and put bread in a mixing bowl. Add sautéed onion, pork, salt, pepper, nutmeg, ½ cup ale. Mix well, blend in egg yolks, then fold in beaten egg whites. Form mixture into the shape and size of pullet eggs. Sprinkle with flour. Heat 2 tablespoons butter in heavy saucepan, add meat balls and white onions, sauté, shaking the pan occasionally until meat and onions are lightly browned. Drain off excess fat, add potatoes, bay leaf, garlic, thyme and enough half ale and half broth to reach to top of meatballs. Cover tightly and cook gently until potatoes are done. If gravy is too thin, drain it off into another pan and reduce quickly over high flame.

Pork Pot

For Four to Six

2 lbs. lean pork (loin,
    tenderloin, or very lean
    meaty ribs) cubed
2 lbs. potatoes, peeled,
    sliced ½ inch thick
2 large onions, sliced
1 medium carrot, peeled,
    sliced thin

1 stalk celery, white part,
    sliced thin
¼ cup dry white wine
1 bay leaf
pinch of thyme
1 tbsp. juniper berries,
    crushed
salt and pepper to taste
¼ cup beef broth

Cover bottom of heavy saucepan with a layer of potato slices, then add meat, cover with sliced onion and another layer of potatoes. Add carrot, celery, also thyme, bay leaf and juniper berries tied in a piece of cheesecloth. Season with salt and pepper, add wine and broth. Cover tightly and simmer very slowly for 4 to 5 hours. If you do this dish in a crockpot, simmer it all day.

Meat Loaf Pojarsky

For Four to Six
2 tbsp. shallots, minced
1 large clove garlic, minced
1½ lbs. veal (any cut),
  ground with finest blade
4 large chicken legs,
  skinned, boned, ground
  with the finest blade
1½ cups soft white
  breadcrumbs

4 tbsp. butter
1 egg, beaten
⅓ cup green olives,
  coarsely chopped
2 tsp. paprika
pinch of thyme
pinch of grated nutmeg
⅓ cup dry vermouth
2 tbsp. brandy
salt and pepper to taste

Sauté shallots and garlic in butter until soft but do not brown. Add, together with the butter, to all other ingredients. Blend well and put into a greased loaf pan. Set pan in a larger one, partially filled with water and bake at 350° for about 1 hour and 15 minutes.

Pork Cutlets

For Four
8 very lean pork chops,
  ¼ inch thick
salt and pepper
2 eggs beaten with
  2 tbsp. milk

½ cup flour
1 tbsp. parsley, minced
1 cup fine breadcrumbs
1 cup lard
lemon wedges

Bone chops, remove all fat and pound them thin. Season with salt and pepper. Dredge in flour, dip in beaten egg, sprinkle with parsley and roll in breadcrumbs. Shake off excess crumbs. Heat lard in a skillet, sauté cutlets until golden on one side — about 4 minutes — turn and cook the other side. Drain on paper towel, garnish with lemon wedges. Serve with cucumber salad (p. 244) and apple sauce.

Choucroute Garnie Alsacienne

For Six
3 lbs. sauerkraut
2 medium onions
3 tbsp. lard
1 cup dry white wine
  (Riesling preferred)
1 apple, peeled, cored,
  and diced
2 dozen juniper berries,
  crushed and tied in
  cheesecloth

2 cups beef stock
1 lb. piece of smoked pork
  belly or lean bacon
1½ lbs. smoked pork loin
1 large garlic sausage
  (Saucisse à l'ail, Polish
  or Italian types)
6 frankfurters
2 tbsp. Kirsch brandy
pepper to taste

Heat lard in a heavy casserole, add onion and fry until light golden brown. Wash sauerkraut lightly, squeeze out much of the liquid, add to the onions, stir well and continue cooking for 5 minutes, stirring frequently with a long fork. Mix in the diced apple, add the wine, stock and the juniper berries. The liquids should almost cover the sauerkraut. Cover and simmer for 2 hours. Stir a few times with the fork. Then add the smoked pork belly, cover it with sauerkraut and continue cooking for another 1½ hours. Add a bit more wine and stock if needed. About half an hour before serving stir in Kirsch, place the smoked pork loin, frankfurters and sausages on top, cover again and finish cooking. Serve with boiled potatoes.

Pichelstein Stew

For Six
3 tbsp. butter
1½ lbs. beef, round or
  chuck, cut in 1-inch
  cubes
1½ lbs. lean pork shoulder,
  cut in 1-inch cubes
4 large potatoes, peeled,
  sliced
1 large onion, sliced

1 medium head white
  cabbage, shredded
1 large clove garlic,
  chopped
1 cup beef broth
1 tbsp. vinegar
salt and pepper to taste
1 tsp. grated lemon rind
1 tsp. marjoram
3 carrots, peeled, sliced

Melt butter in a dutch oven or heavy casserole, add alternate layers of diced meats and vegetables. Season layers with salt, pepper and a sprinkling of lemon rind and marjoram. Add beef broth and vinegar, cover and simmer over very low heat for 2½ to 3 hours until meat is done. Do not stir while cooking but shake pan occasionally to prevent sticking.

Sauerkraut and Sausages ⇨

For Six
4 cups sauerkraut
2 cups beer
2 cups water
1 medium onion, chopped
1 bay leaf
salt to taste
12 peppercorns
½ tsp. caraway seed
12 small boiled potatoes, peeled
½ lb. frankfurters
½ lb. bratwurst
  (or other sausage)
½ lb. smoked sausage
  (Polish kielbasy or other)

In a kettle or Dutch oven combine sauerkraut, beer, water, onion, bay leaf, salt, peppercorns and caraway seed; bring to a boil. Prick sausages with a fork and add to the kettle. Cook uncovered over low heat for 10 minutes. Add potatoes, cover and simmer 15 minutes until sauerkraut is done.

⇦ Stuffed Mushrooms

For Four
½ lb. ground veal
8 large firm mushrooms
4 tbsp. butter
½ cup soft white
  breadcrumbs
1 tbsp. parsley, minced

1 tsp. grated onion
salt and pepper to taste
¼ cup chicken broth,
  or water
1 tbsp. flour
¼ cup sour cream
paprika

Trim mushrooms, remove and chop stalks. Heat 2 tablespoons butter in a skillet, add veal and sauté while stirring with a fork, for about 3 minutes until light brown. Break up any clumps. Add chopped mushroom stalks, sauté 3 minutes longer. Remove from fire, blend in breadcrumbs, parsley, onion, salt and pepper. Shape into 8 meat balls the size of the mushroom caps. Return meat balls to skillet, cover and cook gently for 10 minutes, turning them once. Heat remaining butter in another skillet, sauté mushroom caps over moderate heat, turning them a few times, until cooked — about 6 or 7 minutes. Remove caps and keep warm. Deglaze skillet with chicken broth, add this broth to the cooking meat balls. Remove meat balls and keep warm. Stir in flour, cook until sauce has consistency of heavy cream. Blend in sour cream, bring to a simmer but do not let boil. Place meat balls on a hot serving dish, top each with a mushroom cap, spoon sauce over it, sprinkle with a little paprika and serve.

Cabbage ◊ Cacciatore

For Six
1½ lbs. lean ground beef
1 cup onions, chopped
1 cup celery, chopped
1½ tsp. salt
pepper to taste
1 tsp. paprika
1 clove garlic, crushed
1 medium head cabbage (about
    1½ lbs.) cut into 6 wedges
2 cups canned tomato sauce
½ tsp. basil
½ tsp. oregano
1 cup grated mozarella cheese
3 cups hot cooked rice

In an ovenproof skillet sauté beef, onions, celery, salt, pepper, paprika and garlic until meat is no longer pink and vegetables are tender crisp, stirring frequently to crumble meat. Arrange cabbage wedges on top of meat mixture.

Blend tomato sauce, basil, oregano, pour over cabbage wedges. Cover tightly and bake at 350° for 45 minutes or until cabbage is tender. Remove cover; sprinkle with cheese, return to oven for 5 minutes. Serve over bed of rice.

Alsatian Meat Stew (Beckenoff)

For Six to Eight
1 lb. boned pork shoulder, cubed
1 lb. boneless lamb shoulder, cubed
1 lb. beef chuck, cubed
4 medium white onions, sliced
2 leeks, white part only, sliced
3 cloves garlic, minced
pinch of allspice
bouquet garni (sprig of thyme, parsley and one bay leaf, tied together)
4 cups dry white wine (Riesling type)
2 lbs. potatoes, peeled, sliced ¼ inch thick
salt and pepper to taste
1 tsp. meat extract (Bovril or other)

Put meat cubes in a bowl, add onions, leeks and garlic, mix well. Add salt, pepper, allspice, bouquet garni. Cover with wine and marinate in the refrigerator for 24 hours. Put half the potatoes in a heavy saucepan or kettle, also half the onions from the marinade. Put meats on top, cover with the rest of potatoes and onions. Remove and discard bouquet garni and pour remainder of the marinade and the remaining vegetables into the casserole. Stir in the meat extract. Cover and cook in a 350° oven for 3 hours. Then skim off any fat, ladle most of the liquid into a saucepan and reduce it quickly over a hot fire by one third. Pour it back over meat and serve.

Picadillo (Mexican Hash)

For Six

1 lb. ground lean pork
1 lb. ground lean beef
2 tbsp. oil
1 medium onion, chopped
1 clove garlic, chopped
2 tomatoes, peeled, sealed, and chopped
¼ cup beef broth
1 tart green apple, peeled, cored and grated
1 tbsp. sugar

3 tbsp. blanched almonds, slivered
3 tbsp. chopped black olives
2 tbsp. chili powder
pinch of cinnamon
pinch of allspice
pinch of cumin
1 tbsp. vinegar
salt and pepper to taste
¼ cup raisins, soaked in water and drained

Brown meats and onion in oil. Add the tomatoes and beef broth, blend well. When mixture starts to simmer, add all other ingredients, mix well. Bring to a boil and simmer for about 30 minutes. Stir occasionally and add a little more broth if hash gets too dry. Serve with rice or beans.

Stuffed Peppers

For Four

6 large green peppers
½ lb. veal, ground
½ lb. pork, ground
1 egg, lightly beaten
⅓ cup raw rice
½ small onion, grated
1 clove garlic, minced
1 tbsp. parsley, chopped
salt and pepper to taste
1 cup tomato sauce (canned)
1 cup beef or chicken broth
3 tbsp. tomato paste
1 tbsp. paprika
2 tbsp. sugar
1 tbsp. lemon juice

Cut stem end off the peppers, seed and blanch them for a couple of minutes in boiling water. Combine meats, egg, rice, onion, garlic, parsley, salt and pepper. Fill the peppers with stuffing. Stand them upright and close together in a saucepan. Combine all other ingredients and add to the pan. The liquid should come up to about 2 inches from the top of the peppers. Add more tomato sauce and broth if needed. Cover and cook slowly for about one hour. Baste a few times. Correct seasoning. The sauce should have a tangy sweet-sour taste.

Polynesian Kraut Kebabs

For Four to Six

6 cups undrained sauerkraut
(about 48 oz.)
1 can (20 oz.) pineapple
chunks in pineapple juice,
undrained
brown sugar
½ cup ketchup

2 tbsp. soy sauce
1 lb. frankfurters,
cut into 1 inch pieces
2 medium green peppers
cut into chunks
2 tbsp. salad oil
1 cup chopped green onion
parsley for garnish

Drain kraut, reserving 2 tablespoons kraut liquid; set aside. Drain pineapple chunks, reserving the juice.

In small saucepan, measure 3 tablespoons brown sugar and 2 tablespoons reserved pineapple juice. Stir in 2 tablespoons kraut liquid, ketchup and soy sauce; heat to boiling, stirring constantly. Reduce heat and simmer 10 minutes.

While sauce is simmering, prepare 12 kebabs: alternately thread pineapple chunks, franks and green pepper chunks on twelve 10-inch skewers. Place on rack of broiler pan; brush kebabs with sauce and broil 5 minutes, brushing occasionally with additional sauce. Turn kebabs, brush with additional sauce and broil 5 more minutes or until franks are heated through.

While kebabs are broiling, heat salad oil in large skillet; add onion and drained kraut; cook, stirring constantly, until onion is tender. Stir in ½ cup brown sugar and ½ cup pineapple juice, Continue cooking until hot.

Spoon hot kraut mixture onto large serving platter; arrange kebabs on top. Garnish kraut mixture with parsley.

Savory Meat Loaf

For Eight

2 lbs. ground lean beef
1 lb. ground lean pork
1 lb. ground veal
1 medium onion, chopped
2 tbsp. butter
¾ cup mushrooms,
chopped

2 cups soft white
breadcrumbs
½ cup dry red wine
3 tbsp. soy sauce
1 tbsp. paprika
1 tbsp. Dijon mustard
salt and pepper to taste

Sauté onion in butter until soft. Add mushrooms and sauté 5 more minutes. Blend well with all other ingredients. Put in a loaf pan and bake at 350° for about 1½ hours.

Note: This mixture freezes very well. Put in loaf pans and freeze. When ready to use, put frozen in a preheated 350° oven and bake about 45 minutes per pound.

Tripe Normande

For Eight

¼ lb. salt pork, cut
into thin slices
5 lbs. fresh honeycomb
tripe
2 calves' feet, split in half
3 medium carrots, peeled
and halved
2 medium Spanish onions,
stuck with 2 cloves each
2 cloves garlic
pinch of nutmeg
pinch of allspice

pinch of rosemary, thyme,
small bay leaf, tied
in cheesecloth
2 stalks celery and
3 leeks, white part only,
halved lengthwise
tied together
6 cups dry white wine
3 cups chicken broth
salt and white pepper
¼ cup calvados brandy
or applejack

Wash tripe well and soak, together with the calves' feet, in cold water for 3 or 4 hours, changing the water occasionally. Drain and let dry. Line the bottom of a heavy saucepan with a tight-fitting lid, with the salt pork slices. Cut the tripe in 2-inch long strips and place on top of salt pork along with the calves' feet. Add carrots, onions, garlic, herbs, celery, leeks, nutmeg, allspice, salt and pepper. Then cover with wine and chicken broth. Bring to a boil on top of the stove, cover and seal the edges of the pot with aluminum foil or dough. Put in 325° oven and cook for about 8 hours. Then remove tripe, put it in an earthenware serving casserole. Take the meat off the calves' feet and cut it in pieces, add to the tripe. Strain all the liquid through a fine sieve. Discard all the vegetables. Reduce liquid on top of the stove to about 4 cups. Skim off all the fat and add the calvados. Correct the seasoning and pour it over the tripe. Then simmer for half an hour before serving.

Cooking it the day before and reheating before serving improves the flavor.

Kraut and Frankfurter Loling

For Four to Six

1 cup sliced onion
1 cup slivered green pepper
1 cup diagonally sliced celery
1 tbsp. salad oil
6 frankfurters, sliced diagonally
1 can (11 oz.) mandarin orange segments
about 1½ cups water
¼ cup vinegar
¼ cup sugar
1 beef bouillon cube
1 tsp. soy sauce
½ tsp. salt
½ tsp. MSG (opt.)
¼ tsp. ginger
⅛ tsp. each: pepper and fennel seed
1 tbsp. cornstarch
3½ cups undrained sauerkraut
cooked rice

In large skillet over medium heat, cook onion, green pepper and celery in oil until crisp-tender, about 3 minutes. Remove from skillet; set aside. Lightly brown frankfurter slices in same skillet. Drain syrup from oranges; reserve. Combine orange syrup with enough water to measure 1¾ cups; add to frankfurters. Stir in vinegar, sugar, bouillon cube and seasonings. Bring to boil. Blend cornstarch with ¼ cup water. Stir into boiling mixture; boil 1 minute. Reduce heat to simmer. Drain and wash kraut; add to frankfurters with vegetables and orange segments. Cover; heat to serving temperature. Serve over cooked rice.

Stuffed Cabbage

For Four

8 large cabbage leaves
1 lb. chopped beef
½ cup raw rice
1 medium onion, grated
¼ cup peeled, grated parsnip
1 tbsp. parsley, minced
1 tbsp. dill, chopped
salt and pepper to taste
¼ cup lemon juice
1 cup tomato sauce (canned)
1 clove garlic, mashed
⅓ cup brown sugar
beef broth
1 egg

Blanch the cabbage leaves with boiling water. Combine meat with rice, onion, parsnip, parsley, dill and egg; season with salt and pepper. Place a portion of this stuffing on each cabbage leaf, roll them up, tuck in the ends and fasten with toothpicks. Put close together in a heavy casserole. Combine lemon juice, tomato sauce, garlic and brown sugar; blend and add to the stuffed leaves, with enough broth to barely cover the rolls. Cover and cook on top of stove at moderate heat for half an hour. Then put in a preheated 350⁰ oven, bake for 30 to 40 minutes longer until the rolls are nicely browned. Turn once during baking. Add more broth if needed.

Ragout of Pig's Trotters

For Four
4 pig's trotters (feet)
   cut lengthwise in half
large onion, stuck with
   4 cloves
salt and pepper to taste
4 tbsp. butter

4 tbsp. flour
½ bottle dry white wine
2 cloves garlic, minced
4 carrots, peeled and sliced
1 lb. fresh broad beans or
   lima beans
¼ tsp. allspice

Put pig's trotters in a saucepan, cover with water, add the onion, salt and pepper. Cover and simmer for about 3 hours. Let the trotters cool in the water, then drain and bone them. Reserve the cooking liquid.

Heat the butter in a casserole and stir in the flour. Blend well, then add 2 cups of the cooking liquid and the wine. Stir over medium heat until it comes to a boil, then add the boned trotters, garlic, carrots and beans. Season with allspice. The sauce will be quite thin in the beginning but will thicken during cooking time. Simmer for 45 minutes, then correct seasoning.

Serve with mashed potatoes.

Scrooch

For Six to Eight
3 lbs. brisket of beef (or
   lean, meaty shortribs)
2 lbs. shoulder or neck
   of lamb, cut into
   large pieces
1 turnip, peeled, halved

4 qts. water (or half water
   and half beef broth)
2 large onions, sliced
2 lbs. potatoes, peeled,
   sliced ½ inch thick
salt and pepper to taste
1 carrot, peeled

Put meats in a heavy saucepan or kettle, add water, salt; bring to a boil. Skim off scum, add onion, carrot and turnip; cover and simmer for one hour. Add a cup of ice water — skim off fat, cover again and simmer 45 minutes longer. Add potatoes, pepper, more salt if needed and continue simmering until potatoes are cooked and meat is done. Serve soup first, then meat, potatoes and vegetables.

Devilled Lamb Kidneys

For Four
12 lamb kidneys
1 qt. water
¼ cup white vinegar
½ cup oil
1 tsp. Dijon mustard

dash of Tabasco sauce
½ tsp. thyme
½ tsp. oregano
1 tbsp. lemon juice
salt and pepper to taste

Clean kidneys, remove outer membrane and trim away fat. Split almost all the way through but do not separate halves. Soak for two hours in water and vinegar. Drain and pat dry. Blend all other ingredients, pour over kidneys and let them marinate for about ½ hour. Broil kidneys under a hot broiler or over charcoal for about 2 minutes on each side.

Calf Liver Paprika

For Four
1¼ lbs. calf liver
3 tbsp. butter
1 medium onion, minced

1½ tsp. paprika
1 tbsp. flour
½ cup chicken broth
salt and pepper to taste

Cut liver into strips about 2 inches long and ¾ inch wide. Heat butter in a skillet, sauté onions until golden brown. Stir in paprika, add livers and sauté over fairly high heat for 3 to 4 minutes until browned. Stir while sautéeing. Sprinkle with flour, add broth and stir. Simmer for a minute or two. Season with salt and pepper and serve.

Italian Boiled Dinner (Bollito Misto)

For Eight to Ten

3 lbs. beef (brisket
   or flanken)
1 3-lb. smoked beef tongue
3 lbs. boneless veal
   (shoulder or breast)
   tied in a roll
1 3-lb. chicken, trussed
1 lb. Italian garlic sausage

2 carrots, peeled
2 onions, stuck with
   1 clove each
3 stalks celery, with
   green tops
1 parsnip, peeled
1 bay leaf
salt and pepper to taste
10 boiled potatoes

Put beef tongue in a large saucepan or kettle, cover with water, bring to a boil and boil for 10 minutes. Pour off water, add enough boiling water to cover the tongue. Cover and cook gently for 45 minutes. Add beef, veal and all vegetables except potatoes. Cook slowly for another 1½ hours. Skim off scum frequently. Add chicken and sausage, season with salt and pepper and continue cooking until all meats are tender. Remove meats, pare and peel tongue. Slice meats and arrange on a hot serving platter, spoon some of the broth over the sliced meat, garnish with hot boiled potatoes.

Philadelphia Pepper Pot

For Eight

3 lbs. cleaned honeycomb
   tripe
2 lbs. meaty veal shanks
1 tsp. whole peppercorns
1 tsp. whole allspice
5 whole cloves
1 tbsp. salt
4 tbsp. butter
1 large carrot, peeled,
   chopped

1½ cups chopped onion
1 cup celery, chopped
½ tsp. thyme
1 tsp. marjoram
½ cup flour
3 large potatoes, peeled,
   diced
hot red crushed pepper
   to taste
black pepper to taste

Put tripe and veal shank in dutch oven or heavy saucepan, cover with 2 inches of water. Add peppercorns, allspice, cloves and salt, bring to a boil and simmer covered for about 3 hours until tripe is tender. Remove tripe and veal and reserve cooking liquid. Remove veal from bone and cut veal and tripe into small strips. Strain cooking liquid and reserve 8 cups. Chill the liquid well and remove fat from top. In a kettle or saucepan heat butter and sauté onions, celery and carrot until soft, stir in flour and sauté while stirring until flour is light brown. Add warmed cooking liquid gradually, stir while simmering until the broth thickens. Add meat and all other ingredients and simmer covered for another hour or more. Correct seasoning and serve.

Note: Don't be too sparing with the pepper. Pepperpot, as the name indicates, should be hot and pungent.

Hotchpot

For Four to Six

1½ lbs. shin beef,
   boneless, in one piece
1 lb. smoked sausage
¼ lb. smoked lean bacon,
   in one piece
2 cups beef broth
2 cups water
salt and pepper to taste
1 large bay leaf

2 cloves
4 medium carrots, peeled,
   sliced
2 leeks, white part only,
   sliced
1 small head white
   cabbage, shredded
4 medium potatoes,
   peeled, quartered

Put beef, sausage, bacon, broth, water, salt, pepper, bay leaf and cloves in a saucepan, bring to a boil, skim off scum, cover and cook gently for about 2½ hours. Add carrots, leeks, cabbage and potatoes and cook covered until vegetables are cooked. Slice meats and put on a serving platter, surround with vegetables. Serve broth separately.

Kidney Hash

For Four

1 lb. veal or beef kidneys
4 tbsp. butter
¾ lb. lean pork, shredded
6 medium potatoes, peeled, sliced thin

1 large onion, sliced thin
1½ tbsp. fresh dill, chopped
salt and pepper to taste
pinch of cayenne pepper
1½ cups ale
1 cup beef broth

Trim fat off kidneys, wash in cold water and pat dry. Slice kidneys quite thinly. Heat butter in a skillet, add sliced kidneys and shredded pork; sauté, stirring often until meats are lightly browned. Add onion and continue to sauté until onion is quite soft. Add potatoes and dill, season with salt, pepper, cayenne, mix in ale and broth, cover and cook over medium heat for about 45 minutes until kidneys are soft. Most of the liquid should be absorbed by this time. If too liquid, cook uncovered for a few minutes longer.

Baked Calf Liver

For Six to Eight

2 lbs. calf liver in one piece
3 or 4 strips of smoked bacon
2 cups dry red wine (approx.)
pinch of ground cloves
pinch of mace
2 tbsp. bacon fat

6 small white onions, peeled
1 cup chicken broth
1 clove garlic
1 tbsp. minced shallots
1 stalk celery, sliced
1 tbsp. butter
1 tbsp. flour
salt and pepper to taste

Wash liver, dry well and lard with bacon strips sprinkled with ground cloves and mace. Put liver in a bowl, pour wine over it, season with salt and pepper. Marinate for about 3 hours, turning the liver a few times in the bowl. Drain liver. Heat bacon fat in a saucepan or casserole, put in the liver and the onions, sauté quickly until liver is browned on all sides. Add remaining marinade, broth and vegetables. Bring slowly to a boil, cover and bake in 350° oven for about 1 hour until tender. Remove liver and keep hot. Strain sauce, return sauce to pan. Combine butter and flour and stir into sauce. Return liver to pan, spoon sauce over liver and continue to simmer until sauce has thickened. When serving, carve liver into thin slices.

Meat Loaf en Croustade

For Four

½ lb. ground beef
½ lb. sausage meat
½ cup finely chopped onion
2 loaves "brown-and-serve" French bread
⅓ cup beef broth

1 egg, lightly beaten
2 tbsp. Dijon mustard
2 tbsp. parsley, minced
pinch of oregano
salt and pepper to taste
1 clove garlic, minced
2 tbsp. melted butter

Break up sausage meat and sauté it in a skillet for about 5 minutes over medium heat. Add ground beef and onion, sauté until meats and onion are lightly browned. Cut a slice off one end of each loaf of bread, hollow out with a fork or spoon, leaving 2 shells. Combine the crumbs you took out of the bread with broth, egg, mustard, parsley, oregano, salt and pepper; mix well with browned meats and onion. Fill the bread shells with this mixture, replace the sliced off bread caps and fasten with skewer or toothpicks to the loaves. Combine minced garlic and melted butter and brush the loaves with the mixture. Bake in 400° oven for 15 to 20 minutes until golden brown.

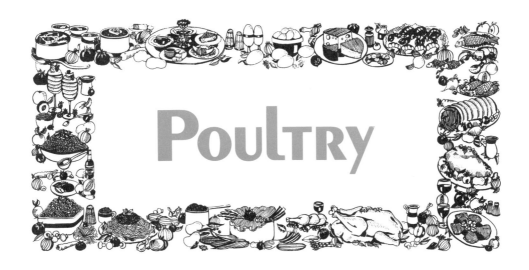

Mexican Chicken

For Six

1 frying chicken (3 lbs.)
    cut in 6 pieces
1/3 cup flour
2 tbsp. oil
2 tbsp. butter
1/2 lb. cooked ham, cut
    into thin slivers
1 cup dark seedless raisins
salt and pepper to taste

1/8 tsp. ground cloves
1/4 tsp. ground cumin
2 cloves garlic, crushed
1 cup dry white wine
1 cup chicken broth
1/2 cup pimiento-stuffed
    olives, halved
1 tbsp. capers, drained
1/2 cup toasted slivered
    almonds

Shake chicken with flour in a large paper bag. Heat oil and butter in a heavy casserole over medium heat. Fry chicken pieces until golden brown. Pour off excess fat, sprinkle ham and raisins over chicken. Combine salt, pepper, cloves, cumin, garlic, wine and chicken broth. Pour over chicken, cover and simmer for about 1 hour or until chicken is tender. Add olives and capers, cook uncovered to heat through. Sprinkle almonds on top just before serving.

Braised Young Turkey

For Six

1 young turkey (5 lbs.)
salt and pepper
4 tbsp. lard
3 carrots, minced
1 small turnip, minced
2 stalks celery, minced

2 onions, minced
1 clove garlic, minced
thin sheets of fresh pork fat
bouquet garni*
2 tomatoes, quartered
3 cups chicken broth
3 tbsp. beurre manié*

Wipe the turkey inside and out with a damp cloth, season inside and out with salt and pepper. Heat the lard in a casserole and brown the turkey on all sides. Remove and keep warm. Put the carrots, celery, turnip and onions in the casserole, add a little more lard if necessary and cook until the vegetables are soft and golden. Season with salt and pepper, add garlic and mix well. Remove the vegetables from the casserole with a slotted spoon.

Line the bottom and sides of the casserole with the sheets of pork fat and put turkey in the casserole. Add the vegetables, bouquet garni, the tomatoes and the broth. Cover the turkey with another sheet of pork fat.

Cover the casserole, bring the liquid to a boil and then put the casserole in a preheated 350° oven for about 1¾ hours. Remove the turkey, put it on a serving dish and keep hot. Skim the fat off the liquid in the casserole, strain through a fine sieve, let stand for 5 minutes and skim fat off again. Return sauce to low heat, stir in beurre manié. You should use 1 tablespoon of beurre manié for each cup of braising liquid. Simmer for 10 minutes, correct seasoning and serve the sauce separately in a sauceboat. Garnish platter on which turkey is served with watercress.

*See Glossary

Chicken à la Crème

For Four
5 tbsp. butter
1 chicken (3 lbs.)
   cut in pieces
1½ tbsp. flour
pinch of nutmeg and
   powdered ginger

salt and white pepper
¾ cup chicken broth
¾ cup dry white wine
1 cup crème fraîche*
   or heavy cream
2 egg yolks
1 bouquet garni*

Sauté chicken pieces in butter for about 20 minutes over gentle heat. Turn them occasionally but do not let them brown. Then sprinkle with flour, salt and pepper, turn them a few more times, cover and simmer for 10 minutes. Add the wine, chicken broth, bouquet garni, nutmeg and ginger and simmer covered for 15 minutes or until the chicken is tender. Remove the chicken pieces and keep them hot. Blend cream into the sauce and cook, barely simmering, for 10 minutes. Beat egg yolks with a whisk until they are light colored and creamy, blend a half cup of the cream sauce into them and then add them to the sauce. Blend well, correct seasoning, pour over the chicken and serve.

*See Glossary

Circassian Chicken

For Four
1 3-lb. chicken, cut into
   serving pieces
8 cups water
2 onions, quartered
2 stalks celery
1 carrot, peeled
3 sprigs parsley

salt and pepper to taste
2 slices stale white bread,
   crust removed
1 cup shelled walnuts
2 tbsp. grated onion
1 clove garlic, crushed
1 tsp. paprika
1 tbsp. oil

Place chicken in a saucepan, add water, onion, celery, carrot, parsley, salt and pepper. Bring to a boil, skim off scum, cover and cook until chicken is tender. Remove chicken, discard skin, bone and slice meat. Strain chicken broth, return broth to pan and reduce quickly to about 2 cups. Soak bread in ½ cup reduced broth, squeeze dry and crumble. Put walnuts twice through a meat grinder; combine soaked bread, ground nuts, grated onion and garlic and put through the grinder again. Add, while beating, one cup of concentrated chicken broth, a little at a time, until the mixture has the consistency of mayonnaise. Add more broth if too thick. A simpler way to proceed is to put nuts, bread and other ingredients in a blender or food processor and blend until smooth. Add salt and pepper if needed. Combine chicken meat with half of the sauce, put in serving dish. Pour remaining sauce over the top. Combine oil and paprika, heat in a small skillet until bright red and pour oil over the chicken.

Braised Duck

For Four to Five
1 duck (5 lbs.)
1 tbsp. soy sauce
1 tbsp. sherry
1 tsp. cornstarch
1 clove garlic, mashed
1 tbsp. hoisin sauce
2 tbsp. oil
3 scallions, chopped
2 thin slices fresh ginger
   root, minced
½ cup onion, sliced thin

1 clove garlic, chopped
1 tsp. sugar
3 tbsp. soy sauce
2 tbsp. sherry
2 cups chicken broth
1 cup water
½ cup celery, sliced
½ cup water chestnuts,
   diced
1 tbsp. cornstarch
2 tbsp. water

Wipe duck with a damp cloth, cut in quarters or smaller pieces. Blend soy sauce, sherry, cornstarch, mashed garlic and hoisin sauce, rub into duck pieces and let stand for an hour. Heat oil in a heavy saucepan, brown the duck pieces on all sides. Remove duck and drain off all fat. Add scallions, ginger, onion and garlic, stir-fry for a few seconds, return duck to pan, add sugar, soy sauce, sherry, chicken broth and water, cover and simmer for about one hour or until duck is cooked. Half an hour after starting to simmer the duck, add celery and water chestnuts. When duck is cooked, remove to hot platter, skim fat off the sauce, add cornstarch diluted in water and stir to thicken.

Breast of Chicken Piccata

For Four
4 tbsp. butter
1 tbsp. cooking oil
2 whole chicken breasts
flour
salt and pepper to taste

3 tbsp. freshly squeezed
   lemon juice
1 tbsp. butter
3 tbsp. parsley
thin slices of lemon

Have chicken breasts boned, and halved, flatten the halves between sheets of wax paper, and sprinkle the breasts lightly with flour. Heat butter and oil in a skillet. When foaming, sauté chicken breasts for 2 to 3 minutes on each side until nicely browned. Remove and keep warm. Add lemon juice, salt and pepper to skillet, deglaze to dissolve all brown particles. If needed, add a spoonful of water or dry white wine. Add one tablespoon butter, parsley, blend, return chicken breasts to pan and heat through for one minute. Put meat on a hot serving platter. Pour pan juices over the breasts and top each with a slice of lemon.

Roast Stuffed Capon

For Six
1 capon or chicken,
   about 6 to 7 lbs.
salt and pepper to taste

Stuffing:
½ cup butter
3 eggs, separated
4 chicken livers,
   cut in pieces
2 rolls soaked in milk
   and squeezed dry

¼ cup butter, softened
1 cup chicken broth or
   water
2 tbsp. flour

½ cup fresh mushrooms,
   chopped
¼ cup light cream
1 pinch nutmeg, grated
1½ tbsp. parsley, chopped
salt and pepper to taste

Prepare the stuffing: cream ½ cup butter, add egg yolks one at a time and blend well. Mix in livers, mashed rolls, and all other ingredients, folding in stiffly beaten egg whites last.

Season bird inside and out with salt and pepper. Pack stuffing lightly into the cavity of the bird, close the opening and truss. Rub the bird with softened butter and put in a roasting pan. Add remaining butter to the pan. Roast at 350° for about 1½ hours until bird is done. Baste frequently with chicken broth. When done, remove bird to serving platter, skim most of the fat off the pan juices. Stir flour into the pan juices, add a little more broth if needed and make a pan gravy.

Stuffed Goose or Turkey Neck

For Four
1 goose or turkey neck
½ cup ground veal
½ cup ground beef
½ cup chopped cooked
   giblets
1 clove garlic, minced
2 medium onions, minced
1 hard roll soaked in water
   and squeezed dry
2 tbsp. fat

1 tbsp. flour
½ cup chicken broth
3 tbsp. dry breadcrumbs
¼ tsp. marjoram
1 tsp. paprika
salt and pepper to taste
2 eggs, lightly beaten
water
2 tbsp. vinegar
1 bay leaf
1 tbsp. salt

Blend ground meats, giblets, garlic, onions and roll. Heat 1 tablespoon fat in a skillet. Add flour and cook while stirring until flour is light brown. Add hot broth and stir until smooth and thickened. Add meat mixture, breadcrumbs, marjoram, paprika, salt and pepper, blend well and simmer for 15 minutes, stirring once in a while. Remove from stove, cool and blend in eggs. Fill the neck loosely and tie or sew up ends. Heat remaining fat in a skillet and brown the stuffed neck on all sides. Place in a saucepan, add enough water to come half-way up the stuffed neck, add bay leaf, vinegar and salt. Let come to a boil, cover and simmer for about 40 minutes. Slice for serving.

Basque Chicken

For Four

1 tbsp. butter
3 tbsp. olive oil
1 frying chicken
¼ lb. fresh mushrooms,
  sliced
1 medium onion, chopped
2 cans (8 oz. each) tomato
  sauce
½ cup dry white wine
10 small white whole
  onions, peeled

2 sprigs parsley
1 clove garlic, minced
salt and pepper to taste
½ cup small pimiento-
  stuffed green olives
1 green pepper, cut
  in strips
2 medium ripe tomatoes,
  peeled and cut
  into wedges
hot cooked rice

Heat butter and 2 tablespoons olive oil in a heavy casserole. Truss and fry the chicken on all sides until golden brown. Remove from pan. Sauté mushrooms, onion and garlic in the same pan until light brown. Add tomato sauce, wine, whole onions, parsley. Return chicken to pan, sprinkle with salt and pepper. Cover and simmer for about 1 hour or until chicken is tender, basting the chicken occasionally with the sauce. Add olives for the last 15 minutes of cooking time. When done, place chicken on a platter and keep warm. Simmer sauce uncovered for 5 minutes. Heat 1 tablespoon oil in a small skillet, sauté green pepper strips for 2 minutes, add tomato wedges and cook until hot. Arrange on platter around the chicken. Using a slotted spoon lift mushrooms, onions and olives from the sauce and arrange on the platter. Serve with the sauce and rice.

Paprika Chicken

For Four

⅔ cup onion, minced
2 tbsp. lard or butter
1 frying chicken,
  about 3 lbs., cut up
1 large ripe tomato, peeled,
  seeded and chopped
½ tbsp. paprika
salt and pepper to taste
¾ cup chicken broth (or water)
¼ cup sour cream
1½ tbsp. flour
1 medium green pepper,
  seeded and sliced

Heat lard in a heavy casserole, add onion, cover and cook slowly until onion is very soft. Do not let brown. Add chicken, tomato, cover and cook 10 minutes longer. Stir in paprika, chicken broth, salt and pepper, cover and cook over gentle heat for half an hour. Remove cover and reduce sauce by one third. Combine flour and sour cream, blend well into the sauce, correct seasoning, cover and simmer until chicken is done. Garnish with green pepper.

Chicken Cacciatore

For Four

one 4-lb. frying chicken,
    cut in pieces
flour
4 tbsp. oil
2 thick slices of meaty
    bacon, diced
½ cup onion, chopped
1 clove garlic, minced

½ cup sliced mushrooms
1 tbsp. chopped parsley
¼ cup carrot, chopped fine
1 bay leaf
1 tsp. basil
2 cups canned tomatoes,
    measured, drained
½ cup dry white wine
salt and pepper to taste

Dredge chicken in flour. Heat oil in saucepan and sauté chicken pieces until browned. Remove and keep warm. Add bacon, onion and garlic to saucepan, sauté until onions are soft and transparent, add mushrooms and cook one minute more. Add parsley, carrot, bay leaf, basil and tomatoes; season with salt and pepper, blend and bring to a boil. Add chicken pieces and wine, cover and simmer for half an hour or until chicken is tender.

Stuffed Cornish Hens

For Four

2 fresh cornish hens or
    small young chickens
2 hard rolls, soaked in
    milk and squeezed dry
¼ cup diced smoked bacon
½ cup minced fresh
    mushrooms

1 small onion, minced
¼ lb. chicken livers, diced
3 tbsp. softened butter
3 hard-boiled eggs,
    coarsely chopped
1 tsp. marjoram
1 tbsp. parsley, minced
salt and pepper to taste

Wipe hens inside and out with a damp cloth, dry, season inside with salt and pepper. Sauté bacon until light brown, add onion and mushrooms, sauté for 2 minutes, add chicken livers, sauté 2 or 3 minutes longer while stirring. Remove from fire, blend with rolls and 2 tablespoons butter, eggs, marjoram and parsley, season with salt and pepper. Stuff the birds, truss and sew up opening. Brush with remaining butter and roast in a 350° oven for about 1 hour or until done.

Honey Chicken

For Four

3 lb. frying chicken cut
    in serving pieces
½ cup sherry
2 tbsp. soy sauce
2 tbsp. honey
1 tsp. vinegar
salt to taste

1 tsp. fresh ginger,
    shredded
2 scallions, white part
    only, chopped
1 clove garlic, minced
2 tbsp. oil
1 tbsp. cornstarch

Heat oil in a saucepan, sauté chicken pieces until well browned on all sides. Remove chicken, pour off oil from pan. Combine all other ingredients except cornstarch, add to pan, stir well and let come to a simmer. Return chicken to pan, cover and simmer for about 45 minutes. Five minutes before chicken is done, dilute cornstarch with a little water, add to pan and stir until thickened.

Steamed Chicken Breast

For Four

2 whole chicken breasts,
    boned and skinned
½ cup bamboo shoots
8 water chestnuts
6 Chinese mushrooms
2 tbsp. oil

1 tsp. sugar
1 tbsp. soy sauce
1 tbsp. sherry
salt and pepper to taste
2 tsp. cornstarch
1 tbsp. water

Cut chicken into 1½ inch cubes. Soak mushrooms in warm water for ½ hour, drain, discard stems and slice caps. Slice bamboo shoots and water chestnuts ⅛ inch thick. Blend oil, sugar, soy sauce, sherry, salt, pepper, cornstarch, and water. Blend well with all other ingredients. Put in serving dishes. Place in steamer and cook for 15 minutes.

Chicken Sautéed with Riesling

For Four

1 frying chicken, 2½ to
  3 lbs. cut in pieces
1 tbsp. cooking oil
¼ lb. firm mushrooms,
  sliced
3 tomatoes, peeled,
  seeded and chopped

4 tbsp. butter
1½ cups Riesling or other
  dry white wine
2 tbsp. brandy
salt to taste
pinch of cayenne pepper
1 clove garlic, minced
3 tbsp. parsley, chopped

Heat oil and butter in casserole. Add chicken and sauté until pieces are browned on all sides. Add mushrooms and tomatoes, cook gently for about 5 minutes. Add the wine and brandy, salt and cayenne pepper. Bring to a boil, cover and simmer for 25 minutes. Remove chicken pieces, put on hot serving dish and keep hot. Skim fat off the pan juices, add parsley and garlic and reduce slightly over high heat. Correct the seasoning and pour sauce over chicken.

Chicken in Wine Batter

For Four

2 boned chicken breasts,
  halved
salt and pepper to taste
⅓ cup flour
2 tbsp. white wine or
  white vermouth

2 tsp. oil
3 egg whites, stiffly
  beaten
1 cup lard or shortening
lemon wedges
parsley

Season chicken pieces with salt and pepper. Combine flour, oil, wine, egg whites and blend well. Heat fat in a skillet, dip chicken in the batter, fry chicken until golden brown on one side, turn and brown the other side. Drain on paper towel, garnish with lemon wedges and parsley.

Chicken and Peaches ◁ Cantonese

For Six

2 whole skinned and boned chicken
    breasts (about 1 lb.)
1½ tsp. salt
¼ tsp. pepper
1½ tbsp. oil
1 large onion, sliced
1 cup ketchup
1 can (16 ounces) sliced peaches
    (drain; reserve syrup)
2 tbsp. soy sauce
1 large green pepper, cut in squares
3 cups hot cooked rice

Cut chicken in thin strips, sprinkle with salt and pepper, stir-fry in oil about 2 minutes. Add onion, continue cooking until onion is tender crisp. Blend ketchup, peach syrup with enough water to make two cups liquid, and soy sauce. Pour over chicken. Cover and simmer 20 minutes. Add green pepper and peaches. Replace cover and continue cooking 10 minutes longer. Serve over beds of rice.

Fried Chicken

For Four

2 young broiler chickens
    (or Cornish hens)
lemon juice
salt and pepper to taste
¾ cup flour
lemon wedges

2 eggs, lightly beaten
    with 2 tbsp. water
¾ cup fine dry white
    breadcrumbs
½ cup margarine (approx.)
¼ cup cooking oil (approx.)

Cut chicken into serving pieces. Sprinkle with lemon juice, salt and pepper. Dredge the pieces in flour, shake off excess flour, then dip in beaten eggs and finally roll in breadcrumbs. Shake off excess crumbs. Set aside for 1 hour before cooking.

Heat margarine and oil in a heavy skillet. The fats should be about ¾ inch deep. Fry chicken, a few pieces at a time, until golden on one side, turn and repeat. Drain on paper towel and garnish with lemon slices when serving.

Note: Best results for all breaded and fried foods are achieved by making the breadcrumbs yourself. Cut crust off good white bread, dry and rub through a fine sieve to have breadcrumbs of uniform size. Ready-bought crumbs are brown and turn to an even browner and not too appetizing color when fried.

Chicken Casserole

For Four

1 frying chicken (3 lbs.)
   cut in serving pieces
¼ cup oil
2 tbsp. butter
flour, seasoned with salt,
   pepper and paprika
5 strips lean bacon, diced
2 carrots, peeled and sliced
1 small onion, sliced

1 can green chili peppers,
   cut in strips
1 small bay leaf
1 tbsp. parsley, minced
¼ tsp. rosemary, crumbled
⅛ tsp. thyme
1 lemon, thinly sliced
1 cup dry white wine
1 cup tomato juice

Dredge chicken pieces in seasoned flour. Heat oil and butter in a skillet and sauté chicken pieces until browned on all sides. Remove chicken and place in a casserole. Add all other ingredients except lemon, wine and tomato juice. Sprinkle with 2 tablespoons of the seasoned flour. Arrange sliced lemon on top of chicken, add wine and tomato juice, cover and bake in 350⁰ oven for about one hour or until chicken is tender. Correct the seasoning of sauce and serve.

Chicken à la Marseillaise

For Four

1 frying chicken (3 lbs.)
   cut in 8 pieces
2 tbsp. Pernod or Ricard
⅛ tsp. ground Spanish
   saffron
8 tbsp. olive oil
salt and pepper to taste
2 onions, chopped

For the Rouille Sauce:

1 clove garlic, mashed
4 small hot red peppers

4 cloves garlic, mashed
6 tomatoes, peeled, seeded
   and chopped
1 tbsp. parsley, chopped
1 small head fennel, white
   part only, chopped
4 potatoes, peeled and
   thickly sliced
4 slices French bread

¼ cup olive oil
1 chicken liver
1 tbsp. butter

Reserve the chicken liver. Marinate the chicken in 3 tablespoons of olive oil, Pernod and saffron, salt and pepper for about 30 minutes. Turn the pieces occasionally. Heat 3 tablespoons olive oil in a casserole, add onions and garlic and sauté them just until light golden. Add the tomatoes and cook, stirring occasionally for 5 minutes. Add fennel, parsley, chicken pieces and their marinade, and enough boiling water to just cover the chicken.

Cover and cook over low heat for 10 minutes. Add potatoes, simmer covered for 15 more minutes or until chicken and potatoes are almost cooked. Uncover casserole and continue cooking until the liquid has reduced and slightly thickened. Line a soup tureen or bowl with bread slices, sprinkle the remaining 2 tablespoons of oil over them. Put chicken, vegetables on top and pour sauce over them.

To make the Sauce Rouille: Process garlic cloves, hot peppers and olive oil in a blender. Sauté the chicken liver quickly in butter, mash and add to the mixture. Add 2 slices of potatoes from the stew, also 6 tablespoons of gravy, blend again.

Braised Stuffed Turkey

For Eight

10 lb. turkey
1 lb. veal, ground
½ lb. sweet Italian sausage
⅓ cup bacon, diced
2 eggs, lightly beaten
½ cup grated Romano
   cheese
1 cup boiled chestnuts,
   peeled and mashed
turkey giblets, boiled
   and chopped

1 cup bread croutons
¼ cup dry vermouth
salt and pepper to taste
pinch of grated nutmeg
4 tbsp. butter
3 slices prosciutto ham
½ tsp. rosemary
1 pinch thyme
1 tsp. juniper berries
¾ cup dry white wine
1 tbsp. flour
1 cup chicken broth

Strip the sausage meat out of the casing, break it up and blend with veal, bacon, eggs, croutons, cheese, chestnuts, giblets, vermouth, salt, pepper and nutmeg. Stuff the turkey with this mixture and close the opening. Heat butter in a large heavy pot or Dutch oven, put the turkey in the pot and brown on all sides. Then put prosciutto over the turkey breast, add rosemary, thyme, juniper berries and wine, cover and cook over gentle heat for about 4 hours or until done. Baste quite frequently. When done, remove turkey to hot serving dish. Blend flour into sauce and add enough chicken broth to make a gravy. Simmer until thickened.

Chicken Pörkölt

For Four

1 frying chicken about
   3½ lbs, cut up
1 cup chopped onion
1 tbsp. lard or butter
1 clove garlic, mashed
1 tbsp. tomato puree

1 tbsp. paprika
salt to taste
2 firm ripe tomatoes,
   peeled, seeded, chopped
1 large green pepper,
   seeded and diced

Heat lard in a heavy saucepan, add onion and sauté for a few minutes until onion is soft and transparent; do not let brown. Add tomato puree, garlic, paprika and salt; mix, add chicken pieces, cover and cook gently for 15 minutes. Add tomatoes and green pepper, cover again and cook 30 minutes longer or until chicken is done. There should be enough juice in the pan even without any addition of liquid. However, if necessary, add a few tablespoons of broth or water during cooking.

Chicken Teriyaki

For Four

2 whole chicken breasts,
   boned
½ cup soy sauce
½ cup mirin*
   (or dry sherry)
½ cup soy sauce

1 clove garlic, minced
2 tsp. sugar
salt to taste
pinch of cayenne pepper
1 tsp. grated fresh ginger
3 tbsp. sesame or
   cooking oil

Cut whole chicken breasts in half, and cut the halves crosswise in two. Place chicken in a bowl. Place 1 tablespoon oil and all other ingredients in a saucepan and bring to a boil. Remove from heat immediately and pour over chicken pieces. Coat the pieces well with the sauce, let stand for half an hour. Turn the pieces in the marinade a couple of times.

Drain chicken and pat dry, reserve the marinade. Heat 2 tablespoons oil in a heavy skillet, put in chicken pieces, skin side down; sauté until browned, turn and brown the other side. Drain off oil, add half the marinade to the skillet, cover and simmer over low heat for about 15 minutes until the chicken is almost cooked. Uncover, cook for 5 to 7 minutes longer until the chicken looks nicely glazed and the liquid in the skillet has thickened.

The chicken can also be prepared in the oven. Oil a baking dish, put chicken pieces into it, bake in 400° oven for 15 minutes, turn and bake another 10 minutes. Discard oil in the pan, coat the chicken with ample marinade, return to oven. Turn heat down to 350° and bake for another 15 minutes or so until the chicken is tender and well glazed. Baste a few times while baking.

*See Glossary

Turkey Casserole

For Six

1 small young turkey
   (about 6 lbs.) cut in
   serving pieces
1 tbsp. paprika
2 large cloves garlic,
   crushed
salt and coarsely ground
   pepper to taste
1 tsp. Dijon mustard
½ cup wine vinegar
2 tbsp. lemon juice

2 bay leaves
4 tbsp. olive oil
4 tbsp. butter
½ cup chopped onions
2 cups chicken broth
2 green peppers, seeded
   and sliced
¼ cup canned pimientos,
   sliced
12 large pitted olives,
   sliced

Place the turkey pieces in a bowl. Blend paprika, garlic, salt and pepper, mustard and lemon juice and rub this mixture into the turkey pieces. Add vinegar and bay leaves, mix again and let stand for two or three hours. Then drain the turkey, sauté in combined oil and butter until golden brown on all sides, add onions, stir and sauté 2 or 3 minutes longer. Add chicken broth, cover and cook slowly for about 2 hours or until meat is tender. Add all other ingredients and simmer 15 more minutes.

Chicken and ◁Cashew Nuts

For Four
2 whole chicken breasts,
  skinned and boned
1½ tbsp. cornstarch
3 tbsp. sherry
3 thin slices, ginger root, minced
2 stalks celery, white part only,
  minced
3 scallions, cut in ¼ inch lengths
⅓ cup onions, chopped
1 clove garlic, minced
4 tbsp. soy sauce
2 tbsp. sherry
1½ tsp. sesame oil
2 tsp. sugar
⅓ cup chicken broth
4 tbsp. oil
⅓ cup roasted cashew nuts
2 tsp. cornstarch
1½ tbsp. water

Cut chicken breast in medium cubes. Put the cubes in a bowl and mix them with the combined 1½ tablespoons cornstarch and 3 tablespoons sherry. Heat 3 tablespoons oil in a wok and stir-fry chicken cubes for about 3 minutes until chicken takes on color. Remove chicken and keep warm. Add remaining oil to wok, combine ginger, celery, scallions, onion and garlic and stir-fry for 2 minutes. Add cashews, stir for a few seconds. Return chicken to wok, add combined soy sauce, sherry, sesame oil, broth and sugar and stir until heated through. Dilute cornstarch with water, add to wok and stir until thickened.

Pungent Chicken

For Four
2½ lb. chicken, cut
  in serving pieces
2 tbsp. oil
1 large onion, sliced thin
3 large cloves garlic, halved
1 cup chicken broth

1 cup white vinegar
2 tbsp. sugar
1 tbsp. shredded fresh ginger
½ tsp. ground coriander
½ tsp. turmeric
½ tsp. hot red pepper flakes
salt to taste

Heat oil in a saucepan, add onion and sauté until light golden, add garlic and sauté for another minute. Add all other ingredients, mix well, bring to a boil, then cook gently for about half an hour until chicken is tender. Serve hot with rice, or chilled with vegetable relish.

Rolled Breast of Chicken ▷

For Four
2 tbsp. onion, minced
2 cloves garlic, minced
2 tbsp. oil
4 sweet Italian sausages
¼ cup fresh white breadcrumbs
1 tbsp. parsley, chopped
1 tsp. tarragon
salt and pepper to taste
2 large whole chicken breasts
2 tbsp. butter
½ cup dry white wine

Have chicken breasts skinned, boned and halved, and then cut horizontally in half. You will then have 8 pieces of thin chicken, the shape and size of half a chicken breast.

Heat oil in a skillet, add onion and garlic and sauté for 1 minute. Strip sausage meat out of the casing, add to skillet and cook for about 8 minutes until well browned. Break up any lumps. Remove sausage, onions and garlic with a slotted spoon, and discard all but 1 tablespoon of fat. Mix sausage, onion, garlic with breadcrumbs, parsley, tarragon, salt and pepper and put a pat of this stuffing on each of the chicken pieces. Roll them up, tuck in the ends and secure with toothpicks or tie with thread. Add butter to skillet, sauté the chicken rolls for 2 or 3 minutes until browned on all sides. Remove rolls to a hot serving platter and remove thread or toothpicks. Add wine to skillet, deglaze quickly and pour sauce over chicken.

Orange Roasted Chicken

For Six
1 (5 lb.) roasting chicken
¼ cup butter, melted
salt and pepper
½ tsp. dried rosemary

2 oranges, cut in half
¼ cup cornstarch
2 cups orange juice
1 cup chicken broth
1 tbsp. brown sugar

Brush chicken with butter; season with salt, pepper and rosemary. Place oranges in chicken cavity. Roast in 325⁰ oven about 2½ hours. Remove chicken from pan. Sprinkle cornstarch into pan. Stir and cook over medium heat just until smooth; remove from heat. Gradually stir in orange juice, chicken broth and brown sugar until smooth. Bring to boil over medium heat, stirring constantly; boil 2 minutes. Serve sauce with chicken.

Chicken Tetrazzini

For Six

12 oz. spaghetti
1 medium onion, chopped
¼ cup butter
¼ cup flour
1½ cups chicken broth
1 cup cream
salt and pepper to taste

½ cup dry vermouth
¾ cup grated Parmesan
   cheese
½ lb. mushrooms, sliced
2 tbsp. butter
3 cups cooked chicken
   meat, cut up

Cook spaghetti *al dente*. Drain.

Meanwhile, in saucepan sauté onion in ¼ cup butter until almost tender; stir in flour. Gradually add broth and cream. Cook over low heat, stirring constantly, until sauce boils. Add salt, pepper, vermouth and ¼ cup of the cheese; set aside. In large skillet sauté mushrooms in 2 tablespoons butter until brown. Combine spaghetti, mushrooms and chicken in 2½ quart shallow casserole; pour sauce on top. Sprinkle with remaining cheese. Bake in 375⁰ oven for 20 minutes or until bubbling.

Chicken Granada

For Six

3 lbs. chicken pieces
   (breasts and thighs)
2 tsp. paprika
2 tsp. garlic salt
2 tsp. celery salt
1 cup rice
1½ cups hot chicken broth
2 tsp. lemon juice
½ tsp. Tabasco sauce
2 tbsp. parsley, chopped
salt and pepper to taste
⅓ cup sliced stuffed Spanish olives

Season chicken pieces with paprika, garlic and celery salts. Put in a shallow casserole and bake, skin side up, in a 425⁰ oven for 20 minutes. Remove chicken from casserole, add all other ingredients except olives, mix well, place chicken on top of rice, cover and bake at 350⁰ for 30 minutes or until chicken is tender and all liquid is absorbed. Garnish with sliced olives.

Duck à la Vasco da Gama

For Four
1 duck (5 lbs.)
⅓ cup sugar
¼ cup vinegar
2 cups chicken broth, or
  stock made with duck
  giblets and back

salt and pepper to taste
2 tbsp. cornstarch
  diluted in 2 tbsp. water
2 tbsp. red currant jelly
juice of 1 orange
2 tbsp. curaçao
6 oranges

Season the duck cavity with salt and pepper and truss the bird. Prick the lower breast and thighs with a fork to allow fat to escape. Roast the duck in a preheated 350° oven for 1¼ hours or until the juice runs clear when the thigh is pricked with a fork.

While the duck is roasting make the sauce: In a heavy saucepan make a light caramel by stirring the sugar over low heat until it melts. Add the vinegar and hot chicken broth. Stir and simmer for 3 minutes, then add cornstarch and simmer for 5 minutes. Finally stir in the currant jelly, orange juice and curaçao. Keep hot over low heat.

Prepare the oranges: Peel the zest (skin) from four of the oranges. (There must be no white membrane.) Cut zest into julienne strips, blanch them in boiling water to cover for 3 minutes and drain. Using a very sharp knife cut off the white part from these four oranges, cut out the sections so that they are skinless. Set aside both the orange strips and the sections until the duck is ready. Use the remaining two oranges to make baskets as shown in illustration on opposite page.

When the duck is fully cooked, place it on a hot serving dish, arrange the orange sections around it and put an orange basket at each end. Sprinkle the orange strips over the bird and coat with the sauce.

Broiled Savory Chicken

For Four
2 broiling chickens, split,
  breastbone removed
1 tbsp. salt
2 tbsp. paprika
¼ tsp. crushed hot red
  pepper

3 tbsp. oil
1 clove garlic, crushed
3 tbsp. hot chili peppers
  (canned) diced
½ cup lime juice
1 onion, sliced paper thin
sprigs of parsley

Have butcher flatten the chicken halves with a cleaver. Wipe chicken with a damp cloth. Combine salt, paprika, hot pepper and oil, and rub into the chicken. Place chicken in a shallow dish. Combine garlic, chili peppers and the lime juice, pour over chicken. Place in refrigerator and marinate overnight. Turn the chicken a couple of times.

Remove from refrigerator a couple of hours before cooking. Broil over charcoal, basting with the marinade and turning it frequently until done. Garnish with onion slices and parsley.

Roast Stuffed Duck

For Four
1 duck, about 5 lbs.
salt
3 large potatoes
6 small white onions
1 tbsp. butter

¼ cup light cream
½ tsp. marjoram
salt and pepper to taste
1 tbsp. flour
½ cup water or chicken
  broth

Boil potatoes, peel and rice. Peel onions, boil until soft. Combine riced potatoes, cooked onions, butter, cream and marjoram, season with salt and pepper.

Wipe duck inside and out with a damp cloth. Season outside with salt. Stuff duck with potato mixture, truss and close opening. Put in roasting pan, add ½ cup of hot water and roast at 350° for 1½ to 2 hours until meat is soft. Skim off fat frequently and baste often with pan juices. Add more water to pan as needed. Remove cooked duck, skim off all fat from pan, stir in flour, add water or broth, blend and simmer for a few minutes until gravy has thickened.

Chicken Piemontese

For Four

2 tbsp. dried Italian
   mushrooms
½ cup hot water
one 4-lb. frying chicken,
   cut in serving pieces
2 tbsp. butter
1 tbsp. olive oil
2 tbsp. brandy

¾ cup chopped onion
1 large clove garlic, minced
1 small green pepper,
   seeded and diced
½ cup diced celery stalk
½ tsp. basil
½ tsp. rosemary
salt and pepper to taste
½ cup tomato puree

Wash mushrooms, put in a bowl and soak in half cup of hot water for an hour before starting to cook. Heat butter and oil in a saucepan, sauté chicken pieces until nicely browned, then pour brandy into the pan and flame. Remove chicken and keep warm. Put onion and garlic in the pan, sauté for two minutes, then add mushrooms and the water they soaked in, along with all other ingredients. Stir well, bring to a boil, return chicken to pan. Cover and simmer for about 45 minutes until chicken is done. If sauce is too thin reduce quickly before serving.

Roast Duck Cantonese

For Six

1 duck (5 lbs.)
salt
1 large clove garlic, minced
1½ tsp. minced fresh
   ginger root
2 scallions, minced
2 tbsp. soy sauce

2 tbsp. sherry
1 cup chicken broth
¼ tsp. allspice
3 tbsp. honey
2 tbsp. soy sauce
1 tbsp. vinegar
½ cup chicken broth

Wipe the duck, inside and out, with a damp cloth, then dry with paper towels. Rub the duck lightly, inside and out, with salt. Let stand for 15 minutes, then dry again. Combine garlic, ginger, scallions, 2 tablespoons soy sauce,

sherry, chicken broth and allspice in a saucepan. Let come to a boil, take off heat and cool slightly. Sew up the neck cavity of the duck to make it as leakproof as possible. Stand duck, neck down, in a bowl and pour the hot liquid in the cavity. Truss the opening tightly. Place duck on a rack in a roasting pan, cover bottom with an inch or so of water. Put duck in a preheated 375° oven for 20 minutes. Combine remaining soy sauce, honey, vinegar and chicken broth. Reduce heat to 325° and roast duck 1½ hours, basting every 15 minutes with the honey mixture. When done, remove from oven, let stand 10 minutes, then remove skewers and let liquid run from cavity into a bowl. Carve and spoon the sauce over the portions.

Chicken Curry

For Four
2½ lbs. chicken, cut
   in serving pieces
salt to taste
4 tbsp. butter
1 large onion, sliced
   paper thin

2 cloves garlic, minced
1 tsp. curry powder
pinch of cayenne pepper
½ tsp. powdered turmeric
¼ tsp. powdered cardamom
1 tsp. grated fresh ginger
2 cups coconut milk*

Season chicken with salt. Heat butter in a skillet or saucepan, add onion and sauté gently until onion is soft and translucent. Remove onion slices with a slotted spoon and reserve. Add garlic, curry, cayenne, turmeric, cardamom and ginger; mix and sauté gently for 2 minutes. Add chicken and sauté until lightly browned on all sides. Add onion slices and coconut milk, cover and simmer for about 25 minutes or until chicken is tender. Uncover the skillet, cook a few minutes longer to reduce the sauce. Serve with rice, chutney or any condiments desired.

*See Glossary

Turkey Mole

For Eight
1 small young turkey
   (about 7 lbs.)

For the sauce:
4 large tomatoes, peeled
   and seeded
2 green peppers, seeded
   and chopped
4 cloves garlic, chopped
1 fried stale tortilla
   (or 1 slice white toast)
½ cup blanched almonds
¼ cup raisins
¼ cup peanuts

1 tbsp. salt
⅓ cup olive oil
1 onion stuck with 2 cloves

2 tbsp. sesame seed
½ tsp. coriander seed
½ tsp. anise seed
¼ tsp. ground cinnamon
¼ tsp. allspice
1½ tbsp. chili powder
2 ozs. unsweetened
   chocolate, grated
salt and pepper to taste
2 cups broth

Disjoint turkey and cut into serving pieces. Put the pieces in a saucepan, barely cover with water, add salt and onion stuck with cloves, bring to a boil and cover. Cook gently for about 1 hour, or until bird is nearly cooked. Remove turkey pieces, drain. Reserve 2 cups of the broth.

Heat half the olive oil in a skillet and sauté the turkey pieces until they are browned on all sides.

Put all other ingredients, except oil and broth in a blender and blend at medium speed until a paste is formed. Add a little water if necessary.

Heat the remaining oil, add the chocolate mixture, blend well and simmer for a minute, stirring constantly, add broth and blend well. The sauce should have the consistency of heavy cream. Place turkey pieces in a heavy saucepan, spoon sauce over it and cook gently for another hour or until tender.

Roast Goose

For Four to Six
1 young goose (about 8 lbs.)
salt and pepper
pinch of ginger (opt.)

Stuffing:
2 large onions, chopped
2 large tart apples, cored,
   peeled and chopped
1½ tsp. salt

1 clove garlic
2 tbsp. flour
1 cup hot water

3½ to 4 cups dry
   breadcrumbs
½ tsp. pepper
   (or to taste)
½ tsp. marjoram

Wipe the goose inside and out with a damp cloth. Season inside and out with salt, pepper and ginger, and rub with garlic. Combine all stuffing ingredients, stuff the goose, truss and close the cavity. Place the bird on a rack in a roasting pan, breast side down. Add ½ cup water to the pan and roast in 325° oven for about 3½ to 4 hours or until the meat on breast and legs is tender. After 2 hours of roasting turn the goose breast side up. Remove accumulated fat from pan every hour or so. If the goose is fat, it does not need any basting. When the bird is done, remove to a serving platter; remove all but 2 tablespoons of fat from roasting pan, stir in flour, add hot water, stir until smooth, and simmer for a couple of minutes to make pan gravy.

Coq au Vin de Pomerol ⇨

For Six

2 tbsp. oil
4 tbsp. butter
20 tiny white onions
¼ lb. bacon, cut into
  thin strips
1 chicken (4 lbs.)
¼ cup brandy
1 bottle Pomerol or
  good Burgundy wine

salt and pepper to taste
1 tbsp. sugar
4 tbsp. flour
2 cloves garlic, mashed
bouquet garni* (parsley,
  tarragon, small bay leaf)
10 mushroom caps
2 tbsp. minced parsley
  and chives

Heat half the oil and half the butter in a casserole, sauté the onions until they are about to take on color, add the bacon strips. Blend and cook over low heat until onions are tender and the bacon transparent.

Cut the chicken in eight pieces. Remove onions and bacon with a slotted spoon and reserve. Brown the chicken pieces in the casserole on all sides. Season with salt and pepper, sprinkle with brandy and flame. Heat the wine and sugar in a separate saucepan. Sprinkle the flour over the chicken and then add the hot wine to the casserole, along with the garlic and the bouquet garni. Simmer covered over low heat for about 40 minutes.

Sauté the mushroom caps in the remaining butter and oil in a skillet for about 5 minutes. Reserve them with the onions and bacon.

When the chicken is fully cooked, discard the bouquet garni, add mushrooms, onions and bacon. Heat through, transfer everything to serving platter, sprinkle with parsley and chives. Garnish the platter with fried slices of bread.

*See Glossary

Chicken Taos ◁ with Rice

For Six

12 pieces (about 2 lbs.)
  choice chicken parts
¼ cup flour
salt and pepper to taste
¼ cup butter
1 cup chopped onions
1 clove garlic, minced
2 tbsp. Worcestershire sauce
1 cup chili sauce
1½ cups chicken broth
½ cup dry sherry
3 cups hot cooked rice

Roll chicken in combined flour, salt and pepper. Brown in butter. Push chicken to one side. Add onions and garlic; sauté until transparent. Stir in remaining ingredients except rice. Bring to a boil, cover, reduce heat and simmer for 35 minutes. If desired, thicken sauce with 2 tablespoons flour blended with ¼ cup water. Serve chicken and sauce over bed of fluffy rice.

Pheasant in Sour Cream

For Four to Six

2 young pheasants
¼ lb. salt pork
1 small carrot, peeled
  and sliced
½ parsley root, peeled
  and sliced
2 stalks celery, white part,
  sliced

1 tbsp. onion, minced
4 tbsp. butter
1 cup chicken broth
1 small pinch thyme
½ small bay leaf
1 cup sour cream
1 tbsp. flour
salt and pepper to taste

Clean pheasants inside and out with a damp cloth. Salt cavity lightly, season outside with salt and pepper. Truss the birds and cover breasts with slices of salt pork.

In a small roasting pan sauté carrot, parsley root, celery and onion in butter until vegetables start to take on color. Add thyme and bay leaf. Place pheasants on top, add ⅓ cup broth and roast in 375° oven for about an hour, until birds are tender. Timing depends on the size and age of the birds. Baste frequently with pan juices and add more broth to the pan as needed. Five minutes before serving remove birds to hot platter, remove trussing strings. Skim fat off pan gravy. Blend sour cream, flour and ½ cup broth, add to pan gravy and simmer for a few minutes. Strain sauce and serve separately.

Braised Chicken

For Four

1 3½-lb. chicken
3 tbsp. flour
6 tbsp. butter
½ cup dry white wine
1 small clove garlic, crushed

4 medium-sized ripe
  tomatoes
½ tsp. dried rosemary,
  crushed
salt and pepper to taste

Wash chicken, dry inside and out, and truss. Sprinkle with flour. Heat butter in a heavy saucepan, sauté chicken until nicely browned on all sides. Add all other ingredients, cover and cook gently for about 1 hour or until chicken is tender.

Chicken Livers Paprika

For Four

1 lb. chicken livers
1 medium onion,
  thinly sliced
4 tbsp. butter

½ tbsp. paprika
pepper to taste
¾ cup sour cream
1 tbsp. flour
salt to taste

Trim livers and cut in half. Heat butter in a skillet, sauté onion slices until light brown. Add chicken livers, paprika and pepper; sauté, stirring frequently until the livers are browned. When blood starts to run out of the livers they are done. Blend sour cream and flour, add to the livers, stir well and heat through. Simmer for 2 minutes. Season with salt just before serving.

Chicken Livers Marsala

For Four

1 lb. chicken livers
salt and pepper
1 tsp. fresh sage
  (½ tsp. dried)

4 tbsp. butter
2 slices lean bacon, diced
¼ cup dry marsala wine
toast triangles

Trim livers and cut them in half. Season with sage, salt and pepper. Heat butter in skillet, add diced bacon, sauté for one minute, then add chicken livers and cook over medium flame for 3 or 4 minutes, turning them once or twice. When browned, remove to a hot serving platter, add marsala to skillet, stir to deglaze pan and simmer sauce for 2 minutes. Arrange livers on toast triangles, pour the sauce over them and serve.

Bean Sprout Salad

For Four

1 lb. fresh bean sprouts
2 tbsp. soy sauce
1 tbsp. mirin*
1 tbsp. oil

salt to taste (if needed)
1 tsp. toasted sesame seed*
3 tbsp. rice (or cider)
  vinegar

Wash bean sprouts, drain, put in a bowl. Cover with boiling water and let stand for a minute. Drain well, cover with ice water and let stand for 5 minutes. Drain. Blend all other ingredients and toss with bean sprouts.

*See Glossary

Cauliflower Nicoise

For Four to Six

1 firm cauliflower
6 tbsp. olive oil
1½ tbsp. white wine
  vinegar
1 tbsp. lemon juice
12 ripe black olives,
  coarsely chopped

6 anchovy filets, chopped
3 tbsp. pimiento, chopped
2 tbsp. chopped parsley
1 tbsp. capers, drained,
  chopped
salt and pepper to taste
sliced, peeled tomatoes

Wash cauliflower, separate florets and trim off stems. Cook in boiling salted water for about 5 minutes, drain well and chill. Combine all other ingredients except sliced tomato, mix with cauliflower and let marinate for 2 or 3 hours. Put in a serving bowl, garnish with sliced tomatoes and serve.

Mexican Corn

For Four

1½ cups fresh sweet corn,
  cut from cob
2 medium ripe tomatoes,
  peeled, seeded and
  chopped
½ cup chopped green
  pepper
3 tbsp. minced onion

2 tbsp. butter
1 tbsp. flour
1 tbsp. chili powder
salt and pepper to taste
1 cup sharp cheddar
  cheese, grated
½ cup pitted ripe
  olives, sliced

Heat butter and sauté onion and pepper until tender. Add flour, chili powder, salt and pepper, stir and simmer for a minute. Add corn, tomatoes, bring to a simmer and cook for a few minutes until the corn is done. Add a little water if mixture is too dry. Stir in grated cheese and olives, stir and heat until cheese melts and serve.

Spanish Rice ◁ Salad

For Six to Eight
3 cups cooked rice
  (cooked in chicken broth)
1 cup diced green peppers
1 cup chopped celery
3 tbsp. minced onion
¼ cup chopped pimiento
½ cup Italian salad dressing
4 tomatoes, peeled and cut into
  wedges

Combine rice, green peppers, celery, onion and pimiento. Mix well. Chill. When ready to serve, pour dressing over rice-vegetable mixture. Toss lightly. Spoon onto salad plate and surround with tomatoes.

French Potato Salad

For Four
6 medium potatoes (the
  waxy kind, like russets)
salt and pepper to taste
⅓ cup olive oil
4 tbsp. hot water
  (or chicken broth)
3 tbsp. vinegar
1 tsp. Dijon mustard
2 tbsp. grated onion
2 tbsp. parsley, chopped
2 tsp. capers, squeezed
  dry and chopped

Boil potatoes until cooked but still somewhat firm. Peel and slice thin. Sprinkle with oil, vinegar, season with salt and pepper, turn carefully with a wooden spoon and fork. Mix mustard with hot water, add, along with onion, capers and parsley, to potatoes. Blend carefully once more and let stand for an hour or two. Do not refrigerate. This potato salad should be served at room temperature.

Mixed Vegetable Salad ▷

For Eight
1 cup diced cooked
  potatoes
1½ cups cooked sliced
  carrots
1½ cups cooked whole or
  cut green beans (fresh,
  frozen or canned)
1½ cups cooked green peas
  (fresh, frozen or canned)
1 cup sliced celery
1 cup sliced or diced
  cooked beets
1 small onion, chopped
2 hard-boiled eggs,
  chopped
¾ cup small Spanish
  stuffed green olives
Boston lettuce
¾ cup mayonnaise
¼ cup chili sauce
1 tsp. lemon juice

Chill vegetables, eggs and olives separately, then arrange in lettuce-lined salad bowl. Combine remaining ingredients. Just before serving, toss salad with dressing.

Asparagus Milanese

For Four
2 lbs. fresh asparagus
salt and white pepper
  to taste

4 to 5 tbsp. butter
1 tbsp. lemon juice
¾ cup grated Parmesan
  cheese

Trim asparagus, snap off tough ends, peel and tie in bundles. Fill a narrow high pan with enough water to cover two thirds of the bundled asparagus, but leave the upper third and tips out of the water. Bring water to a boil, add asparagus and cover. Cook for 10 to 15 minutes, depending on the thickness of the stalks, until the tip of a knife pierces the stalks easily. Do not overcook. Drain and cool the cooked stalks.

Butter the bottom of an oblong baking dish, place a row of asparagus in the dish, sprinkle with salt, pepper, Parmesan and dot with butter. Cover this layer with another row of asparagus, arrange the tips to face away from those in the bottom row. Sprinkle again with salt, pepper, Parmesan, dot with butter. Repeat until all asparagus have been used. Sprinkle top layer with a good amount of cheese, dot with butter and sprinkle with lemon juice. Bake in 425° oven for about 15 minutes until top is golden brown.

Celeriac a la Grecque (Knob Celery)

2 large firm celery
  knobs
juice of 1 lemon
2 carrots, peeled, diced
2 medium onions, diced
5 tbsp. olive oil
2 cups dry white wine

4 black peppercorns,
  crushed
salt to taste
6 coriander seeds
1 bouquet garni*
1 lemon peeled, sliced
1 cup water

Peel the knob celery, cut in ¾-inch dice, sprinkle with lemon juice to prevent discoloring. Let stand for 15 minutes.

Heat 2 tablespoons oil in a saucepan, add carrots and onion and cook gently for 10 minutes. Add the celery, mix well. Add wine and water, salt, peppercorns, coriander, bouquet garni and sliced lemon. Cover and cook over medium heat for about 15 minutes until celery is barely tender.

Drain the vegetables and discard the bouquet garni. Boil the cooking liquid over high heat until it is reduced to about 1 cup. Remove from fire, add the remaining olive oil and the cooked vegetables and let stand for 2 hours. Chill well before serving.

*See Glossary

Braised Lettuce

For Four
4 heads Boston or bibb
  lettuce
4 very thin slices of
  salt pork
1 thinly sliced onion

1 large carrot, thinly sliced
3 cups beef broth
1 tbsp. meat extract
  (Bovril or similar)
2 sprigs parsley
pepper to taste

Trim off outer lettuce leaves, wash well and blanch heads in boiling water for 5 minutes. Remove, drain and wash under cold running water. Squeeze gently to remove water, shape the heads neatly and wrap a slice of salt pork around each head. Put onions and carrot in a heavy saucepan, place lettuce on top, add parsley, pepper, beef broth and meat extract. Bring to a boil, cover and cook in a pre-heated 350° oven for 1 hour. Remove the lettuce, squeeze into uniform shapes. Reduce sauce very quickly and spoon some of it over the lettuce. Finish with a pat of butter on each.

The hearts of romaine are also excellent when braised. After blanching, fold each in half and then proceed as above.

Broccoli Palermo

For Four

1 bunch broccoli
1 Bermuda onion, sliced thin
1 sweet red pepper, seeded and cut into narrow strips
½ cup minced prosciutto ham
¼ cup olive oil
½ cup Provolone cheese, diced fine
salt and pepper to taste
⅔ cup dry white wine
12 pimiento-stuffed green olives, sliced

Wash broccoli and trim off coarse stems. Put in a bowl, pour boiling water over broccoli, let stand for 2 minutes, drain and cool. Cut broccoli in thin slices.

Put one tablespoon olive oil in a saucepan, cover the bottom of the pan with a thin layer of sliced onions, a few sliced olives and a sprinkle of prosciutto. Then add a layer of broccoli, season with salt and pepper, sprinkle with oil and diced cheese. Repeat until all ingredients have been used up. Place pepper strips on top, pour remaining oil over the top; add the wine, cover and cook gently for about half an hour until broccoli is done.

Eggplant Imam Bayildi

For Four

2 medium sized eggplants
1 large onion, quartered and then thinly sliced
2 tomatoes, peeled, seeded and coarsely chopped
½ cup parsley, chopped
1 clove garlic, minced
1 large green pepper, seeded and chopped
½ cup olive oil
salt and pepper to taste
1 tbsp. lemon juice
1 cup water

Cut eggplants lengthwise in half, salt the cut surface and let stand for 15 minutes.

Heat oil in a skillet, sauté onion and pepper until they are soft, add tomato, parsley, garlic and lemon juice, season with salt and pepper, mix well and sauté for 5 minutes.

Rinse eggplant, pat dry. Remove vegetables from skillet and sauté eggplant lightly on both sides in the remaining oil. Make 2 slits down the cut side of each eggplant half, spread the slits and stuff with the sautéed vegetables. Put eggplants in a casserole, add water, cover tightly and cook for about 45 minutes over medium heat until eggplants are soft. Add a little more water during cooking if needed. Serve cold.

Potatoes au Gratin

For Six

2 lbs. waxy potatoes
2½ cups milk
½ cup light cream
1 large egg
salt and pepper to taste
pinch of mace
¾ cup Gruyère cheese, grated
¼ cup Parmesan, grated
1 clove of garlic
3 tbsp. butter

Peel the raw potatoes, grate them on the coarse side of a vegetable grater (or use a mechanical shredder or food processor) into a pan filled with cold water. Drain potatoes. Fill the pan again with water, wash the potatoes well and drain again. Simmer them in milk for about 5 minutes, taking care not to scorch the milk. Drain and reserve the milk. Beat the egg until light and creamy, add salt, pepper, mace and half of the mixed grated cheeses. Slowly add milk and cream and whisk until well blended. Mix in the potatoes. Rub the inside of a shallow baking dish with the garlic, butter it well and fill with potato mixture. Even the surface, sprinkle with remaining cheese and dot with butter. Bake in preheated 400⁰ oven for 25 minutes until golden brown.

Olive Potato Salad

For Eight

1 lb. shrimp, cooked
   and peeled
3 lbs. potatoes, cooked,
   peeled and sliced
¾ cup chopped stuffed
   green olives
½ cup chopped ham
¼ cup chopped Spanish
   onion

½ medium cucumber,
   peeled and diced
½ cup olive or
   salad oil
⅓ cup wine vinegar
salt and pepper
tomato slices
cucumber slices
whole stuffed green olives

Reserve 8 shrimp for garnish; chop remainder. In large bowl, combine chopped shrimp, sliced potatoes, chopped olives, ham, onion and diced cucumber. Add oil, vinegar and salt and pepper to taste; toss gently to mix well. Cover and chill until serving time. Turn salad into serving dish; garnish with reserved shrimp, tomato slices, cucumber slices and whole olives.

Avocado Salad Acapulco

For One

¼ cup diced cooked lobster meat
¼ cup shredded heart of romaine
   lettuce
1 tsp. capers
2 tbsp. mayonnaise
salt and freshly ground pepper
½ large avocado
juice of ½ lemon
1 round slice lobster meat
   from the tail
1 tsp. minced parsley
paprika

Mix the diced lobster with the shredded romaine and the capers, combine the salad with the mayonnaise and season with salt and pepper.

Cut the desired number of avocados lengthwise in half, remove the pits. Fill each cavity with the lobster salad, sprinkle with lemon juice and top with round slice of lobster meat. Sprinkle with chopped parsley and paprika. Serve well chilled.

Cucumber Salad

For Four
3 medium cucumbers
1½ tbsp. salt
1 clove garlic, mashed

1 tsp. paprika
2 tbsp. olive oil
1 tbsp. vinegar
1 tsp. fresh dill, chopped

Peel cucumbers, slice as thin as possible. Put in a bowl, add salt and garlic and mix very well. Chill for 2 or 3 hours. Press handfuls of sliced cucumbers, express and discard as much moisture as possible. Add olive oil, vinegar and dill, mix well. Sprinkle with paprika and serve.

For a variation, prepare cucumbers as above, but instead of oil and vinegar, blend with ½ cup of yoghurt.

Three Bean Salad

For Six
1 can chick peas, drained
1 can lima beans, drained
1 can kidney beans, drained
1 small onion, minced
⅓ cup canned pimento, diced
3 scallions, chopped

2 anchovy filets, mashed
1 clove garlic, mashed
salt and pepper to taste
½ tsp. oregano
½ tsp. basil
1 tbsp. parsley, minced
5 tbsp. olive oil
1½ tbsp. vinegar

Put peas, beans, onion, pimento and scallions in a bowl. Blend all other ingredients, pour over vegetables and mix well. Let stand for an hour or so before serving.

Mashed Potatoes Milanese

For Four

4 cups boiled potatoes
5 tbsp. butter
⅓ cup milk

⅔ cup grated Parmesan
    cheese
salt and pepper to taste

Mash hot potatoes, add butter and milk, whisk until they are quite fluffy. Add salt and pepper and ½ cup of Parmesan. Whisk until well mixed. Put mixture in a buttered gratin or soufflé dish. Do not fill to the top since the potatoes will fluff up during baking. Sprinkle top with remaining cheese and bake in 375° oven for about 15 minutes until nicely browned.

Fried Plantains

For Four

2 plantains (cooking
    bananas) or under-ripe
    bananas
¼ cup lemon juice
3 eggs

¼ cup flour
3 tbsp. milk
½ tsp. salt
⅛ tsp. pepper
½ tsp. chili powder
oil for frying

Peel plantains and cut lengthwise in half. Brush each half with lemon juice.

Prepare batter: beat egg yolks until creamy, beat egg whites stiff. Mix flour, salt, pepper, chili powder with the egg yolks, fold in egg whites.

Put oil about 1 inch deep in a heavy skillet, heat over medium flame. Coat plantain halves with batter and fry them, two at a time until browned on both sides. Drain and serve.

Eggplant with Vegetable Stuffing

For Six

2 cups cooked rice
3 medium eggplants
1 large tomato, peeled,
    seeded and chopped
1 medium onion, grated
1 clove garlic, crushed
4 tbsp. parsley, chopped
1 green pepper, seeded
    and chopped

1 tbsp. pine nuts
1 tbsp. currants
1 tsp. mint, chopped
1 tsp. sugar
1 tsp. lemon juice
salt and pepper to taste
2 large firm tomatoes,
    peeled and sliced
water
3 tbsp. butter

Cut eggplants lengthwise in half and hollow out with a sharp knife and a spoon, leaving a shell about ¼ inch thick. Discard pulp. Mix all ingredients except sliced tomatoes, water and butter, stuff the eggplant shells ¾ full. Place the sliced tomatoes in the bottom of a saucepan, arrange eggplants on top, sprinkle with a little more salt and dot with butter. Add enough water to half cover eggplant, bring to a boil, cover tightly and cook gently for half an hour. Uncover and continue cooking for 15 minutes until sauce has thickened. Serve hot or cold.

Mexican Succotash (Colache)

For Six

¼ cup butter
1 lb. zucchini, sliced
1 green pepper,
    seeded and diced
¼ cup canned pimiento,
    diced

½ cup chopped onion
2 large tomatoes, peeled,
    seeded and coarsely
    chopped
1½ cups fresh corn,
    cut off the cob
salt and pepper to taste

Sauté onion in butter until light golden, add all vegetables, salt and pepper, cover and simmer until vegetables are tender. If liquid is needed during cooking, add a little chicken broth or water.

◊ Moussaka

For Six
2 medium eggplants
5 tbsp. olive oil
1 large onion, chopped
¾ lb. ground beef or lamb
1 tbsp. tomato paste
pinch of cinnamon
1 tomato, peeled, seeded
    and chopped
2 tbsp. parsley, chopped
salt and pepper to taste
¼ cup beef broth (or water)
2 tbsp. butter
2 tbsp. flour
1 cup hot milk
1 egg yolk
pinch of grated nutmeg

Cut stem end off eggplant, discard. Slice eggplant thinly, sprinkle with salt and put in a colander, weigh down with a heavy plate and let drain for 1 hour. Squeeze, rinse with cold water, pat dry.

Heat 3 tablespoons oil in a skillet, sauté eggplant slices on both sides until light golden. Remove from skillet and reserve. Add remaining oil to skillet, add onion, sauté until light golden, add meat, cook while stirring until browned. Stir in tomato paste, cinnamon, chopped tomato and parsley, season with salt and pepper, add broth, cover and simmer for 15 minutes. Put a layer of eggplant slices in a baking dish, spread some of the meat mixture on top, another layer of eggplant and continue until all ingredients are used up. Finish with a layer of eggplant.

Melt butter in a small saucepan, add flour, stir and cook for 2 minutes — do not let brown. Gradually add hot milk, stir constantly and simmer while stirring until mixture is smooth. Add nutmeg. Mix egg yolk with a little of this white sauce, remove sauce from fire and blend in egg yolk until smooth. Season with salt and pepper. Pour over eggplant and bake at 350⁰ for about 50 minutes until the top is golden brown.

Green Peas à la Francaise

For Four

3 tbsp. butter
⅓ cup lean salt pork,
    blanched and diced
1 heart of romaine lettuce,
    washed and shredded
12 very small white onions

¾ cup chicken broth
2 cups green peas
1 tsp. sugar
small pinch of thyme
2 sprigs of parsley
salt and pepper to taste

Heat butter in a saucepan, add the diced salt pork and sauté, stirring often, for 10 minutes. Add the shredded lettuce and sauté 5 minutes longer. Then add all other ingredients, cover pan and simmer for 6 minutes. Uncover, and cook until the liquid has evaporated and the onions and peas are cooked. Shake the pan occasionally.

Sub Gum Vegetables ⊳

For Four
1 green pepper
1 carrot
1 medium onion
3 stalks celery (white part
   only) sliced ½ inch thick
5 medium firm, fresh mushrooms
4 water chestnuts
½ cup bamboo shoots
3 scallions
½ cup bean sprouts, washed and
   dried
1 thin slice ginger root, shredded
1 clove garlic, minced
4 tbsp. oil
½ tsp. salt
3 tbsp. water
2 tbsp. soy sauce
1 tbsp. sherry
1 tsp. sugar
¼ tsp. sesame oil
1 tbsp. cornstarch
2 tbsp. water

Remove seeds and membrane from pepper, cut into 2 inch diamond shapes. Slice carrot into ¼ inch rounds. Cut onion lengthwise in half and the halves in ½ inch strips. Cut bamboo shoots and water chestnuts in ¼ inch slices, scallions into 1 inch pieces. Slice mushrooms ¼ inch thick.

   Heat 2 tablespoons oil and salt in wok, stir-fry pepper and onion for half a minute. Remove and keep warm. Add another tablespoon of oil and stir-fry mushrooms and celery for 1 minute. Add bean sprouts and stir-fry 1 minute more. Remove from pan and keep warm. Add another tablespoon of oil to wok, fry carrot, bamboo shoots, ginger root, scallions, garlic and water chestnuts for 2 minutes. Add water, soy sauce, sherry, sugar and sesame oil, bring to a boil, return all vegetables to wok, heat to boiling and cook covered for 2 minutes. Dilute cornstarch with water, stir in until thickened.

Parmesan Potatoes

For Four
4 large potatoes, peeled
  and diced small
2 tbsp. butter
1 tbsp. beef extract
  (Bovril or other)
3 tbsp. water

salt and pepper to taste
pinch of grated nutmeg
pinch of thyme
⅓ cup beef broth
4 tbsp. melted butter
½ cup grated Parmesan
  cheese

Heat 2 tablespoons butter in a saucepan, add potatoes, stir well, cover and cook for about 10 to 15 minutes, until just soft. Blend beef extract with water, add to potatoes; also broth, salt, pepper, nutmeg and thyme; blend well. Put potatoes in a buttered baking dish, cover top with melted butter, sprinkle with Parmesan and bake at 425⁰ for about 12 minutes until top is golden brown.

Sunomono (Pickled Cucumber)

For Four
1 firm cucumber
3 tbsp. rice (or cider) vinegar

1 tbsp. water
salt to taste
2 tsp. sugar
½ tsp. grated fresh ginger

Peel cucumber, cut lengthwise in half, scoop out seed. Cut crosswise in very thin slices. Blend all other ingredients and mix with sliced cucumber. Let stand for one or two hours. Serve chilled as a side dish with meats or fish.

Eggplant Parmigiana

For Four
2 medium eggplants
2 eggs beaten with 2 tbsp. milk
2 cups fine dry white breadcrumbs
1½ cups Italian tomato sauce (below)

¾ cup olive oil
1 tsp. basil
½ tsp. oregano
4 tbsp. grated Parmesan cheese
½ lb. mozarella cheese, thinly sliced
salt and pepper to taste

Combine ⅔ cup breadcrumbs with basil, oregano and Parmesan and reserve. Slice eggplants about ½ inch thick. Dip in beaten egg and coat with unflavored breadcrumbs. Fry slices in hot oil until browned on both sides. Remove from pan, drain on paper towel. Place a layer of slices in the bottom of a baking dish, spread tomato sauce over it, season with salt and pepper and sprinkle with the breadcrumb-cheese mixture. Repeat until all eggplant slices have been used. Cover top with tomato sauce and sliced mozarella and bake in 400° oven for about 15 minutes until cheese has melted and is bubbly.

Italian Tomato Sauce

Six Cups
3 tbsp. olive oil
1 cup minced onion
2 cloves garlic, minced
2½ cups canned Italian tomatoes
½ cup tomato paste (small can)
1½ cups chicken broth (or water)

1 tsp. dried basil
¼ tsp. thyme
½ tsp. rosemary
1 bay leaf
1 tsp. sugar
1 tsp. vinegar
salt and pepper to taste
½ cup dry white wine (opt.)

Heat oil in a saucepan, add onion and garlic and sauté until onion is soft. Add all other ingredients, stir well and simmer for 45 minutes. Strain and reheat before serving.

Tomatoes Provençale

For Four
4 ripe, firm tomatoes
salt and pepper to taste
1 tbsp. parsley, chopped

1 large clove garlic, crushed
¾ cup dry white breadcrumbs
6 tbsp. olive oil

Halve the tomatoes, squeeze out gently the seeds and most of the water. Season the halves with salt and pepper. Mix parsley, garlic and breadcrumbs and spread some on the tomato halves. Then sprinkle them with olive oil. Arrange on baking dish and bake in 450° oven for about 10 minutes until browned or finish browning them under the broiler.

Mushrooms à la Lyonnaise

For Four

1 lb. firm mushrooms,
   sliced
3 tbsp. butter
1 tsp. lemon juice
1 clove garlic, chopped

1 tbsp. onion, minced
1 large tomato, peeled,
   seeded and chopped
1 tbsp. parsley, chopped
salt and pepper to taste

Heat butter, add sliced mushrooms, lemon juice, garlic and onion. Mix and sauté for a minute, then add tomato, and cook until liquid has evaporated. Stir in parsley, season with salt and pepper and serve.

Japanese Spinach Salad

For Six

2 lbs. fresh spinach
¼ cup sesame seeds
¼ cup Japanese soy sauce

2 tsp. sugar
2 tbsp. rice vinegar
2 tbsp. peanut oil

Wash spinach, remove wilted leaves, trim off coarse stems. Cook in a small amount of water until barely tender — a minute or so. Drain well, chill. Toast sesame seeds in a skillet until they are light brown and start popping. Remove from fire, crush with the back of a spoon and combine with all remaining ingredients. Add to the cooked spinach, mix lightly and serve.

Gazpacho Salad

For Four to Six
1¼ cups beef broth
1½ envelopes unflavored
    gelatine
⅔ cup water
¾ cup sliced Spanish
    stuffed green olives
1 cup diced cucumber,
    unpeeled
1 cup diced tomato

½ cup diced green pepper
½ cup diced celery
¼ cup sliced scallions
1 can (4 oz.) pimiento,
    drained and chopped
⅛ tsp. salt
⅓ cup Italian dressing
hard-boiled egg slices
sliced stuffed green
    olives

Combine broth and gelatine in saucepan; let stand 5 minutes. Stir over low heat until gelatine dissolves. Add ⅔ cup water and chill until mixture is the consistency of unbeaten egg white. Combine sliced olives, vegetables and salt with dressing; fold into chilled mixture. Turn into 1½-quart mold; chill until firm. Unmold and garnish with egg and olive slices.

Onion and Tomato Salad

For Four
1 large sweet onion
    (Bermuda or Spanish)
1 tbsp. salt
3 firm ripe tomatoes,
    peeled, seeded and cut
    in thick slices
4 tbsp. oil

3 tbsp. lemon juice
2 tbsp. parsley, chopped
pepper to taste
rolled filets of anchovy
1 small green pepper,
    seeded and sliced into
    rings

Peel onion, cut lengthwise in half, slice halves crosswise very thin. Sprinkle with salt, let stand for half an hour, then knead the onion slices for a couple of minutes with your hands. Place in a strainer, rinse well with cold water, drain and squeeze with your hands to remove most of the liquid. Put onions in a flat serving bowl, arrange tomato slices on top. Blend oil, lemon juice, parsley and pepper, pour over tomatoes. Garnish with anchovy rolls and pepper rings before serving.

Curried Potato Salad

For Six
¼ cup simple vinaigrette
    dressing (p. 315)
1 tsp. curry powder
    (or to taste)
4 cups diced cooked
    potatoes

½ clove garlic, mashed
½ cup diced celery
⅔ cup diced green pepper
¼ cup sliced scallions
½ cup mayonnaise
3 hard-boiled eggs

Combine garlic and curry powder with the vinaigrette, pour over the cold diced potatoes and blend gently. Chill for 2 hours. Combine with all other ingredients except eggs, place in a serving bowl, garnish with quartered eggs.

Tomato Salad

For Four
4 large firm ripe tomatoes
1 medium onion, minced
1 tbsp. salt

2 tbsp. parsley, chopped
3 tbsp. oil
1½ tbsp. vinegar
pepper to taste

Peel tomatoes, slice them about ½ inch thick, put in a deep plate, mix gently with minced onion, sprinkle with salt and let stand for an hour. Drain off liquid, sprinkle with parsley. Blend oil, vinegar and pepper, pour over tomatoes, let stand for 15 minutes before serving.

Note: The salad can be chilled, of course, but the flavor of real ripe tomatoes comes through best when not too cold.

Spring Salad with Asparagus Tips

▷

For each person:
1 large artichoke heart
6 asparagus tips, peeled
6 leaves Boston or other
   lettuce
1 thin slice of liver
   pâté (opt.)
2 tbsp. pine nuts
6 leaves of Belgian endive,
   cut in strips

½ cup finely shredded
   red cabbage
1 small celery heart,
   cut in thin strips
¼ cup shelled walnuts
1 tbsp. parsley, chopped
1 lemon
mayonnaise
oil and vinegar salad
   dressing

This salad is served to each person on two plates.

Cook the artichoke hearts and the asparagus in boiling salted water until just tender. Line 2 plates with lettuce leaves. Trim the artichoke heart, remove the inner leaves and the "choke" and put it in the center of one plate. Top with a slice of liver pâté. Around it arrange the asparagus tips, pine nuts and Belgian endive. On the other plate place the strips of celery heart, the red cabbage and the walnuts. Sprinkle with parsley. Scoop out the lemon, fill the shell with mayonnaise, and put it in the middle of the plate. Serve with oil and vinegar dressing on the side to be used liberally on both plates.

Potatoes in Dill Sauce

For Four
1½ lbs. small new
   potatoes
4 tbsp. butter
2 tbsp. flour
1¼ cups chicken broth
   (or water)

1 egg yolk
⅓ cup plain yoghurt
1 tsp. lemon juice
½ cup fresh dill,
   minced
salt and pepper to taste

Wash potatoes, boil in water until just done, peel and keep hot. Heat butter in a saucepan, stir in flour and cook while stirring until light brown. Add dill, mix well and gradually add broth, stirring until the sauce is smooth and has thickened. Beat egg yolk until light, add while beating, a little of the hot sauce. Blend egg mixture into yoghurt. Remove sauce from fire, blend in yoghurt and egg mixture, season with salt and pepper, add lemon juice. Return potatoes to sauce, heat through without letting the sauce boil.

Caesar Salad

For Four
2 firm heads romaine
   lettuce
¼ cup minced parsley
¼ cup grated Parmesan
   cheese
6 slices bacon, sautéed
   until crisp

1 cup diced bread,
   fried in the bacon
   fat until golden brown
10 anchovy filets, coarsely
   chopped
3 hard-boiled eggs,
   quartered

Wash, dry and chill the lettuce. Blend all the dressing ingredients in a large salad bowl. Break the lettuce into pieces, put on top of the dressing in the bowl. Scatter the fried bread croutons and the broken up slices of bacon on top, sprinkle with grated cheese and parsley. Toss the salad, garnish with egg quarters and sprinkle the egg with chopped anchovy.

Dressing:
½ cup olive oil
½ tsp. Dijon mustard
¼ tsp. dry mustard
½ tsp. sugar
2 tbsp. white wine vinegar

1 small clove garlic,
   mashed
1 tbsp. lemon juice
salt and ample pepper
   to taste

◁ # Garden Salad

For Six

1 lb. firm ripe tomatoes, sliced
2 large green peppers, seeded and cut in rings
2 medium cucumbers, peeled and sliced thin
3 tbsp. oil

1 large sweet onion, sliced thin
2 tbsp. vinegar
½ tsp. sugar
1 tsp. dill, chopped
1 tbsp. parsley, chopped
salt and pepper to taste

Combine oil, vinegar, sugar, dill, parsley, salt and pepper. Put the vegetables in a bowl, blend with dressing.

Mushroom Salad

For Six to Eight

2 lbs. firm fresh mushrooms
1 cup green peppers, minced
1 small onion, minced
1 small clove garlic, mashed with salt (opt.)

1 tbsp. vinegar
1 tbsp. lemon juice
salt and pepper to taste
¾ cup sour cream
1 tbsp. parsley, minced
1 tsp. paprika

Trim mushrooms, blanch for 2 minutes in boiling water, drain well. If mushrooms are small, leave whole — quarter or halve them if they are large. Mix with onion, garlic and green pepper, then add lemon juice, vinegar, season with salt and pepper. Blend well with sour cream, sprinkle with parsley and paprika when serving.

Cucumber Salad ▷

For Four

2 large cucumbers
1½ tbsp. salt
1 clove garlic, crushed
½ tsp. sugar
4 tbsp. white wine vinegar
1 tsp. paprika

Peel cucumbers and slice them very thin. Put in a bowl, add garlic, mix well with salt and let stand for one or two hours. The cucumbers will have released quite a bit of liquid. Press them well and discard the liquid. Blend with sugar and vinegar, sprinkle with paprika and chill for an hour.

Note: Sour cream or plain yoghurt can be blended into the cucumbers with or instead of the vinegar.

Rice/Pasta

To flavor plain boiled rice, cook it in meat broth; add tomato paste or juice; add various herbs or spices to the cooking water — herbs whose flavor will complement the dish you serve the rice with — tarragon with chicken for instance; or add orange juice to the cooking water if the rice is to be served with pork or ham — grated lemon rind when fish is the main course.

A little lemon juice in the cooking water will keep the rice whiter.

Rice yields: 1 cup uncooked white rice yields 3 cups cooked, enough for 4. 1 cup brown rice yields 3 to 4 cups cooked.

To Cook Pasta

Always use a sufficient amount of water — at least 5 quarts. Have water boiling briskly in a large pot, add about 2 tablespoons of salt for each pound of pasta. Cooking time depends on the thickness and size of the pasta.

As a general suggestion, the cooking time for

Spaghettini: 10 to 12 minutes

Spaghetti: 15 to 18 minutes

Noodles: 10 to 12 minutes, depending on size and thickness

Macaroni: 15 to 20 minutes

Pasta should never be overcooked, but served "al dente" — cooked, but a bit chewy. The best test whether that stage has been reached is to take a strand of pasta out of the pot and bite into it. If it gives a slight resistance to the teeth but has no raw dough taste, the pasta is cooked. Remove pot from fire, add quickly enough cold water to stop the boiling, but not enough to cool the pasta, drain well and serve with sauce of your choice.

Note: 8 ounces of pasta will be sufficient for 3 to 4 people.

Plain Cooked Rice

Cooking perfect rice is very simple and easy and the result so much better than any "convenience" product can provide.

There are probably nearly as many ideas about how to cook a perfect rice as there are rice varieties. Each country in the world has different methods. Some boil rice in a great amount of water, some with very little liquid, some steam the rice, others cook it in the oven. There are those who wash the rice before boiling; in Italy and Spain rice is usually sautéed in butter or oil before the cooking liquid is added — and so on.

For plain boiled rice, I prefer to wash the rice. Place it in a strainer and wash under cold running water, working it with your hands for a minute or so. This removes some of the surface starch.

To cook plain rice:
Boiling Method
1 cup rice
2 cups water or broth
salt to taste

Put washed rice in a saucepan (the pan should not be too large). Add the liquid. The liquid should stand about 1 inch over the rice. Bring to a boil. Stir once, cover and lower heat. Cook over gentle heat for about 15 to 16 minutes until liquid is absorbed and rice is tender. Do not stir while cooking. Remove from heat, let stand covered for 2 or 3 minutes before serving.

Sauté Method
1 tbsp. fat or butter
1 cup rice
2 cups broth

Heat fat, add unwashed rice and sauté while stirring constantly until grains are well coated with fat, become translucent and just start to take on color. Be careful not to scorch the rice. Add liquid, let come to a quick boil, cover and cook over low heat until done.

Rice Pilaf
Wash rice, cook in meat broth until done. Remove from fire, top with a few pats of butter, cover and place in a 325⁰ oven for a few minutes until the rice is dry.

Creole Rice Omelette

For Six

6 eggs, beaten
¼ cup water
½ tsp. salt
1 tbsp. butter

3 slices (4″ x 4″) Swiss
   cheese
¼ cup stuffed olives,
   sliced

Creole Sauce:

¼ cup minced onion
¼ cup slivered green pepper
2 tbsp. butter
salt and pepper to taste

1 can (8 oz.) tomato
   sauce
1½ cups hot cooked
   rice

Combine eggs, water and salt, Melt butter in 10 inch skillet until hot. Pour in egg mixture. Stir rapidly with a fork until it begins to set. Smooth surface of eggs. Spoon on sauce; top with cheese. Continue cooking until just set and cheese melts. Garnish with sliced olives.

For Creole Sauce: Sauté onion and green pepper in butter until tender crisp. Add tomato sauce and seasonings; simmer 5 minutes. Stir in cooked rice.

Rice Parmesan

For Six

3 cups hot cooked rice, cooked in
   chicken broth
1 can (4 oz.) sliced mushrooms,
   drained
1 cup cooked green peas
2 tbsp. butter, melted
salt and pepper to taste
⅓ cup grated Parmesan cheese
3 tbsp. chopped parsley

Combine hot rice, mushrooms, peas, butter and seasonings. Heat until vegetables are hot, about 3 or 4 minutes. Add Parmesan cheese, toss lightly. Garnish with chopped parsley.

Basic Risotto and Cheese

For Four to Six

6 cups chicken broth
5 tbsp. butter
2 tbsp. minced onion
1 small clove garlic,
   minced

1½ cups rice
¼ tsp. saffron
½ cup grated Parmesan
   cheese
salt and pepper to taste

Heat the chicken broth and keep it simmering. Heat 4 tablespoons butter in a heavy saucepan, add onions and garlic and sauté until onion is transparent and limp. Do not let brown. Add the unwashed rice and stir until the rice is well coated with butter and translucent. Add ½ cup hot broth and cook while stirring, until the liquid is absorbed.

Then add another half cup of liquid, keep stirring; when that has been absorbed add more and continue cooking while stirring, taking care that no rice sticks to the bottom of the pan. After using 2 or 3 cups, add saffron to remaining broth, season with salt and pepper and continue the cooking procedure as above until the rice is cooked but still firm. About 20 to 25 minutes should do it. There might be some broth left over — the exact quantity of broth needed for a risotto is hard to measure; it depends on the quality of the rice, cooking temperature and other factors.

About 5 minutes before the rice is ready to be served, add the remaining tablespoon of butter and the cheese, blend well and finish cooking. The risotto should be creamy but not runny.

Risotto Milanese

For Six

6 cups chicken broth
6 tbsp. butter
2 tbsp. minced onion
2 tbsp. beef marrow
   (opt.)

1½ cups rice
¾ cup dry white wine
¼ tsp. saffron threads
salt and pepper to taste
⅔ cup Parmesan cheese,
   grated

Heat chicken broth and keep simmering. Combine saffron with a little hot chicken broth and reserve. Heat 3 tablespoons butter in a heavy saucepan, add onion and diced beef marrow and sauté until onion is limp and translucent. Add rice and stir until rice is well coated with butter and translucent. Add wine and saffron; cook and stir until liquid is nearly absorbed, then continue cooking as for Basic Risotto (above). When rice is nearly done, stir in remaining butter and the grated cheese and finish cooking.

Fish Risotto

For Four

1 lb. cod or halibut
salt
1 tbsp. lemon juice
4 tbsp. butter
2¾ cups chicken broth
   or water

2 tbsp. grated onion
1¼ cups rice
1 tbsp. tomato paste
salt and pepper to taste
¼ cup grated Parmesan
   cheese
1 tbsp. chopped parsley

Skin fish, remove bones and cut into bite-sized cubes. Sprinkle with a little salt and lemon juice and let stand for half an hour. Heat butter in a saucepan, add onion and sauté for 2 or 3 minutes. Add rice and sauté while stirring until rice is well coated with butter and translucent. Add fish, broth, tomato paste, salt and pepper; bring to a simmer, cover and cook in oven at 325° for about half an hour until rice is done. Remove from oven, mix half of the cheese lightly into the rice, using a fork, sprinkle top with remaining cheese and parsley and serve.

Eight Precious Fried Rice

For Six

4 cups cooked rice, cold
3 eggs, beaten with
   1 tbsp. water
3 tbsp. oil
3 scallions, chopped
8 medium raw shrimp,
   shelled, deveined
   and chopped
½ cup raw diced chicken
   breast
½ cup diced lean pork

½ cup smoked ham,
   diced
4 fresh mushrooms,
   chopped
2 water chestnuts, thinly
   sliced
2 bamboo shoots, diced
½ cup cooked peas
1 tbsp. soy sauce
1 tbsp. sherry
1 tsp. salt

Heat oil in wok, add scallions, stir-fry half a minute. Add pork, stir-fry 2 minutes until all traces of pink have disappeared. Add chicken, ham and mushrooms, fry for 1 minute. Add shrimp, water chestnuts and bamboo shoots, stir-fry for another minute. Add rice, blend well and fry 1 minute. Add peas, soy sauce, sherry and salt, blend and fry until hot. Add eggs, blend quickly and stir-fry until they are just starting to set.

Indonesian Fried Rice (Nasi Goreng)

For Six

4 cups boiled rice
4 eggs
salt and pepper to taste
5 tbsp. oil
1 cup shrimp, peeled,
   diced
1 clove garlic, minced

1 cup cooked pork
   or beef, cut in
   julienne strips
1 medium onion, minced
cayenne pepper to taste
3 scallions, chopped
1 cucumber, thinly sliced

Beat eggs, season with salt and pepper. Heat 1 tablespoon oil in a skillet and make an omelette with 2 eggs. Do not fold, slide onto a plate and reserve. Repeat process and make another omelette with remaining eggs. Heat 2 tablespoons oil in a wok. Stir fry onion and garlic until lightly browned and soft. Add shrimp and meat and stir fry for 2 minutes. Add cayenne pepper, scallions, the remaining oil and rice. Mix well and stir fry until mixture is very hot. Put rice mixture on a heated serving dish, garnish with shredded omelette and cucumber slices.

Simple Chinese Fried Rice

For Four

4 cups cold cooked rice
1 cup cooked meat (roast
   pork, chicken or other;
   or cooked shellfish) diced
1 cup fresh vegetables,
   sliced or diced
2 eggs, lightly beaten

4 scallions, cut in small
   pieces
4 tbsp. oil
2 tbsp. soy sauce
1 tbsp. sherry
½ tsp. sugar
salt and pepper to taste

Heat 2 tablespoons oil in a wok, add scallions, stir-fry a few seconds, add vegetables and stir-fry a minute or two until they are somewhat softened. Add meat or shellfish, blend well and fry until hot. Remove vegetables and meat from wok and keep warm. Add remaining oil to wok, heat until quite hot, add rice (be sure that the grains are separate and that there are no lumps), stir-fry quickly until all grains are coated with oil. Return meat and vegetables to wok, blend well with a spoon or spatula. Mix in soy sauce, sherry, sugar, salt and pepper. Fold in eggs and cook until they just begin to set. Serve immediately.

Barbecued One-Dish Meal ▽

For Six

1 lb. smoked link sausage
1 can (16 oz.) cut
    green beans
1 tbsp. bacon drippings or
    vegetable oil
1 tsp. prepared mustard

1 cup chopped onions
¾ cup ketchup
2 tbsp. brown sugar
1½ tsp. liquid smoke (opt.)
2 bouillon cubes
3 cups cooked rice

Cover and cook sausage in ½ cup water about 5 minutes. Remove from water and cut in 1-inch pieces. Drain beans, reserving liquid. Sauté onions in bacon drippings. Add ½ cup bean liquid and remaining ingredients except rice. Simmer to 10 minutes. Stir in rice. Season to taste. Cover and continue simmering 20 minutes.

◁   # Paella

For Six

¼ cup olive oil
1 frying chicken (2½ lbs.)
    cut in pieces
1 lb. chorizo sausages, parboiled
    and cut in 1 inch pieces
¾ cup onion, chopped
2 cloves garlic, crushed
1½ cups rice
2 cups chicken broth
2 cans (5 oz. each) whole baby clams
¼ tsp. Spanish saffron
salt and pepper to taste
1 package frozen artichoke hearts,
    partially thawed
2 ripe tomatoes, peeled and cut in
    thin wedges
1 cup small whole pimiento-stuffed
    green Spanish olives
1 lb. shrimp, peeled, deveined, and
    cooked for about 3 minutes

Heat oil in a 4-quart paella pan or a 13-inch skillet. Add chicken and chorizos and sauté until chicken is browned on all sides. Remove chicken and sausage and pour off all but 2 tablespoons of the fat. Add onion and garlic, sauté until soft, then add rice and sauté over gentle heat for about 2 or 3 minutes until rice is coated with oil and transparent. Stir constantly. Add chicken broth, the juice from the clams, the saffron, salt and pepper. Bring to a boil, stir well and return chicken and chorizos to pan, stir and simmer for about 25 minutes, stirring occasionally. If needed, add more broth to prevent sticking.

Stir in artichoke hearts, olives and tomatoes, cook for 5 minutes then add shrimp and drained clams, stir and cook for 5 more minutes until all ingredients are hot.

Basic Fried Rice

For Four

4 cups cooked rice, cold
3 eggs, lightly beaten
    with 1 tbsp. water
salt to taste

2 tbsp. oil
3 scallions, cut in
    ½ inch pieces
2 tbsp. soy sauce
1 tbsp. sherry

Stir rice with a fork to separate grains and break up lumps. Heat oil in wok, add salt and stir-fry scallions for 30 seconds. Add the rice and stir-fry until hot and each grain is coated with oil. Add eggs and stir-fry quickly until well blended and the eggs are nearly set. Blend in soy sauce and sherry. Serve piping hot.

Vegetarian Fried Rice

For Four

1 clove garlic, minced
½ cup fresh mushrooms,
    sliced
½ cup bean sprouts,
    washed and blanched
½ cup onions, chopped
½ cup green peppers,
    diced small

¼ cup pimento (canned),
    chopped
2 scallions, chopped
2 eggs, beaten
4 cups cooked, cold rice
4 tbsp. oil
2 tbsp. soy sauce
1 tsp. salt
pepper to taste

Heat 2 tablespoons oil in a wok, add garlic and stir-fry for a few seconds; add onions and bean sprouts, fry for 2 minutes; add peppers and scallions, fry for 1 minute; add mushrooms and pimento and stir-fry 2 more minutes. Remove vegetables and keep warm. Add remaining oil to pan and heat. Break up rice so that there are no chunks and the grains are separated, add to pan along with soy sauce, pepper and salt. Stir-fry until well heated. Return vegetables, stir well and heat through. Fold in beaten eggs and stir until they are about set.

Island Rice

For Four

3 tbsp. butter
3 tbsp. minced onion
1 small clove garlic,
    minced
2 tsp. grated orange peel
½ tsp. ground ginger

¼ tsp. sage
salt and pepper to taste
½ cup orange juice
2 cups chicken broth
1 cup long grained rice
1½ tbsp. chopped parsley

Heat butter in a saucepan, add onion and garlic and sauté until light golden. Add orange peel, ginger, sage, salt and pepper, orange juice and chicken broth. Bring to a boil. Add rice and parsley, stir once to mix; cover tightly and simmer for 20 minutes until rice is tender and liquid has been absorbed. Serve with ham or roast pork.

Rice and Mushrooms (Song-i-pahb)

For Six to Eight

2 cups Carolina rice
1 cup sliced fresh
    mushrooms
1 cup thinly sliced onion
½ cup shredded or
    ground lean sirloin or
    round steak

3 cups cold water
2 tbsp. light soy sauce
pepper to taste
1½ tbsp. oil
1½ tbsp. toasted sesame
    seed*
salt to taste

Place rice in a strainer, wash under running water until water runs clear, drain and place in a saucepan. Heat oil in a wok or skillet, sauté mushrooms, onion and beef for 2 minutes while stirring. Add all other ingredients except rice and water and sauté another minute. Combine with rice, add water, mix well, bring to a rapid boil. Cover tightly, reduce heat to a bare simmer and cook for 30 minutes. Do not uncover while cooking.

*See Glossary

Plain Curried Rice

For Four

2 cups chicken broth
2 tsp. curry powder
(or to taste)
½ tsp. turmeric

salt to taste
1 cup long grain rice
½ cup seedless raisins
(plumped in hot water)
1 tbsp. butter

Heat chicken broth in a saucepan, add curry powder, turmeric and salt, bring to a boil and simmer for 5 minutes. Add the dry rice, cover and cook gently for about 20 minutes until rice is tender and liquid has been absorbed. Add raisins and butter, toss lightly with a fork and serve.

Bayou Jambalaya

For Six

1 tbsp. bacon fat or lard
1 cup chopped onion
½ lb. small breakfast
sausages
½ lb. smoked ham
(not cooked), cut
in 1-inch strips
1 large tomato, peeled,
seeded, chopped
(or ¾ cup canned)

½ green pepper, chopped
1 clove garlic, crushed
¼ tsp. hot red pepper
flakes (or to taste)
1½ tbsp. chopped parsley
¼ tsp. thyme
½ bay leaf
2 cups chicken broth
¾ cup long grain rice
12 shucked oysters, drained
salt and pepper to taste

Heat fat in a saucepan, add onion, sausages and ham. Sauté until well browned. Add tomatoes, green pepper, garlic, red pepper, parsley, thyme and bay leaf. Stir and sauté 5 minutes longer. Add broth, bring to a boil, cover and simmer 2 or 3 minutes.

Wash rice under running cold water, add to the boiling sauce, stir well, cover and cook gently for 15 to 18 minutes until rice is tender. Add oysters and simmer uncovered until their edges curl. Correct seasoning and serve.

Broccoli and Rice Quiche   ⇨

For Six

3 cups hot cooked rice
1½ cups (6 oz.) grated
    sharp cheddar cheese
6 eggs
1 tsp. salt
½ cup chopped onions

2 packages (10 oz. *each*)
    frozen chopped broccoli
½ cup milk
¼ tsp. pepper
1 can (4 oz.) sliced
    mushrooms, drained

Combine rice, ¾ cup of the cheese, 2 eggs, slightly beaten, and ½ teaspoon salt. Press firmly and evenly over bottom and sides of a greased 12-inch pizza pan or two 9-inch pie pans. Set aside. Add onions to broccoli and cook according to package directions. Drain well. Beat remaining eggs slightly. Stir in milk, pepper, mushrooms, and remaining salt. Add to broccoli and mix well. Spoon into crust. Bake at 375° for 20 minutes. Sprinkle with remaining cheese. Bake 10 minutes longer. Cool a few minutes before cutting into wedges.

⇩ # Brown Rice Lyonnaise

For Six

1 cup sliced onion
2 tbsp. oil
3 cups cooked brown rice (cooked in
    chicken broth)
¼ cup canned pimientos, diced
salt and pepper to taste

Heat oil in a skillet, sauté onion until golden brown, add rice and pimiento, season with salt and pepper. Sauté while stirring occasionally over low heat until rice is thoroughly heated.

Plain White Rice Pilaf

For Four

1 cup long grain rice
1¾ cups broth or water (approx.)
4 tbsp. butter
salt and pepper to taste

Place rice in a sieve, rinse well under cold running water, working it for a minute or so with your hands.

Place broth and butter in a saucepan, bring to a boil, add rice, salt and pepper. The liquid should stand about 1 inch over the rice. Bring to a boil again, cover tightly and cook rapidly for 5 minutes. Turn heat as low as possible, simmer rice for about 20 minutes longer, until all liquid has been absorbed and rice is cooked. Never stir while rice is cooking. Remove lid, cover pan with a napkin, replace lid and let stand in a warm place for 15 minutes before serving.

Curried Rice au Gratin

For Six
3 cups hot cooked
    long grain rice
1 ½ cups grated sharp
    cheddar cheese

3 tbsp. butter
½ tsp. curry powder
pinch of cayenne pepper
1 cup diced white bread,
    crumbled

Toss rice with half the cheese, spoon into a buttered baking dish, top with remaining cheese. Bake at 350° for 10 to 15 minutes until cheese melts. Meanwhile heat butter in a skillet, stir in curry and cayenne, add breadcrumbs and brown very lightly while stirring. Remove rice from oven, sprinkle with curried crumbs.

Saffron Chicken Pilaf

For Four
1 frying chicken (2½ lbs.)
salt and pepper to taste
3 tbsp. butter
1 large onion, thinly
    sliced
3 tbsp. currants

3 tbsp. chopped walnuts
¾ cup green peas
2 tbsp. chopped parsley
¼ tsp. Spanish saffron
    threads
1 cup long grain rice
2 cups chicken broth

Cut up chicken, remove and discard skin. Bone the chicken and cut meat into even strips. (You may prefer to buy chicken breasts and thighs instead of a whole chicken.) Season meat with salt and pepper.

Heat butter in a heavy saucepan, sauté onions until light golden brown, add chicken and sauté 1 minute. Add currants, walnuts, peas, parsley and saffron, mix well and sauté while stirring for 2 minutes. Add rice, cook and stir one minute longer until rice is coated with butter. Add hot chicken broth, bring to a boil, stir and mix with a long tined fork, cover tightly and cook over low heat for about 20 minutes until all liquid has been absorbed and rice is tender. Place pan in a preheated 275° oven for 15 minutes before serving.

Stuffed Tomatoes

For Six
6 large, very firm
    tomatoes
salt
1 large onion, grated
¾ cup olive oil
¼ cup parsley, chopped
3 tbsp. fresh dill, chopped

¼ cup currants
¼ cup pine nuts
½ cup raw rice
salt and pepper to taste
1 tsp. lemon juice
¼ cup chicken broth
    (or water)

Slice a cap off the stem end of the tomatoes, scoop out pulp. Sprinkle inside of tomatoes with a little salt, save caps.

Sauté onion in 3 tablespoons oil until quite soft. Remove from fire, mix well with ⅓ cup oil, parsley, dill, currants, pine nuts and rice, season with salt and pepper and add lemon juice. Stuff the tomatoes with this mixture — do not fill too full since rice will expand in cooking. Cover tomatoes with sliced off caps, place in a deep baking dish or casserole, add remaining oil and broth to pan. Cover tomatoes with a plate to weigh them down, cover pan and cook gently for about 30 minutes until rice is cooked.

Serve well chilled.

Lemon Pilaf

1 cup celery, sliced
6 to 8 scallions, sliced
(green and white parts)
3 cups cooked long
grain rice

2 tbsp. butter
1 tbsp. grated lemon peel
½ tsp. lemon juice
salt and pepper to taste
1 tbsp. parsley, chopped

Heat butter in a skillet, sauté celery and scallions until soft. Add all other ingredients except parsley, toss lightly with 2 forks and sauté over low heat for a few minutes until hot. Stir in parsley, sauté one more minute. Serve with meats, chicken or fish.

Portuguese Rice and Chicken Livers

For Four
½ lb. chicken livers
2 tbsp. butter
salt and pepper to taste
4 tbsp. olive oil
⅔ cup minced onion
1 large clove garlic,
minced
1½ cups long grain rice

3 cups chicken broth
¾ cup tomato sauce
½ tsp. oregano
½ tsp. marjoram
pinch of thyme
1 tsp. vinegar
3 tbsp. minced parsley
pinch of cayenne pepper

Sauté chicken livers in butter for about 3 minutes until browned, but still a little pink inside. Season with salt and pepper, chop coarsely and keep warm.

Heat oil in a heavy saucepan, add onion and garlic and sauté until soft. Add rice, stir and sauté until rice is well coated with oil, translucent and just starts to take on color. Add hot broth and hot tomato sauce to rice, mix well and bring to a boil. Add all other ingredients except livers, mix well, cover and cook over medium heat for 10 minutes. Stir lightly with a fork, reduce heat, cover again and simmer for about 10 more minutes until liquid has been nearly absorbed. Mix in chicken livers, cover again and continue cooking until rice is dry and tender. Add more broth during cooking if needed.

Farmer's Paella

For Six
½ lb. smoked ham,
cut into strips
1 frying chicken, cut up,
parboiled for 10 minutes
½ lb. lean boneless lamb,
cubed
¼ lb. chorizos (Spanish
sausages), sliced

1 small onion, sliced
3 cloves garlic, sliced
1 bay leaf
¼ tsp. Spanish saffron
threads
½ tsp. crushed red pepper
2 cups long grain rice
6 to 8 cups chicken broth
salt and pepper to taste

Wash rice under running cold water. Put rice, 6 cups of broth and all other ingredients in a large saucepan or paella pan, mix well. Bring to a boil, cook over medium heat uncovered, stirring from time to time to keep food from sticking. Add more broth as the liquid evaporates. When rice is just about cooked, put pan in a 350° oven to finish cooking and dry out the rice.

Note: If Spanish sausages are not available, use sweet or hot Italian sausages instead.

◁

Macaroni Zucchini Casserole

2 cups elbow macaroni
  (8 oz.)
2 tbsp. butter or margarine
2 tbsp. flour
salt and pepper to taste
2 cups milk

1 cup cubed cheddar cheese
  (about 4 oz.)
1 cup cubed Swiss cheese
  (about 4 oz.)
1½ lbs. zucchini, sliced
  and cooked

Add macaroni to rapidly boiling water, cook uncovered, stirring occasionally, until tender. Drain.

Meanwhile, melt butter in saucepan; blend in flour, salt and pepper. Gradually add milk; cook, stirring constantly, until sauce boils 1 minute. Reduce heat. Add cheese; stir and heat until cheese melts. Spread half the macaroni over bottom of 3 quart casserole; top with half the zucchini and half the sauce. Repeat layers. Bake in 350° oven for 30 minutes. Sprinkle with buttered breadcrumbs, if desired.

Pilaf a la Grecque ▷

For Six
1 lb. lean ground beef
1 cup chopped onion
1 clove garlic, chopped
1 cup sliced celery
1½ cups thinly sliced carrots
1 can (16 oz.) tomatoes
1 tsp. oregano
salt and pepper to taste
1 package (10 oz.) frozen chopped
  spinach
3 cups cooked rice
lemon wedges optional
⅓ cup grated Parmesan cheese

Combine meat, onions, celery and carrots. Sauté until meat is lightly browned. Add tomatoes, seasonings and spinach. Cook over low heat until spinach has thawed and separates easily. Stir in rice; cover and simmer 15 to 20 minutes. Remove from heat; serve with lemons and Parmesan cheese.

Brown Rice

Brown rice takes longer to cook then white rice because of the higher fiber and oil content of the bran layer. Brown rice also requires more liquid in cooking because of the longer cooking time.

Brown rice expands during cooking like white rice, but the outside bran coating "explodes" and bran adheres to the cooked rice grain. Even when cooked the bran never gets as tender as the inner part of the grain and stays somewhat "crunchy".

To cook Brown Rice:

1 cup brown rice   salt to taste (about 1 tsp.)
2½ cups water or broth   1 tbsp. butter or oil

Combine ingredients in a saucepan, cover tightly. Bring to a rapid boil, stir once or twice and cover. Reduce heat and simmer for about 45 minutes until rice is tender and liquid absorbed.

Brown Rice and Curried Peas

For Four

1 cup brown rice	½ tsp. paprika
2 tbsp. butter	1 medium onion,
1 cup yellow split peas	sliced thin
1 scant tsp. curry powder	1 clove garlic, minced
¼ tsp. turmeric	salt and pepper to taste

Wash peas, drain, put in a saucepan with all other ingredients except brown rice and butter. Cover with about 2 inches of water, stir well and cook gently until peas are soft and the sauce is thickened. Add more water if needed and stir occasionally while cooking.

Cook brown rice (see above), drain, stir in butter. Put rice in a bowl, pour split pea sauce over it and serve.

Brown Rice and Mushrooms

For Six

2 cups sliced fresh	1 small clove garlic, minced
mushrooms	2 tbsp. oil
½ cup minced scallions	3 cups cooked brown rice
(green and white part)	(cooked in beef broth)
	salt and pepper to taste

Heat oil in a skillet, sauté mushrooms, scallions and garlic until soft. Stir in rice, season with salt and pepper and heat through, stirring a few times with a fork.

Stuffed Macaroni Marinara

For Four

1 lb. ground lean pork	¼ tsp. oregano
1 small onion, chopped	½ tsp. basil
1 egg	salt and pepper to taste
¼ cup milk	12 jumbo macaroni shells
½ cup soft white	2 cups marinara sauce
breadcrumbs	(p. 313)
	½ cup dry red wine

Sauté pork in a skillet over medium heat until lightly browned. Add onion and cook 2 minutes, stirring frequently. In a small bowl beat egg, milk, breadcrumbs, oregano, basil, salt and pepper until well blended. Stir egg mixture into pork and blend. Cook macaroni *al dente* and stuff shells with pork mixture.

Combine marinara sauce and wine, pour a small amount in a 9-inch square pan. Place shells in pan, pour remaining sauce over shells. Cover with foil and bake in 350⁰ oven 40 minutes or until hot and bubbly.

Spaghetti with Mussels ◇

For Four

3 doz. mussels, scrubbed
4 shallots, minced
1 small onion, minced
1 clove garlic, mashed
1 tsp. parsley, minced
1 cup dry white wine

3 peppercorns, crushed
2 tbsp. butter
2 tbsp. flour
½ cup heavy cream
2 egg yolks
1 lb. spaghetti
1 cup grated Parmesan cheese

Put the shallots, onion, garlic, and parsley into a kettle with the wine and the crushed peppercorns. Add the mussels, cover tightly and cook over high heat until the mussel shells are open, about 5 minutes. Remove from heat and cool to lukewarm. Drain the mussels and reserve all the liquid. Shell the mussels, being careful to save all the liquid that drains from the shells, and keep them barely warm. Boil the mussel liquid over moderate heat for 5 minutes and strain it twice through a very fine sieve or a triple layer of damp cheese cloth.

Heat the butter in a saucepan, stir in the flour and cook until golden. Stir in the strained liquid and simmer for 10 minutes. Beat together the heavy cream and the egg yolks and stir into the sauce off the heat. Return it to low heat, but do not let it boil or it will curdle.

Cook the spaghetti al dente. Drain carefully and toss quickly with the sauce. Add the reserved mussels and serve immediately with the grated cheese on the side.

Fettucine
◁ Alfredo

For Eight to Ten

¼ cup salt
8 to 12 qts. boiling water
2 lbs. medium egg noodles
1 lb. sweet butter, softened
4 cups freshly grated
   Parmesan cheese
1 cup heavy cream
   at room temperature
pepper to taste

Add ¼ cup salt to rapidly boiling water. Gradually add noodles. Cook uncovered, stirring occasionally, until tender. Drain in colander.

Place butter in hot 4-quart casserole; add noodles and toss gently. Add cheese and toss again. Pour in cream; toss. Sprinkle with freshly ground pepper.

Macaroni Milanese

For Four
½ lb. macaroni
6 tbsp. butter
½ cup grated Swiss
  cheese
2 cups simple tomato
  sauce
pinch of grated nutmeg

1 slice cooked ham
  (½ inch thick), diced
2 thick slices cooked
  tongue, diced
2 large, firm mushrooms,
  minced and sautéed
  in butter
salt and pepper to taste

Cook macaroni until tender — about 11 to 12 minutes. Drain and mix with butter, cheese, heated tomato sauce and nutmeg. Add all other ingredients, toss and serve very hot.

Simple Tomato Sauce
2 cups canned Italian
  tomatoes, measured
  with their juice
⅓ cup celery, white
  part, minced

½ cup olive oil
1 medium onion, minced
⅓ cup carrots, minced
salt and pepper to taste
1 tsp. vinegar
1 tsp. lemon juice

Heat oil in a saucepan, sauté onion over medium flame until soft but not browned. Add carrot and celery, sauté 2 minutes longer, stirring a few times. Add all other ingredients, simmer uncovered for about ½ hour, stir often. Rub through a sieve, heat through and serve.

Pastichio

For Eight
1. Meat filling
¾ cup chopped onion
4 tbsp. butter
1½ lbs. chopped lean beef
  (or half beef, half lamb)
salt and pepper to taste

2 tbsp. tomato paste
½ cup beef broth
  (or water)
small pinch powdered
  cinnamon

2.
1 lb. elbow macaroni
3 eggs, beaten

salt to taste
⅔ cup grated Parmesan
  cheese

3. Cream Sauce
6 tbsp. butter
⅔ cup flour

4 cups hot milk
salt and pepper to taste
3 eggs, lightly beaten

Heat butter in a saucepan, add onion and sauté until light golden. Add meat and sauté, stirring, until nicely browned. Add salt, pepper, tomato paste, broth and cinnamon; blend well and simmer for 10 minutes.

Prepare cream sauce: Melt butter in a saucepan, add flour, cook while stirring until light golden. Gradually add milk, while stirring, and stir until mixture is smooth and thickened. Season with salt and pepper, take off fire and cool. When cool, blend in beaten eggs.

Boil macaroni until just done. Drain well. Cool until lukewarm. Add eggs, salt, toss to mix well. Put half the noodles in a buttered 9 x 13 pan, sprinkle with grated cheese, spread meat mixture on top, sprinkle with cheese, cover with remaining macaroni. Bake at 350° for 10 minutes. Remove from oven, cover with cream sauce, sprinkle with remaining cheese and bake for another half hour until top is well browned.

Fettucine Ostia

For Four
½ cup butter
1 medium onion, minced
1 clove garlic, minced
1 can (14 oz.) Italian
  plum tomatoes
¾ cup sliced fresh
  mushrooms
salt and pepper to taste

½ tsp. dried rosemary,
  crushed
¼ cup dry red wine
1 tsp. sugar
½ tsp. lemon juice
1 lb. fettucine
¼ cup grated Parmesan
  cheese

Heat 2 tablespoons butter in a saucepan, add onion and garlic and sauté for about 5 minutes until soft but not browned. Add tomatoes with their juice, mushrooms, salt, pepper, rosemary, wine, sugar and lemon juice, mix, cover and simmer for 30 minutes. In the meantime cook fettucine in salted, boiling water for about 7 minutes until just done (al dente), drain well, put in a serving dish and toss with remaining butter. Cover with tomato sauce and sprinkle with cheese.

Lasagne Sorrento Style

For Eight
1 lb. lasagne

For the sauce:

4 tbsp. olive oil
½ cup onion, minced
¾ lb. lean pork, chopped
½ cup beef or chicken
  broth
2 cloves garlic, minced

2 cups tomato puree
4 cups canned Italian
  tomatoes, mashed
1 tbsp. sugar
1 tbsp. wine vinegar
1 tsp. crushed rosemary
salt and pepper to taste

Heat oil in a saucepan, sauté onion and garlic until limp, add pork and sauté, stirring a few times for 15 minutes. Add all other ingredients, cover and simmer for an hour.

Bring water in a large pot to a boil, salt and add a spoonful of oil. Cook lasagne *al dente*, drain well, spread out on a towel and cool.

Prepare the Filling:

1½ lbs. ricotta cheese
1 lb. mozarella, sliced thin
1 cup Parmesan cheese,
  grated

3 tbsp. parsley, chopped
2 tbsp. fresh basil leaves,
  chopped (or 2 tsp.
  dried basil)

Cover bottom of a square baking pan with a coating of the sauce. Cover with a layer of lasagne, top with pieces of ricotta, sprinkle with parsley and basil, top with some slices of mozarella, another layer of sauce and a sprinkle of Parmesan. Continue in the same order until all ingredients are used up. Top with sauce and grated cheese. Bake in 400° oven for about 25 minutes.

Macaroni Swiss Cheese Casserole

For Four to Six

6 tbsp. butter or margarine
½ cup chopped onion
½ cup chopped green
  pepper
4 cups cooked elbow
  macaroni
½ cup chopped Spanish
  stuffed green olives

½ cup sliced celery
3 tbsp. all-purpose flour
½ tsp. dry mustard
salt and pepper to taste
3 cups milk
3 cups grated Swiss cheese
  (¾ lb.)
green olives, sliced
  for garnish

In a large saucepan, melt 3 tablespoons butter. Add onion, green pepper and celery; sauté over medium heat, stirring constantly, until celery is almost tender, about 5 minutes. Remove vegetables; mix in macaroni and chopped olives. Set aside.

In same saucepan, melt remaining 3 tablespoons butter. Blend in flour, salt, dry mustard and pepper. Cook over medium heat, stirring constantly, until mixture is smooth and bubbly. Reduce heat to low; gradually stir in milk and cook, stirring constantly, until mixture thickens and begins to boil. Remove from heat. Reserve ½ cup cheese; add remaining cheese to sauce. Stir until cheese is melted. Stir macaroni-olive mixture into sauce until combined. Pour into an ungreased 2-quart casserole. Sprinkle top with reserved cheese. Bake in a 400° oven for 20 minutes or until hot and bubbly. Garnish top with olive slices. Serve immediately.

Noodles Smitane

For Six

1 lb. broad egg noodles
2 cups large curd
  cottage cheese
2 cups sour cream
¼ cup grated onion
1 small clove garlic,
  crushed

1 tbsp. Worcestershire sauce
pinch of cayenne pepper
salt to taste
1 tsp. paprika
1 tbsp. butter
⅓ cup grated Parmesan
  cheese

Cook noodles *al dente,* drain well and cool slightly. Mix with cottage cheese and all other ingredients except butter, paprika and Parmesan. Butter a casserole or baking dish, fill with noodles, sprinkle with paprika. Bake at 350° for 30 minutes. Remove from oven, sprinkle with grated cheese and continue baking for another 10 minutes or so until top is browned and bubbly.

Cheese ◁ Enchiladas

Twelve Pieces
1 green pepper, seeded and chopped
1 cup tomatoes, peeled, seeded and
    chopped (or drained canned
    tomatoes)
5 scallions, chopped
1 large clove garlic, crushed
salt and pepper to taste
1 tbsp. chili powder
1 cup shortening or lard
1½ cups sharp cheddar cheese,
    chopped
12 tortillas
½ tsp. oregano

Heat 1½ tablespoons shortening in a skillet, sauté pepper and garlic for a couple of minutes, add tomatoes, scallions, oregano, salt, pepper and chili powder, mix well and simmer for 15 minutes. Add the cheese, blend and heat through. Heat the tortillas to soften them, put cheese filling on each of them, fold them over once and fasten with toothpicks. Fry in hot shortening to brown on both sides. Serve a lettuce and tomato salad, or sliced avocados as a garnish.

Spaghetti with White Clam Sauce

For Four

4 doz. medium clams or	½ cup butter
2 cups canned minced	1 tsp. salt
clams and 3 cups	1 tsp. dried basil leaves
clam juice	freshly ground pepper
1 cup chopped onion	to taste
4 to 5 cloves garlic, minced	1 lb. spaghetti
½ cup chopped parsley	2 tbsp. salt

Wash clams thoroughly. In large pot, cook clams covered in small amount of water just until they open. Remove clams. Strain the broth and reserve 3 cups. Remove clams from shells; chop. In large skillet or Dutch oven sauté onion, garlic and parsley in melted butter until onion is almost tender; add clams and reserved broth, 1 teaspoon salt, basil and pepper. Boil 1 minute.

Meanwhile, gradually add spaghetti and 2 tablespoons salt to rapidly boiling water so that water continues to boil. Cook uncovered, stirring occasionally, until tender. Drain in colander. Serve in shallow bowls topped with clam sauce.

Fried Noodles (Mie Goreng)

For Four
½ lb. thin dried egg
  noodles
½ lb. shrimp, shelled,
  deveined, chopped
4 tbsp. oil
1 medium onion, chopped
2 cloves garlic, minced

3 eggs, lightly beaten
salt and pepper to taste
cayenne pepper to taste
pinch of ground coriander
2 tbsp. light soy sauce
1 cucumber, thinly sliced
2 scallions, chopped

Cook noodles in boiling salted water until just done, but still firm. Do not overcook. Drain noodles, run cold water over them to stop cooking and reserve.

Heat oil in a skillet, sauté onion and garlic until light golden. Add shrimp and sauté 2 minutes longer. Push the foods to one side of the skillet, add the eggs and scramble them until nearly set. Mix them with onion and shrimp, return noodles to skillet and all other ingredients except cucumber and scallions. Mix well, heat through, put on a serving dish or individual plates, sprinkle with scallions and garnish with sliced cucumber.

Lasagne with Clam Sauce

For Eight
4 tbsp. butter
2 cloves garlic, minced
⅓ cup onion, minced
3 cups canned minced
  clams (drained)
3 cups canned Italian
  tomatoes, mashed
½ cup clam juice (drained
  from minced clams)
3 anchovy filets, mashed
4 tbsp. olive oil

2 eggs, lightly beaten
2 cups ricotta cheese
⅔ cup Parmesan cheese,
  grated
2 tbsp. parsley, chopped
1 tsp. oregano
salt and pepper to taste
1 lb. mozarella cheese,
  thinly sliced
1 lb. lasagne, cooked
al dente, drained
  and cooled

Heat butter and oil in a saucepan, add garlic and onion and sauté until light golden brown. Add clams, sauté 2 minutes longer, stir in tomatoes, clam juice and anchovies, mix, cover and simmer for 15 minutes.

Blend eggs, ricotta, ½ cup of Parmesan, parsley, oregano, salt and pepper. Put half of the lasagne in an oiled oblong baking dish, cover with half the clam tomato mixture, half the mixed ricotta and a layer of mozarella slices. Repeat and top with mozarella and a sprinkle of Parmesan. Bake in 400° oven for about 25 minutes until browned and bubbly.

Spaghetti with Chicken Liver Sauce

For Six
4 tbsp. butter
1 cup chopped onion
2 cloves garlic, crushed
⅓ cup chopped parsley
salt and pepper to taste
1½ tsp. oregano
¼ tsp. crushed thyme
1 tsp. Worcestershire

1 can (17 oz.) plum
  tomatoes
1 can (6 oz.) tomato paste
1½ cups beef broth
1 lb. chicken livers, sliced
1 lb. spaghetti
½ cup grated Parmesan
  cheese

Melt 2 tablespoons of the butter in large skillet over medium heat; add onion and garlic and sauté until tender. Reserve 1 tablespoon of the parsley for garnish; add remaining parsley, 1 teaspoon salt, other seasonings, tomatoes, tomato paste and broth to onion mixture. Cover and cook over low heat 30 minutes, stirring occasionally.

Sauté the livers in remaining 2 tablespoons butter for 5 minutes over low heat; add to sauce. Simmer sauce, uncovered, about 5 minutes more, stirring occasionally.

Meanwhile, cook spaghetti until tender. Drain in colander. Blend half of the cheese into chicken liver sauce. Serve with spaghetti sprinkled with reserved cheese and parsley.

Noodles Catalan

For Four
½ cup oil
½ cup chopped onions
1 small green pepper, seeded, diced
1 clove garlic, minced
3 large fresh mushrooms, chopped
1 tbsp. tomato paste
salt and pepper to taste
¼ tsp. Spanish saffron threads
½ tsp. paprika
2 egg yolks, lightly beaten
1 cup heavy cream
½ lb. broad egg noodles
¼ cup grated Parmesan cheese

Cook noodles in boiling salted water for about 10 minutes, drain well and keep hot. Heat oil in a saucepan, add onion, pepper, garlic; sauté very gently for about 10 to 12 minutes until vegetables are soft. Do not brown. Add mushrooms, tomato paste, salt, pepper, saffron and paprika; blend well and sauté 3 more minutes. Add cream, mix and simmer for 3 more minutes. Do not let boil. Remove from fire, cool for a minute or two and blend in egg yolks. Blend the mixture with the noodles, put them in a buttered baking dish, sprinkle with Parmesan and bake at 450° for 10 minutes until very hot and top is brown.

Oysters Tetrazzini

For Six
2 dozen oysters
½ cup clam juice
¼ cup dry white wine
½ cup heavy cream
1½ tsp. minced shallots
5 tbsp. butter
3 tbsp. flour
½ tsp. chervil
¼ tsp. mace
salt and pepper to taste
1 tsp. paprika
1 lb. macaroni or spaghetti
½ cup grated Parmesan cheese

Shuck oysters, strain the oyster liquor and blend with wine, clam juice and cream. Heat the liquids in a saucepan to the simmering point, remove from fire and keep warm.

Sauté shallots in butter until soft, add flour, stir well and cook for a minute or two until smooth and bubbling. Do not let brown. Stir in mace and chervil, add hot liquids gradually and stir until smooth. Season with salt and pepper and keep simmering over a low flame for 6 to 8 minutes until smooth and thickened. Stir often while cooking. Remove from fire, stir in oysters.

Cook macaroni *al dente,* drain well, arrange in 6 buttered ramekins or small baking dishes or large shells. With the back of a spoon make a deep depression in each of the macaroni fillings. Place 4 oysters in each, cover well with the sauce. Sprinkle with paprika and grated cheese, bake in 400° oven for about 10 minutes until top is well browned and the mixture bubbles.

Spaghetti and Meatballs

For Four
½ lb. lean pork, ground
½ lb. veal, ground
¼ lb. cooked ham, ground
1 large clove garlic, minced
2 tbsp. grated onion
2 tbsp. chopped parsley
salt and pepper to taste
⅔ cup white breadcrumbs
1 large egg, lightly beaten
¼ cup milk
¼ cup flour
¼ cup olive oil
1 medium onion, chopped
4 cups canned Italian tomatoes
½ tsp. oregano
½ tsp. basil
½ tsp. rosemary
salt and pepper to taste
½ cup dry white wine
2 tbsp. tomato paste
1 lb. spaghetti

Blend pork, veal, ham, garlic, grated onion, parsley, salt, pepper, egg, breadcrumbs and milk; shape into 8 balls. Heat oil in a saucepan, dredge meatballs with flour and fry until well browned on all sides. Remove meatballs from pan and keep warm. Sauté chopped onion in the same pan until light golden brown. Add tomatoes and herbs, season with salt and pepper and simmer for half an hour. Then add wine and tomato paste, blend well. Return meatballs to sauce and simmer gently for half an hour longer.

Cook spaghetti *al dente,* drain, put in a serving dish. Pour sauce over spaghetti, top with meatballs and serve.

Spaghetti Carbonara

For Four
1 lb. spaghetti
2 tbsp. salt
4-6 qts. boiling water
½ cup butter
½ lb. bacon, chopped
2 cups smoked or cooked
  ham, diced
1 large onion, chopped

2 cloves garlic, chopped
½ lb. mushrooms, sliced
½ cup dry white wine
1 cup (½ pint) heavy cream
2 eggs, well beaten
¼ cup chopped parsley
salt to taste
freshly grated Parmesan or
  Romano cheese

Gradually add spaghetti and 2 tablespoons salt to rapidly boiling water. Cook uncovered, until tender. Drain.

While spaghetti is cooking, melt butter in a large skillet and sauté bacon and ham until golden brown. Add onion and garlic and continue to sauté for 5 minutes. Add mushrooms and sauté for 1 minute. Stir in wine. Beat cream and eggs together until well blended. Stir mixture into skillet. Drain spaghetti and add to sauce with parsley. Stir over low heat. Season to taste with salt. Serve piping hot sprinkled with desired cheese.

Tacos with Meat Filling ▷

For Twelve Tacos
1 lb. ground lean beef
2 tbsp. oil
½ cup minced onion
½ cup minced green pepper
1 clove garlic, crushed
⅔ cup cooked potato, diced
1 cup drained canned tomato,
  chopped
salt and pepper to taste
oil for frying
1 tsp. vinegar
1 tsp. sugar
½ tsp. basil
1 tsp. ground coriander
1 tbsp. chili powder
¼ cup blanched almonds, slivered
¼ cup pitted green olives, chopped
12 tortillas

Fry meat and onions in oil until lightly browned; add pepper and cook until peppers are soft. Add potato, tomatoes, garlic, vinegar, sugar, basil, coriander, chili powder, salt and pepper, mix well and simmer for 10 minutes. Then add almonds and olives and simmer for 10 minutes more. Heat the tortillas to soften, spread some of the mixture on each tortilla, roll up and fasten with toothpicks. Fry in hot oil until they are crisp. Serve with a lettuce and tomato salad and sliced avocados.

Spaghetti Delicado

For Four to Six
1 lb. spaghetti
2½ cups milk
salt and pepper to taste

8 oz. Swiss cheese,
    grated (about 2 cups)
⅔ cup sliced Spanish
    stuffed green olives

Add spaghetti to rapidly boiling water. Cook uncovered until just tender. Drain.

Heat milk to boiling point in same pan. Add spaghetti and cook over medium heat 5 minutes. Add olives and cheese. Toss and cook a few minutes longer, or until cheese melts and sauce thickens slightly. Season with salt and pepper. Turn into warm serving dish. Serve immediately.

Polenta

For Six
1½ cups cornmeal

5 cups water
1 tbsp. salt

Bring water to boil in a heavy saucepan or kettle. Add salt, turn the heat down so that the water is just simmering. Add the cornmeal gradually in a thin stream while stirring with a wooden spoon. Keep stirring constantly and be sure that the water stays at the simmering point.

After all the cornmeal has been added to the water, keep stirring and simmering for about 15 to 30 minutes until the

mixture is so thick that the spoon will stand up in the middle and the mixture comes away from the sides of pot when stirred.

Pour polenta into a serving platter.

In the north of Italy, especially in Lombardy and in the Northeast, polenta is the essential everyday dish and has been so for generations. In most farmhouses and homes it is made fresh every day — prepared in copper kettles. It is often served as a first course — like rice or spaghetti dishes, or served with meat or game.

Polenta Cacciatore

For Six
1½ lbs. veal (shoulder or
    rump) cut in
    1 inch cubes
1 tbsp. butter
1 tbsp. oil
½ cup minced onion

1 clove garlic, minced
3 cups canned Italian
    tomatoes, chopped
½ cup dry white wine
1 tsp. dried basil
salt and pepper to taste
1 recipe polenta (above)

Heat butter and oil in a heavy saucepan, add onion, garlic and meat and sauté until browned. Add tomatoes, wine, basil, salt and pepper, cover and cook for about 45 minutes or until meat is tender.

Put hot polenta on a serving platter, cover with the veal and sauce and serve.

Chicken Lo Mein

For Four
1 large chicken breast,
    boned and skinned
3 tbsp. oil
1 tsp. salt
1 cup Chinese cabbage,
    shredded
1 cup bean sprouts,
    washed and blanched

1 cup celery, sliced thin
2 tbsp. soy sauce
1 tbsp. sherry
½ tsp. sugar
1 cup chicken broth
1 tbsp. cornstarch
3 cups fine egg noodles,
    cooked and drained
3 scallions, minced

Cut chicken breast into thin strips. Pour boiling water over bean sprouts and drain.

Heat oil and salt in a saucepan, add chicken and stir-fry for 2 minutes. Add vegetables, soy sauce, sherry and sugar, stir well, cover and simmer for 3 minutes. Blend cornstarch into broth, add to pan and stir to thicken. Add cooked noodles, stir lightly and heat through. Put on serving platter and sprinkle with scallions.

DESSERTS

Yoghurt Cake

For Six

3 eggs
1 cup sugar
1 cup plain yoghurt

1 cup flour
1 tsp. baking soda
1 tsp. grated lemon peel

Syrup:

2¾ cups water

1¾ cups sugar

Beat eggs with sugar until creamy. Add yoghurt, sifted flour and baking soda, beat with a rotary beater until mixture is smooth. Blend in lemon rind. Pour into a baking dish and bake at 375° for 30 to 40 minutes. Remove from oven. Spoon syrup over hot cake, chill until all the syrup has been absorbed.

Syrup: Boil sugar and water for 10 minutes. Cool before spooning over the cake.

Note: Sweetened fruit juice or syrup drained from canned fruit can be substituted for the sugar in preparing the syrup.

Ricotta Pie

For Six

2 cups flour
pinch of salt
⅔ cup butter
2 tbsp. sherry
1½ lbs. ricotta cheese
4 eggs
⅓ cup sugar

½ tsp. vanilla extract
½ tsp. almond extract
2 tbsp. dark rum
4 tbsp. chopped blanched almonds
2 tbsp. chopped candied citron

Sift together flour and salt into a bowl. Cut in butter and add sherry. Mix gently and add a little water if needed to hold the dough together. Roll out ⅛-inch thick. Line a 10-inch buttered pie plate with the dough, use the remaining dough to cut ½-inch wide strips for lattice to cover the pie.

Rub ricotta cheese through a sieve. Beat eggs and sugar until light and foamy, add vanilla, almond extract and rum, add to cheese, also almonds and citron and whisk until well blended. Pour mixture in the pie shell, place dough strips over the top and pinch the edges together. Bake at 350° for about 45 minutes until the center is firm and the dough golden brown. Cool before serving.

Hazelnut Torte

For Eight to Ten
graham cracker crumbs
2 cups sugar
½ tsp. ground allspice
4 cups hazelnuts or filberts, ground (about 1 lb.)
1 tsp. grated lemon peel

6 eggs, separated, at room temperature
¼ tsp. salt
1 tbsp. light corn syrup
1 tsp. water
1 egg white, slightly beaten

For the garnish:
1 qt. fresh strawberries

1½ cups heavy cream
3 tbsp. kirsch brandy

Grease a 9-inch ring pan and sprinkle with graham cracker crumbs. Set aside. Mix sugar and allspice, mix in filberts and lemon peel. Beat egg yolks until thick and lemon colored. Blend into the nut mixture, working it in thoroughly with your hands. Beat egg whites until frothy, add salt, continue beating until stiff but not dry. Fold into the nut mixture. Turn into the ring pan, bake in 350° oven 35 to 40 minutes or until cake tests done. Cool 5 minutes, loosen with a spatula and turn out onto an ungreased baking sheet. Blend corn syrup and water, brush over top of the cake. Brush entire cake with egg white and bake 5 minutes longer. Serve with strawberry whipped cream: slice berries, reserve one cup for garnish. Whip cream stiff, gradually add kirsch. Fold in the sliced berries, mound in center of the torte, garnish with reserved berries.

Eight Precious Pudding

For Six to Eight
1½ cups rice
1 cup mixed candied fruit
⅔ cup pitted dates
⅔ cup blanched almonds

⅔ cup raisins
1 cup red bean paste*
½ cup sugar
2 tbsp. oil
simple sugar syrup (opt.)

Put rice in a strainer and wash under running water until water runs clear. Put rice in a pan, add 4 cups of water, cover, bring to a boil. Boil for 5 minutes, then reduce heat and cook for 20 minutes, until water has been absorbed and rice is cooked. Blend in sugar and oil. Oil a heatproof bowl

and arrange fruits, raisins and nuts in a neat pattern in the bottom of the bowl. Spoon half the rice into the bowl, being careful not to disturb the fruit pattern. Firm down gently with the back of a spoon. Spread the bean paste on top but don't spread the paste to the edge of the bowl; keep it 1 inch away from the sides. Add remainder of rice to the bowl, pack it down gently, cover bowl with aluminum foil and steam for about 45 minutes. Invert bowl on a serving platter and serve with hot syrup.

*Available in Chinese food markets.

Zuppa Inglese

For Eight
10-inch sponge cake
6 egg yolks, lightly beaten
⅓ cup sugar
3 tbsp. cornstarch
2 cups milk

pinch of salt
1 tsp. grated lemon rind
½ cup dark rum
¼ cup marsala wine
¼ cup crème de cacao liqueur

For the topping:
1 cup heavy cream, whipped

3 tbsp. candied fruit, chopped

Combine sugar, cornstarch, salt and lemon rind, stir into milk, put in a pan and heat. Put egg yolks in top of a double boiler over simmering water, gradually add milk mixture while beating until the custard has thickened. Remove and chill.

Cut the sponge cake in three layers and place one in a shallow dish or bowl. Sprinkle with crème de cacao and spread one third of custard on top. Cover with second layer of cake. Combine rum and marsala and sprinkle second layer with half the mixture and spread second third of custard on top. Cover with third layer of cake, sprinkle with rum mixture and spread last of custard. Cover with whipped cream and sprinkle candied fruit on top. Chill well before serving.

Red Cherry Omelette ◁

For Two
1 cup flour
½ cup plus 1 tbsp. milk
4 eggs, separated
pinch of salt
¼ cup sugar
½ tsp. lemon juice
3 tbsp. melted butter
1 cup pitted cherries
4 tbsp. butter

Mix flour and milk until smooth. Blend in beaten egg yolks, salt, 1 tablespoon butter, sugar and lemon juice. Just before cooking fold in stiffly beaten egg whites and cherries. Heat some of the remaining butter in a pan. Pour batter in — about 1 inch high. Cook one side until light golden, turn and cook the other side. Tear in small pieces with two forks, continue to cook for half a minute.

Make more omelettes until batter is used up. Sprinkle with sugar before serving.

Note: A tablespoon or two of rum may be added to the batter before cooking.

Floating Island

For Four
1¾ cups milk
¼ cup sugar
¼ tsp. salt
3 eggs
1 egg, separated

1 tbsp. orange juice
  concentrate
½ tsp. grated lemon peel
½ tsp. lemon juice
⅛ tsp. cream of tartar
2 tbsp. sugar

In small mixing bowl beat the egg white and cream of tartar until foamy. Add 2 tablespoons sugar, 1 tablespoon at a time, beating constantly until sugar is dissolved* and white is glossy and stands in soft peaks. In small skillet or large heavy saucepan heat milk over low heat until simmering. Drop 4 meringues, using about ⅓ cup each, onto milk. Simmer, uncovered, until firm, about 5 minutes. Using slotted spoon lift meringue from milk, onto paper toweling to drain. Reserve milk for custard. Chill meringues while preparing custard. In same or medium saucepan beat eggs and egg yolk with ¼ cup sugar and salt. Gradually pour reserved warm milk into egg mixture, stirring until blended. Cook and stir over low heat until mixture thickens slightly and just coats a metal spoon. Remove from heat. Stir in orange juice concentrate and lemon extract. Pour into 1-quart shallow serving dish, 9-inch pie plate or 4 (9-ounce) custard cups. Top custard with meringues. Chill.

*Rub just a bit of meringue between thumb and forefinger to feel if sugar is dissolved.

Berry Cake

For Eight
For the cake:

7 eggs
1 cup sugar
1 tsp. vanilla

1 ¾ cups sifted
  all-purpose flour
½ cup clarified butter

For the frosting:
2 egg whites

2 cups confectioners sugar
juice of ½ lemon

For the filling:
2 cups raspberries

1 qt. small strawberries
½ cup superfine sugar

To bake the cake: beat eggs lightly with sugar in a large bowl. Place bowl over, but not touching, simmering water and beat with a wire whisk until mixture feels hot to the finger. Remove from heat and beat with a rotary or electric beater for about 15 minutes until mixture is cool, has tripled in bulk and forms a ribbon when dropped from a spoon. Beat in vanilla. Gently fold in flour alternating with the still liquid but cooled clarified butter, adding a little of each at a time. Butter a 9-inch layer cake pan, dust lightly with flour, pour the batter in and bake on the second rack from the bottom in a preheated 350° oven for 20 to 25 minutes. Turn out immediately onto a wire rack cool. The ingredients in this recipe are sufficient for two 9-inch cake layers.

Pureé raspberries in a blender or through a food mill, put them in a saucepan with the sugar and two thirds of the strawberries. Bring slowly to a boil and simmer for 3 minutes. The strawberries should retain their shape. Drain the fruit, reserving the juice, and cool.

Prepare the frosting: combine egg whites and sugar in a bowl. Blend with a wooden spoon until the entire mixture is smooth, soft and white. Blend in lemon juice.

Put the cooked strawberries between the two layers of cake, frost top and sides with the icing. Decorate with uncooked berries and dribble the reserved juice over the cake.

Apricot Omelette Soufflé

For Four to Six

8 eggs, separated
2 tbsp. sugar
2 tbsp. white wine
  (or water)
pinch of salt

2 tbsp. butter
½ cup apricot preserve
confectioners sugar
3 tbsp. Kirsch brandy
  or light rum

Beat egg yolks with 2 tablespoons sugar, salt and wine until frothy. Fold in the stiffly beaten egg whites. Heat butter in a large skillet or omelette pan, cover the entire bottom with melted butter, pour in egg mixture. Cook very slowly until the bottom is brown and the omelette puffed up. Bake in a 450° oven for 3 or 4 minutes to finish cooking the top without browning it.

Remove from oven, spread with apricot preserve, fold the omelette and turn it out on a hot serving plate. Sprinkle with sugar, pour Kirsch around it and ignite.

Clafoutis

For Six

3 cups dark sweet ripe
  cherries
½ cup sugar
2 egg yolks
1 whole egg

½ cup butter, softened
1 cup flour
2 tbsp. rum
¼ tsp. almond extract
1 cup milk

Beat together the sugar and egg yolks and when they are well blended, beat in the whole egg. Gradually add the butter, beat again, and stir in the flour. Then beat more energetically. Stir in the rum, the almond extract and finally the milk. The batter must be very smooth. Pit the cherries without tearing them apart. Put them in a heavily buttered 8 to 9 inch baking dish. Pour the batter over the cherries. Bake immediately on a lower rack of a preheated 400° oven for about 40 minutes.

Mousse au Chocolat with French Cream ⇨

For Ten
2 pkg. (6 oz. each) semi-
    sweet chocolate pieces
½ cup Marie Brizard
    Anisette cordial
6 eggs, separated
⅛ tsp. cream of tartar
½ cup sugar
French Cream*
chopped pistachio nuts

In top of double boiler, melt chocolate over hot (not boiling) water until just melted; mix in Anisette until smooth. Remove from heat. Beat in egg yolks, one at a time, beating well after each addition. Cool to room temperature. In large bowl, beat egg whites with cream of tartar until soft peaks form. Gradually beat in sugar; continue beating until stiff peaks form. Gently fold chocolate mixture into egg whites. Spoon into 10 individual dishes. Chill thoroughly. Before serving, top with French Cream and pistachio nuts.

To make French Cream: Whip ½ cup heavy cream until stiff; fold in ½ cup sour cream, 1 tbsp. Anisette and 1 tsp. sugar. Refrigerate until serving time.

⇦ Crêpes, Flambees au Grand Marnier

For Six
1 recipe crêpes (p. 295)
¼ cup sugar
¾ cups of Grand Marnier

Make about 24 crêpes. Sprinkle them with sugar, fold them in quarters and put them in a chafing dish. Sprinkle them generously with Grand Marnier, heat the crêpes and flame.

Note: You may add the grated rind of 1 or 2 oranges to the crêpe batter to accentuate the orange flavor.

Banana and Coconut Dessert

For Four
4 ripe firm bananas
1½ cups coconut cream*
2 tbsp. brown sugar
¼ tsp. ground cinnamon
¼ tsp. ground nutmeg

Combine coconut cream, sugar, cinnamon and nutmeg in a saucepan. Simmer for 10 minutes until thickened — do not let brown. Peel bananas and cut each in 4 pieces. Add to coconut cream and simmer for about 5 minutes. Serve hot or well chilled.

*See Glossary

Kaiserschmarren (Emperor's Omelette)

For Two

2 cups milk
1½ cups flour
4 eggs, separated
¼ cup sugar

½ tsp. lemon juice
pinch of salt
8 tbsp. melted butter
2 tbsp. raisins

Blend milk and flour and stir until smooth. Blend in beaten egg yolks, sugar, lemon juice, salt and 4 tablespoons melted butter. Just before cooking fold in stiffly beaten egg whites and raisins. Heat some of the remaining butter in a pan, pour batter in — about 1 inch high. Cook over medium heat until one side is light golden, turn and cook the other side. Tear with two forks in small pieces, continue to cook for half a minute.

Make more omelettes until batter is used up. Sprinkle with sugar before serving.

This omelette is served with a plum compote.

Plum Compote
For Six
2 lbs. Italian plums
1 cup sugar (or to taste)

¼ tsp. ground cinnamon
1 pinch ground cloves
¾ cup water
1 tbsp. cornstarch

Wash plums, remove pit, put in a saucepan. Sprinkle with sugar, add water, cinnamon and cloves. Cover and simmer about 10 to 15 minutes until plums are soft, but still hold their shape. Dissolve cornstarch in a spoonful of cold water, add to plums, mix and simmer for 2 or 3 minutes until juice has thickened.

Apple Fritters

For Six
6 tart cooking apples
1 tbsp. lemon juice
½ cup sugar
pinch of cinnamon

For the batter:
1¾ cups sifted flour
2 tbsp. cooking oil
¼ tsp. salt
⅓ cup milk (or water)

⅓ cup rum
¼ tsp. nutmeg
1 tbsp. chopped raisins
oil for deep frying
confectioners sugar

2 tbsp. melted butter
  or margarine
2 eggs, beaten

Peel and core the apples and chop them coarsely, put them in a bowl and mix with lemon juice, sugar, cinnamon, nutmeg and raisins. Pour rum over it and let stand for 2 hours. Turn and mix several times.

To make the batter, mix flour, oil, melted butter, salt, eggs and milk. Beat well until smooth. Let batter rest for two hours. Then add the apples and their juice to the batter and blend well.

Heat oil to 375° on a frying thermometer and drop big spoonfuls of batter into the hot oil. Fry until golden, remove from fat with slotted spoon and drain on paper towel. Dust with sugar before serving.

Glazed Honey Apples

For Four
2 or 3 firm apples
¾ cup flour
1 egg, beaten
½ cup water

1 cup sugar
2 cups water
½ tbsp. lemon juice
1 tbsp. oil
oil for deep frying

Combine flour, water and egg to make a smooth batter. Prepare a syrup: Put 1 tablespoon oil in a heavy pan, add sugar, water and lemon juice and heat until the syrup reaches the "crack" stage or 275⁰ on a candy thermometer.

Core and pare apples, cut into thick wedges, dip in batter and deep fry; drain on paper towel. Coat well with the hot syrup.

Coat a serving platter with oil to prevent the apple pieces from sticking; put the apples on the platter. Serve with a bowl of ice water.

To eat: Pick up the hot apple slices with chopsticks or small skewers, dip them in the ice water, which will harden the syrup, but the apple inside will be soft and hot.

Note: Banana pieces can be substituted for apple.

Basic Crêpe Recipe

For about 24 crêpes
1½ cups milk
1 tsp. salt
2 tbsp. sugar
½ cup butter

2½ cups sifted all-
    purpose flour
1 tbsp. vegetable oil
4 eggs
½ cup flat beer

Heat the milk, sugar, salt and butter together in a saucepan until the butter has completely melted. Put the flour in a large bowl and make a well in the center. Pour the oil into the well and add the eggs. Mix thoroughly, beating with a wire whisk. Add the milk mixture and then stir in the beer. Strain the batter through a fine sieve and let it rest in the refrigerator for 2 hours before using it.

To fry the crêpe use a heavy iron skillet with sloping sides or a French crêpe pan. These pans come in various sizes and should be used only for making crêpes. Grease the pan very lightly with butter or oil, heat the pan over fairly high heat until the fat is nearly smoking, pour about two tablespoons of batter into the pan, just enough to cover the bottom, and fry for about one minute or until browned. Turn with a spatula, or, with enough dexterity, give the pan a sharp rap and toss the crêpe to turn it. Fry for about 30 seconds on the other side. Crêpes can be cooked well in advance and stacked one on top of the other.

Baked Rice and Wine Sauce

For Four to Six
¾ cup Carolina rice
1 cup milk
1 cup light cream
2 tbsp. butter
¼ cup seedless raisins
1 tbsp. candied orange
    peel, chopped
3 tbsp. sugar

pinch of salt
2 eggs, beaten
¼ cup blanched
    almonds, chopped fine
1 tbsp. butter
¾ cup sugar
¼ cup dry white wine
3 tbsp. rosewater (opt.)

Rinse the rice under cold water, boil in water until soft. Drain well. Combine rice, milk, cream, butter, raisins, orange peel, 3 tablespoons sugar and salt; put in a saucepan, cook over gentle heat, stirring often to prevent sticking and scorching until mixture is quite thick. Remove from fire, cool just a bit, blend in eggs and chopped almonds. Butter a baking dish, pour rice mixture into it and bake at 350⁰ for about 25 minutes, until top is nicely browned.

Remove from oven, cut into wedges but leave mixture in baking dish. Combine wine, rosewater and ¾ cup sugar, boil rapidly for about 10 minutes until syrup has thickened. Pour syrup over baked rice and chill. Serve with whipped cream if desired.

◁ Fruit Compote Anisette

For Ten
2 cups water
1 cup sugar
⅓ cup Marie Brizard
    Anisette cordial
2 tbsp. lemon juice

8 cups fresh cut fruit,
    such as: apples, blueberries,
    grapefruit, grapes, melon
    balls, oranges, pears,
    pineapple, raspberries
    and strawberries

Combine water and sugar in medium saucepan; bring to a boil, stirring constantly. Simmer 3 minutes. Remove from heat; stir in Anisette and lemon juice. Cool to room temperature. Pour over fruit; mix gently, taking care not to break the fruit. Chill at least 4 hours before serving.

Zabaglione

For Four
6 egg yolks

¼ cup sugar
½ cup dry marsala wine

Put egg yolks and sugar in the top of a double boiler and beat with a wire whisk or an electric hand mixer until light yellow and creamy. In the bottom of the double boiler bring water to a simmer, place top over it but do not let touch the water. Continue whisking the egg yolks and gradually beat in the marsala. Beat until the mixture is quite thick, begins to foam and holds its shape.

Remove from heat, spoon into goblets or tulip shaped glasses and serve immediately.

Flan

For Six
⅓ cup light brown sugar
3 cups milk
scant ½ cup sugar
6 tbsp. rum (opt.)
pinch of salt
1 tsp. vanilla extract
6 eggs

Put brown sugar in pan the flan is to be baked in, melt the sugar and stir until sugar starts to turn a deeper brown. Swirl the pan to cover the entire surface with the melted sugar. Remove from heat. Beat the eggs until creamy, beat in sugar, then add salt, milk and vanilla, blend well. Pour the mixture into the caramel lined pan, set the pan in a slightly larger one, half filled with hot water. Bake in a 350⁰ oven for about half an hour or more, until the tip of a knife inserted in the custard comes out clean. Remove from the oven and waterbath, cool. When cool, loosen the edges of the custard with a knife or spatula, place a serving platter on top and invert quickly.

Before serving pour warmed rum over the flan and ignite.

◊ # Strudels

Making strudel dough is a rather difficult undertaking; it takes long experience to master the art. There are, however, easier ways to enjoy home-made strudels. Many supermarkets and specialty stores, especially in areas with a population of Greek or Austro-Hungarian origin, carry factory made and packaged sheets of dough of extreme thinness. They are packaged and sold as phyllo dough for Greek and Middle-Eastern dishes, or as strudel dough. The pastry is nearly identical, though the size of packaged strudel dough sheets is larger than that of phyllo pastry.

Strudel and phyllo dough can be stored in the freezer for a considerable length of time. A word of caution, however, defrosting should be done slowly in the refrigerator. If thawed at room temperature, the outside leaves tend to become mushy and sticky and cannot be separated.

When using a stack of dough sheets, place on a moistened towel since they dry out very fast. Cover with a damp towel, removing sheets one at a time.

To prepare and fill Strudels:

Put one sheet of dough on a slightly dampened towel, brush with melted butter or shortening and sprinkle with a few very fine breadcrumbs. Place another sheet on top, grease. Sprinkle two-thirds of the sheet with sugar and breadcrumbs and then cover the same area with the desired filling. Roll up strudel like a jelly roll starting from the side covered with the filling. Pinch and seal ends, brush with butter and bake at 325° for 30 to 40 minutes until browned.

Fillings

Apple Strudel

For Six
2 lbs. apples, peeled and chopped
¼ cup raisins
¾ cup sugar
½ tsp. cinnamon
¼ tsp. nutmeg
½ cup breadcrumbs
¼ cup melted butter
½ tsp. grated lemon rind
1 tsp. lemon juice
pinch of salt

Blend all ingredients, then fill and bake strudel following instructions on right.

Cherry Strudel

For Six
1 cup breadcrumbs
4 tbsp. butter
3 cups pitted black cherries
⅔ cup sugar
½ tsp. lemon juice
pinch of salt

Sauté breadcrumbs lightly in butter, mix with all other ingredients. Fill and bake strudel following instructions on right.

Sacher Torte ▷

For Six to Eight
5 oz. semi-sweet chocolate
⅔ cup butter, creamed
¾ cup sugar
1 tsp. vanilla
6 eggs, separated
1 cup flour

Glaze:
½ cup apricot preserve

Icing:
6 oz. semi-sweet chocolate
⅓ cup water
1 cup sugar

Put chocolate in a small saucepan and melt over low heat, stirring constantly. Remove from fire. Beat butter until creamy, add sugar and chocolate, blend well. Add egg yolks, one at a time, beating well after adding each yolk. Fold in sifted flour, vanilla and stiffly beaten egg whites. Pour the batter into a well buttered 9-inch spring form pan and bake in a 350⁰ oven for 1 hour. Test with a straw or toothpick for doneness after 45 minutes. Let the cake cool in the pan, preferably for several hours or overnight. Remove from pan, split the cake in two layers.

Melt apricot preserve, rub it through a strainer. Brush the cut side of one layer with apricot, place the other layer on top and coat sides and top of cake with remaining preserve.

To prepare the icing, combine water and chocolate, melt over low heat and blend well. Add sugar gradually and stir well until icing is smooth and shiny and coats a spoon. Spread the warm icing over top and sides of the cake. Let stand a few hours before serving.

Mexican Corn Pudding

For Four
4 ears of mature
   sweet corn
6 tbsp. sugar
½ tsp. cinnamon

½ tsp. mace
1 tsp. lemon juice
pinch of salt
3 tbsp. butter, melted
2 eggs

Score corn with a fork and scrape with a spoon to remove all the pulp from the kernels. Put the pulp in a bowl and mix with sugar, cinnamon, mace, lemon juice and salt. Beat the egg yolks and add, together with the butter, to the corn and blend. Beat the egg whites until stiff, fold into the corn mixture. Put mixture in a casserole or 1 quart soufflé dish, place dish in a larger pan half filled with water and bake at 325⁰ for one hour or longer, until pudding is firm.

Baklava ▽

About 24 servings
1 lb. blanched almonds, chopped
1 cup sugar
1½ tsp. cinnamon

pinch of clove
pinch of nutmeg
1 lb. phyllo pastry sheets
2 cups butter

For the syrup:
½ cup sugar
1 cup honey
2 cups water

1½ tbsp. lemon juice
rind of ½ lemon, cut in strips

Mix almonds, sugar, cinnamon, clove and nutmeg. Place 8 sheets of phyllo dough in the bottom of an 8 x 14 pan, brushing each sheet with melted butter. Sprinkle top with a generous amount of the almond mixture; place 2 buttered phyllo sheets on top, sprinkle again with nuts and continue alternating sheets of dough and nuts until all the nut mixture is used up. Place remaining phyllo sheets on top, butter each sheet. Using a very sharp knife, cut the baklava in diamond shaped pieces. Place a pan with water in the lower shelf of the oven, put baklava on the middle shelf and bake at 300⁰ for about 3 hours. Add water to the lower pan if needed. Prepare syrup: Combine all ingredients, boil over medium heat for 15 minutes, strain and cool.

When baklava is baked, pour cool syrup over the pastry and cool before serving.

Charlotte ◁ à la Valentin

For Six
3 cups raspberry preserves
3 dozen plain ladyfingers
¾ cup sugar
4 egg whites

Put the raspberry preserves in a heavy saucepan and cook over low heat, stirring constantly, for about 20 minutes or until they are very thick. Make a round cake of about 7 inches in diameter, by overlapping layers of ladyfingers, sticking them together with the preserves. Leave an empty space in the center and pour some of the preserves carefully into this space. Top with a few ladyfingers and then coat the cake with the remaining preserves.

Put the cake on a gold foil doily on a small round cake tin. Beat the egg whites and gradually add the sugar. Beat until very stiff. Pipe the meringue in decorative swirls onto the top of the cake and around the bottom. Bake it in a preheated 500⁰ oven for just long enough for the meringue to turn pale golden. Remove from oven, cool and chill well before serving. If desired, stir a little rum or Kirsch brandy into the preserves before coating the ladyfingers.

Salzburg Soufflé

For Four
⅓ cup butter
8 eggs, separated
3 tbsp. flour

½ tsp. vanilla
½ cup sugar
¼ cup hot milk
confectioners sugar

Cream butter, add egg yolks and flour and beat until light and fluffy. Beat egg whites very stiff, gradually adding sugar and vanilla. The success in making the soufflé depends largely on the stiffness of the egg whites. Fold egg whites into the yolks. Pour milk into a baking dish, pour in egg mixture and bake in a preheated 350° oven for 10 minutes until top is lightly browned. Remove in big spoonfuls to a serving dish, dust with powdered sugar and serve.

Sautéed Apples Normande

For Four
4 large, firm apples
3 tbsp. sweet butter
¼ cup sugar

½ tsp. nutmeg
1 tsp. lemon juice
4 tbsp. calvados
   (applejack)

Slice the peeled and cored apples neatly in ½ inch thick slices. Melt butter in skillet, add apples and sprinkle with sugar, lemon juice and nutmeg. Cook them gently until they are light golden, then turn very carefully and sauté the other side. When done, pour the calvados over the apples, ignite and serve.

Milk Pudding (Dulce de Leche)

For Six
1 cup sugar
6 egg yolks,
   beaten until creamy
3 cups milk
1 cup light cream
⅛ tsp. vanilla

⅓ cup blanched
   almonds, ground or
   pounded fine
¼ cup mango meat,
   diced small
¼ cup crushed, drained
   pineapple

Combine sugar, egg yolks, milk, cream and vanilla in a saucepan; heat slowly, while stirring, until mixture starts to simmer. Add almonds and continue cooking and stirring until the mixture thickens. Add fruit, cook another 2 minutes, pour into a serving bowl and chill well.

Mandarin Orange Cream

For Eight to Ten
2 cans (11 oz. each)
   Mandarin orange
   segments, drained,
   syrup reserved
½ cup orange juice
1 tbsp. grated orange peel

3 cups cooked rice
pinch of salt
½ cup sugar
3 tbsp. Curacao cordial
1 tsp. vanilla extract
1 cup heavy cream,
   whipped

Combine syrup from orange segments, orange juice and enough water to make 2 cups. Add orange peel, rice, salt and sugar. Cook over medium heat until rice is thick and creamy, about 30 minutes, stirring occasionally. Remove from heat, stir in Curacao and vanilla. Chill well. Stir in 1 cup of whipped cream and half of the orange segments. Spoon into serving dishes, top with remaining whipped cream and orange segments.

Viennese Bread Pudding (Scheiterhaufen)

For Six

6 slices of good, firm
  white bread
4 tart apples, peeled, cored
  and sliced
1 tbsp. raisins, soaked in
  warm water and drained
1 tbsp. currants, soaked in
  warm water and drained

2 tbsp. butter, softened
1 tsp. cinnamon
½ tsp. nutmeg
1 pinch powdered allspice
4 egg yolks, lightly beaten
1 cup milk
1 cup light cream
2 tbsp. rum (opt.)
¼ cup sugar

Cut crust off bread, butter the bread and cut into strips. Arrange a layer of bread strips in a small buttered baking dish, cover with a layer of sliced apples, repeat until ingredients have been used up. Finish with a layer of bread. Combine other ingredients, blend with a whisk and pour over the bread pudding. Bake in 350° oven until top is brown and the custard is set. Serve slightly warm.

Creme Caramel

For Six

1 cup sugar, divided
3 eggs
3 egg yolks

2 cups milk, heated
  until very warm
1 tsp. vanilla

In heavy saucepan, over medium heat, melt ½ cup sugar, stirring constantly until a deep golden brown. Remove from heat and *immediately* pour about 1 tablespoon into each of six 6-ounce custard cups. Set aside. Mix eggs, egg yolks and remaining sugar together until well blended. Gradually stir

in milk. Add vanilla. Pour into prepared custard cups over caramel. Set cups in large baking pan. Pour very hot water into pan to within ½ inch of top of custard. Bake in preheated 350°F. oven 45 to 50 minutes or until knife inserted near center comes out clean. Remove promptly from hot water. To serve warm: Cool 5 to 10 minutes at room temperature. Gently loosen custard from cups at sides with spatula and invert on serving plate. To serve cold: Chill in refrigerator and unmold.

Coffee Anisette Cake

For Ten

2¼ cups sifted cake flour
1½ cups sugar
3 tsp. baking powder
1 tsp. salt
½ cup salad oil
4 egg yolks
½ cup strong black coffee
¼ cup Marie Brizard Anisette cordial
½ tsp. grated lemon peel
8 egg whites
½ tsp. cream of tartar

Sift together flour, sugar, baking powder and salt into mixing bowl; make a well in center. In this order, add oil, egg yolks, coffee, Anisette and lemon peel. Beat until satiny. In a large bowl, combine egg whites and cream of tartar; beat until very stiff peaks form. Pour egg yolk batter in thin stream over whites; gently fold together. Turn into 2 ungreased, waxed paper-lined 9-inch layer cake pans. Bake in 350° oven 40 minutes. Cool in pans.

Cream Filling and Frosting

3 cups heavy cream
2 tsp. instant powdered coffee
2 tbsp. sugar
⅓ cup Marie Brizard Anisette cordial

Combine cream, coffee and sugar; whip until stiff. Fold in Anisette.

To assemble cake: Cut each cake into 2 layers. Spread cream on 3 layers; stack together. Top with fourth layer. Frost with remaining cream. Decorate as desired.

Turkish Coffee

For Four

4 heaping tsp. of finely pulverized coffee (Turkish coffee blend)
4 tsp. sugar (or less to taste)
4 demi-tasse cups of cold water

Turkish coffee is usually cooked in a cylindrical enamelled or brass coffee pot with a long handle, available in all houseware stores. Put coffee, sugar and water into the pot, place over low heat and cook until the water starts to boil and foam rises. Remove from heat immediately, wait a few seconds, return pot to fire and let it boil up again. Repeat once more, spoon some of the foam into each cup, then pour the coffee into the cups. Do not stir at any time while cooking.

Kugel Pudding

For Four

½ lb. broad noodles
1 tsp. salt
2 eggs, beaten
4 tbsp. sugar
¼ tsp. lemon juice
¼ tsp. cinnamon
½ tsp. grated lemon rind
⅓ cup slivered almonds

½ cup firm apples, peeled and thinly sliced
½ cup seedless raisins
¼ cup chopped candied citrus peels
5 tbsp. margarine or shortening, softened
½ cup orange juice

Boil noodles in rapidly boiling salted water for 6 to 7 minutes. Drain. Blend with all other ingredients. Put into a well-greased baking dish and bake at 400⁰ for about 45 minutes until top is nicely browned.

Plum Cake

For Four to Six

1 cup butter
4 eggs
1 cup sugar
1 tsp. grated lemon peel
¼ tsp. cinnamon

1 tbsp. rum (opt.)
1½ cups flour, sifted
1 lb. Italian plums (approx.)
confectioners sugar

Beat butter until creamy, add eggs, sugar, lemon peel, cinnamon and rum and beat until light and fluffy. Mix in flour, blend well and spread ¾ inch thick on a greased and floured baking tin. Cover neatly with halved plums and bake at 325⁰ for 20 to 25 minutes. Remove from oven, sprinkle with sugar while still warm. Serve warm or cold.

Note: Other fruit, such as halved apricots, pitted cherries or sliced firm peaches can be used instead of plums. Soaked dried fruit can also be used.

Lokshen Kugel

For Four
½ lb. broad noodles
8 cups boiling water
1 tsp. salt
2 eggs, beaten
4 tbsp. sugar
¼ tsp. lemon juice
¼ tsp. cinnamon
½ tsp. grated lemon rind

⅓ cup slivered almonds
½ cup firm apples, peeled
  and thinly sliced
½ cup seedless raisins
¼ cup chopped candied
  citrus peels
5 tbsp. margarine or
  shortening, softened
½ cup orange juice

Boil noodles in rapidly boiling salted water for 6 to 7 minutes. Drain. Blend with all other ingredients. Put into a well greased baking dish and bake at 400⁰ for about 45 minutes until top is nicely browned.

Frozen Sabayon

For Four
3 large egg yolks
2 tbsp. water
3 tbsp. sugar
⅛ tsp. grated nutmeg

½ cup Marsala wine
3 tbsp. dark rum
1 cup heavy cream,
  whipped

Put all ingredients except cream in top of double boiler. The water in the bottom part should be simmering, not boiling. Blend mixture with a wire whisk until the mixture is warm. Remove from heat and continue whisking until the mixture is frothy and slightly thickened. Cool, then fold in whipped cream. Pour mixture into a mold or serving bowl and freeze. If a mold is used, dip it just before serving for a second or two in hot water, cover with a serving dish and invert.

Finnish Cheese Cake

For Six
2 cups cottage cheese
¼ cup flour
3 eggs, lightly beaten
⅓ cup sugar
2 cups light cream

½ cup toasted almonds,
  chopped
¼ cup candied fruit,
  chopped
2 tbsp. brandy
1 tbsp. butter

Stir cottage cheese in a bowl until lumps are broken up. Add flour, mix well, add all other ingredients except butter, blend until smooth. Pour mixture in a buttered 8-inch baking dish or pie plate, bake at 350⁰ for about 1 hour or until the cake is set and a knife inserted in the center comes out clean.

Danish Blueberry Cream

For Four to Six
2 cups fresh blueberries
2½ cups water
2½ tbsp. sugar

½ tsp. lemon juice
3 tbsp. cornstarch
3 tbsp. water

Rinse berries, drain well. Put berries and water in a saucepan, bring to a boil, simmer for 3 minutes, stir in sugar and lemon juice. Dissolve cornstarch in 3 tbsp. water, blend into simmering berries and cook gently, stirring constantly, until mixture thickens, about 3 minutes. Remove from fire, cool and chill well. Serve with whipped cream if desired.

Note: Other berries such as gooseberries or currants can be prepared the same way.

Dobos Torte ▽

For Six to Eight
6 egg yolks
⅔ cup sugar

Chocolate Cream:
1 cup plus 1 tbsp. butter,
    softened
1 cup confectioners sugar

1 cup flour
6 egg whites, stiffly beaten
    with pinch of salt

½ tsp. vanilla
1 egg, well beaten
3 tbsp. very strong black coffee
4 oz. semi-sweet chocolate

Beat egg yolks and ½ cup sugar until fluffy, adding the yolks one by one while beating. Add flour, blend well and fold in beaten egg whites. Line baking sheets or cake tins with wax paper and grease the paper lightly. Pour the batter on the tins and bake about 10 thin round or square layers, 8 inches or so in diameter. Bake in preheated 325⁰

oven for 8 to 10 minutes. Remove from oven, trim evenly and let cool. Reserve the 3 best layers for the top layers of the torte.

Prepare chocolate cream: Beat butter until creamy; beat in sugar, vanilla and the whole egg. Melt chocolate in top of double boiler, add to beaten butter along with coffee and continue beating until well blended and creamy. Cool, then spread layers with chocolate cream, put layers on top of each other and coat the sides with cream. Do not spread cream on the top layer. Place the top layer on a board covered with wax paper. Prepare caramel icing: Melt ⅓ cup sugar in a heavy skillet until sugar turns a golden color. Spoon immediately on the top cake layer, smooth with a buttered knife blade and score the layer into equal portions. When the caramel has hardened, put the layer on top of the others and chill the torte before serving.

Filled
◁ Lady Fingers

For Eight
½ tsp. grated orange
    or lemon rind
1 doz. lady fingers, split
1 tsp. soft butter
½ cup confectioners
    powdered sugar
2 tsp. orange or
    lemon juice

Blend butter and rind. Alternately add sugar and juice, mixing until smooth. Spread a thin layer of fruit glaze between lady fingers. Sprinkle with more sugar. Serve at once, or store in air tight containers.

French Rice Brulee

⇨

For Eight
2 cups cooked rice
3 cups milk
1½ cups Half and Half
   (cream & milk)
½ cup sugar

9 egg yolks
1½ tsp. vanilla extract
½ tsp. almond extract
¼ tsp. salt
½ cup blanched almonds
½ cup light brown sugar

Put rice in a 7½ x 12 x 2-inch baking dish. Scald milk and cream, but do not boil. Add sugar and stir to dissolve. Beat egg yolks until light in color; add extracts and salt. Stir hot milk gradually into egg mixture. Pour over the rice; stir. The custard should be about 1½ inches deep. Place dish in a larger pan; pour boiling water around it.

Bake at 300° for 1 hour. Near end of baking time, insert knife in center of custard. When knife comes out clean, custard is done. Cool; then refrigerate until thoroughly chilled. Sprinkle with almonds and top with brown sugar. Place under the broiler for a few minutes or just until sugar melts and runs together. Serve immediately or chill again and serve cold. Just before serving, shatter the glaze by tapping lightly with a knife.

Fruit
◁ Dumplings

For Four
1½ lbs. potatoes
1½ cups flour
1 egg
2 tbsp. butter
pinch of salt
1 cup white breadcrumbs
16 ripe Italian (prune) plums,
   or small ripe apricots
16 sugar cubes
4 tbsp. butter
¼ cup sugar mixed with ¼ tsp.
   cinnamon

Boil and mash potatoes. While still warm, mix with flour, egg, butter and salt. Knead well. Roll out to ½ inch and cut into 3-inch squares. Remove the plum pits and replace with a small cube of sugar. Fold dough corners over plums, seal the edges well, and shape into round dumplings. Cook in gently boiling water, stirring once in a while, for about 10 minutes. When the dumplings rise to the surface, they are done.

Sauté breadcrumbs in butter until golden. Drain dumplings, put on a serving dish, pour buttered breadcrumbs over them and sprinkle with cinnamon sugar.

Orange Surprise

For Six

6 large oranges
6 egg yolks
6 tbsp. sugar
1 tsp. lemon juice
4 tbsp. Curacao or
   Grand Marnier cordial

3 tbsp. brandy
1 cup heavy cream,
   whipped
¼ tsp. powdered mace
1 tbsp. grated semi-sweet
   chocolate

Slice a cap off the oranges, scoop out all the pulp and some of the pith. The shell should be still quite firm. (Reserve the pulp for some other use.)

Mix egg yolks, sugar, lemon juice, Curacao, brandy and mace, whisk until light and creamy. Fold in the whipped cream.

Fill the orange shells with the mixture and freeze overnight or longer. (If they are to be kept in the freezer for more than 12 hours, wrap them in foil or plastic film after they are frozen, to prevent drying out.) Before serving, decorate tops with whipped cream and a sprinkle of grated chocolate.

Palacsinta (Hungarian Pancakes)

For Twelve pancakes:
1¼ cups flour
2 eggs
½ cup water

¾ cup milk
1 tbsp. sugar
pinch of salt
3 tbsp. butter

Mix well. Spread each pancake with some of the jam, roll them up and place them side by side in a buttered ovenproof serving dish. Bake in a preheated 350° oven for 10 to 15 minutes.

Sift flour with salt into a bowl. Stir in eggs, milk, water, salt and sugar, blend well to make a smooth pancake batter. Heat an 8-inch skillet and add just enough butter to cover the surface. Ladle some batter into the skillet and cover the bottom thinly by tilting and twisting the skillet. Cook until the top of the batter bubbles, turn the pancake and quickly brown the other side, for just a few seconds. Slide pancake on a warm plate and repeat until all batter is used up, adding butter to the skillet before cooking each pancake.

Cottage Cheese Filling:
For Four to Six

½ cup butter
¾ cup sugar
2 whole eggs
2 egg yolks
3 tbsp. raisins

1 cup cottage or farmer
   cheese forced through
   a strainer
4 tbsp. sour cream
confectioners sugar

Cream the butter, add sugar and eggs, one at a time while beating the mixture. Add egg yolks, cheese, raisins and sour cream, blend well, fill the pancakes and cook as in basic palacsinta. Sprinkle with confectioners sugar when serving.

Basic Filling:
2 tbsp. brandy

1 cup apricot or
   strawberry jam

Peach Cup Foyot

For Four

4 ripe firm peaches
lemon juice
1½ cups raspberries*
3 tbsp. Kirsch brandy

½ cup heavy cream
1 tablespoon sugar
a few drops vanilla
   extract

Dip peaches for a minute in boiling water and slip off the skins. Slice and sprinkle with lemon juice to prevent dis-

coloring. Force berries through a fine sieve, add the Kirsch and sweeten to taste. Whip cream with sugar and vanilla and fold the chilled raspberry puree into the cream. Put the peach slices in serving cups, cover with the whipped cream mixture and chill well before serving.

*If frozen raspberries are used, defrost and strain off the juice before pureeing the berries.

SAUCES

Alli-o-li
(Garlic Mayonnaise)

One Cup
4 cloves garlic, crushed
1 tsp. lemon juice
1 tsp. salt
¼ tsp. white pepper

2 tbsp. soft white
  breadcrumbs
2 egg yolks
1 cup olive oil
1 tbsp. dry sherry (opt.)

Put lemon juice, salt, pepper, garlic, breadcrumbs, and egg yolks in a blender, blend for a few seconds at low speed. Add the oil, drop by drop at first, until the mixture starts to thicken, and then in a thin stream. When mayonnaise has thickened, blend in a spoonful of hot water and the sherry. Serve with broiled seafood or broiled or roast meats.

Avgolemono Sauce
(Egg and Lemon Sauce)

One Cup
3 eggs, separated
salt and white pepper
  to taste

juice of 2 small lemons
1 cup hot soup
  or stock

Beat egg whites until fairly stiff but not dry. Beat in egg yolks, one at a time. Add slowly, while beating, lemon juice and the hot soup or stock, a spoon at a time. It is important to add the ingredients quite slowly to avoid curdling. When smooth, season with salt and pepper. The sauce is used in gravies and stews or fricassees. Add the mixture slowly into the hot sauce or stew, beating constantly until the sauce thickens.

Chili Sauce

About Three Cups
1 medium onion, chopped
2 cloves garlic, minced
4 tbsp. olive oil
3 cups chicken broth
⅓ cup tomato puree
1 tbsp. wine vinegar

1 pinch cayenne pepper
salt to taste
½ tsp. oregano
4 to 6 tbsp. chili powder
  (or to taste)
1½ tbsp. cornstarch

Sauté onion and garlic in oil until they just start to take on color. Add chicken broth, tomato puree, vinegar, pepper, salt and oregano, stir well, mix chili powder with a little water and add to sauce. Blend again and simmer for about 45 minutes. Strain sauce through a sieve and return to pan. Correct seasoning. Dissolve cornstarch in a little water, add to sauce and simmer, stirring once in a while until sauce has thickened. Serve with tamales, meat or poultry.

Sauce Gribiche

Three Cups
6 hard-boiled egg yolks
1 tbsp. Dijon mustard
1 tsp. salt
freshly ground pepper
2 cups olive or salad oil
3 tbsp. wine vinegar

1 tbsp. fresh tarragon,
  minced
1 tbsp. parsley, minced
2 tbsp. capers, chopped
1 tbsp. sour pickles, minced
3 hard-boiled egg whites,
  minced

Mash the egg yolks until smooth. Then blend in the mustard, salt and pepper. Add the oil, little by little in the beginning, as though you were making a mayonnaise. As the mixture thickens, add some vinegar from time to time. When the oil is used up, blend in all other ingredients, and finally a spoonful of boiling water. This will insure a smooth, stable mixture. Ideal for cold fish or shellfish.

Marinara Sauce

For Six
¼ cup olive oil
½ cup onion, minced
1 clove garlic, minced
3 cups canned Italian
  tomatoes, chopped

2 anchovy filets, mashed
½ cup dry white wine
½ tsp. oregano
½ tsp. basil
1 tbsp. parsley, chopped
salt and pepper to taste

Heat oil in a saucepan, sauté onion and garlic until light golden, add all other ingredients and simmer for 30 minutes.
    Serve with spaghetti or seafood.

Mexican Green Sauce

About One Cup
3 large ripe tomatoes,
  peeled, seeded
½ small green hot chili
  pepper or to taste (canned
  chili can be used)

1 medium onion, chopped
1 clove garlic, minced
¼ tsp. oregano
¼ tsp. ground coriander
1 tbsp. lime juice
salt and pepper to taste

Place all ingredients in a blender or food processor and blend until smooth. Use with meats, tacos or enchiladas.

Cucumber-Dill Sauce

About Two Cups

1 cup finely chopped
  cucumbers
1½ tsp. salt
1½ tbsp. lemon juice

1 tsp. sugar
½ tsp. dry mustard
1½ tbsp. fresh dill, chopped
1 cup sour cream
pepper to taste

Combine cucumber and salt and let stand for at least one hour. Then drain and squeeze out of cucumbers as much liquid as you can. Blend cucumbers with all other ingredients, chill for one hour. Fold in sour cream just before serving. Serve with broiled fish, such as bluefish, tuna, swordfish and others.

Note: Plain yoghurt can be used instead of sour cream.

Horseradish Sauce with Apples

About One Cup

3 firm apples
1 tbsp. lemon juice
2 tbsp. vinegar
  (1 tbsp. if prepared
  horseradish is used)

1 tbsp. sugar (or to taste)
¼ tsp. salt (or to taste)
3 tbsp. grated fresh horseradish (or 2 tbsp. pre-
  pared horseradish)

Peel and grate apples, mix immediately with lemon juice to prevent discoloring. Blend with all other ingredients. Add more vinegar, sugar or salt if needed.

Sauce Mornay

About Two Cups

Step 1: Sauce Bechamel

3 tbsp. butter
1 tbsp. onion, minced
4 tbsp. flour

3 cups scalded milk
salt and white pepper
  to taste
pinch of grated nutmeg

Melt butter in a saucepan, add onion and sauté while stirring for a few minutes until onion is soft but not browned. Stir in flour and cook, while stirring, until the flour just starts to take on color. Gradually add the scalded milk, stir with a whisk until the mixture is smooth and has thickened. Season with salt, pepper and nutmeg. Strain before using.

Step 2: Sauce Mornay

2 cups hot Sauce Bechamel
2 lightly beaten egg yolks

½ cup grated Gruyere or
  Swiss cheese

Combine egg yolks with a few spoonfuls of Bechamel, then add to the rest of the Bechamel sauce, blend well and bring to a simmer but do not let boil. Simmer for a minute or two, stir in cheese and simmer while stirring until cheese has melted. Correct seasoning.

Pesto

For Six

2 cups of fresh small
  basil leaves
½ cup olive oil
3 tbsp. pine nuts
2 large cloves garlic,
  crushed

1 tsp. lemon juice
salt and pepper to taste
⅓ cup grated Parmesan
  cheese
¼ cup grated Romano
  cheese
2 tbsp. butter

Put basil, oil, pine nuts, garlic, lemon juice, salt and pepper in a blender or food processor and process at high speed until well blended to a smooth paste. Then add grated cheeses, blend at lower speed and finally add the butter and blend again. Just before serving over spaghetti, beat in 2 or 3 tablespoons of hot water.

Spaghetti *al pesto* is one of the greatest pasta dishes. The pesto, a basil sauce, is traditionally prepared by pounding the ingredients in a mortar. A blender or food processor can simplify the preparation considerably.

Ragu Bolognese
(Meat Sauce)

3 tbsp. olive oil
3 tbsp. butter
3 tbsp. minced onion
1 small clove garlic, minced
3 tbsp. celery, white part
  only, minced
1 carrot, peeled and
  minced

½ lb. beef (chuck) ground
½ lb. lean pork, ground
salt and pepper to taste
1 cup dry white wine
2 cups canned Italian
  tomatoes, mashed
½ cup chicken broth
1 cup sliced mushrooms

Heat oil and butter in a heavy saucepan, add onion and garlic, sauté until soft but not browned. Add celery and carrot and sauté 2 or 3 more minutes, stirring occasionally. Add meats, stir well to break up lumps and sauté for 3 or 4 minutes, season with salt and pepper, add wine and tomatoes, blend and simmer for an hour. Add mushrooms and chicken broth and simmer for another hour or so. Stir occasionally.

Sauce Ravigotte

For Four
2 tbsp. minced parsley
2 tbsp. chopped watercress
1 tbsp. minced chives
1 tbsp. minced fresh tarragon (or 1 tsp. dried)
1 tbsp. minced fresh chervil (or 1 tsp. diced)
2 anchovy filets, chopped

1 shallot, minced
1 tbsp. capers, drained and chopped
1½ tbsp. cornichons (or sour gherkins) minced
6 tbsp. olive oil
1 tbsp. wine vinegar
2 tsp. lemon juice
salt and pepper to taste

This should be a fairly thick sauce, to be served with boiled, hot or cold meats.
    Blend all ingredients.

Sauce Remoulade

About Two Cups
2 cups mayonnaise
2 tbsp. capers, drained and minced
2 tbsp. sour pickles, minced (French cornichons preferred)

1 tbsp. onion, grated
1 to 2 tbsp. Dijon mustard (according to taste)
½ tsp. anchovy paste
2 tsp. each of minced fresh parsley, tarragon, chervil (1 tsp. each if dried herbs)

Blend all ingredients well. Served with cold fish or shellfish.

Vinaigrette Sauce

French Dressing
The only real "French dressing" is the vinaigrette, a simple basic oil and vinegar dressing. The variations are numerous.

4 tbsp. oil
2 tbsp. wine vinegar
1 tsp. salt
½ tsp. Dijon mustard

¼ tbsp. freshly ground pepper
touch of crushed garlic (opt.)

Blend well.

To be served with hors d'oeuvres
4 tbsp. vinegar
½ tsp. dry mustard
8 tbsp. olive oil
1 tsp. chives, minced
1 tsp. parsley, minced
pinch of chervil

pinch of tarragon
1 tbsp. capers, squeezed dry and chopped
1 tsp. grated onion
1 hard-boiled egg, chopped
salt and pepper

Mix mustard with vinegar, add the herbs, onion, salt and pepper, blend well, then add oil and egg.

Tarator Sauce

About One Cup
1 cup walnuts or pine nuts, ground
2 slices white bread, crust trimmed off

2 cloves garlic, chopped
2 tbsp. vinegar
salt and pepper to taste
½ cup olive oil

Pound nuts in a mortar until smooth, add garlic, pound until well crushed. Soak bread in water, squeeze dry, add to nut mixture, season with salt and pepper and blend to a smooth paste. Add oil, a little at a time, beating constantly; add vinegar and continue beating until the sauce is very smooth. Serve with fried fish or vegetables.

Note: This sauce is much easier to prepare by using an electric blender or food processor to combine and cream all ingredients.

Sauce Verte

About One Cup
10 spinach leaves, well washed
¼ cup watercress leaves
¼ cup parsley leaves (without stems)
1 cup mayonnaise

Blanch leaves in boiling salted water for 1 minute. Let stand for another minute, drain well and press out all water. Cool and rub through a fine sieve. Blend with mayonnaise. This very attractive and tasty sauce should be served with cold poached fish or shellfish, such as salmon, bass or lobster.

INDEX

This Index is arranged in the same progression as is the book; starting with Appetizers, then Soups, etc. Entries are then listed in alphabetical order. In certain sections, such as Eggs, Seafood, and Poultry subcategories have been added for your convenience.

The page numbers printed in italics indicate color photographs of that entry.